Development Centre Studies

Chinese Economic Performance in the Long Run

SECOND EDITION, REVISED AND UPDATED: 960-2030 AD

OECD

DEVELOPMENT CENTRE OF THE ORGANISATION
FOR ECONOMIC CO-OPERATION AND DEVELOPMENT

ORGANISATION FOR ECONOMIC CO-OPERATION AND DEVELOPMENT

The OECD is a unique forum where the governments of 30 democracies work together to address the economic, social and environmental challenges of globalisation. The OECD is also at the forefront of efforts to understand and to help governments respond to new developments and concerns, such as corporate governance, the information economy and the challenges of an ageing population. The Organisation provides a setting where governments can compare policy experiences, seek answers to common problems, identify good practice and work to co-ordinate domestic and international policies.

The OECD member countries are: Australia, Austria, Belgium, Canada, the Czech Republic, Denmark, Finland, France, Germany, Greece, Hungary, Iceland, Ireland, Italy, Japan, Korea, Luxembourg, Mexico, the Netherlands, New Zealand, Norway, Poland, Portugal, the Slovak Republic, Spain, Sweden, Switzerland, Turkey, the United Kingdom and the United States. The Commission of the European Communities takes part in the work of the OECD.

OECD Publishing disseminates widely the results of the Organisation's statistics gathering and research on economic, social and environmental issues, as well as the conventions, guidelines and standards agreed by its members.

> *The opinions expressed and arguments employed herein do not necessarily reflect the official views of the Organisation, the OECD Development Centre or of the governments of their member countries.*

Also available in French under the title:
L'économie chinoise : Une perspective historique
DEUXIÈME ÉDITION, RÉVISÉE ET MISE À JOUR : 960-2030

THE DEVELOPMENT CENTRE

The Development Centre of the Organisation for Economic Co-operation and Development was established by decision of the OECD Council on 23 October 1962 and comprises 22 member countries of the OECD: Austria, Belgium, the Czech Republic, Finland, France, Germany, Greece, Iceland, Ireland, Italy, Korea, Luxembourg, Mexico, the Netherlands, Norway, Portugal, Slovak Republic, Spain, Sweden, Switzerland, Turkey and the United Kingdom as well as Brazil since March 1994, Chile since November 1998, India since February 2001, Romania since October 2004, Thailand since March 2005 and South Africa since May 2006. The Commission of the European Communities also takes part in the Centre's Governing Board.

The Development Centre, whose membership is open to both OECD and non-OECD countries, occupies a unique place within the OECD and in the international community. Members finance the Centre and serve on its Governing Board, which sets the biennial work programme and oversees its implementation.

The Centre links OECD members with developing and emerging economies and fosters debate and discussion to seek creative policy solutions to emerging global issues and development challenges. Participants in Centre events are invited in their personal capacity.

A small core of staff works with experts and institutions from the OECD and partner countries to fulfil the Centre's work programme. The results are discussed in informal expert and policy dialogue meetings, and are published in a range of high-quality products for the research and policy communities. The Centre's *Study Series* presents in-depth analyses of major development issues. *Policy Briefs* and *Policy Insights* summarise major conclusions for policy makers; *Working Papers* deal with the more technical aspects of the Centre's work.

For an overview of the Centre's activities, please see www.oecd.org/dev

 ISBN: 978-92-64-03762-5 © OECD 2007

Foreword

When historians look back at our period, it is likely that few developments will appear quite so striking as the economic emergence of China. When those historians step back a bit further, though, they will see that this was not an emergence, but a re-emergence. China may well be on course to become the world's largest economy, but it has held that title before – little more than a hundred years ago.

Our knowledge of China's long-term economic development is based in large part on the work of the author of this book, Angus Maddison. In a series of remarkable studies over the years, Mr. Maddison has traced the course of China and the world's economy over the past 2000 years. This is a staggering intellectual achievement, and one with which the OECD is proud to be associated. His work has deepened immeasurably our understanding of the long-term growth of the global economy – the challenges that were met and the opportunities that were missed.

The world faces a new set of economic opportunities and challenges, and China lies at the heart of them. Years of phenomenal growth have made China one of the engines of the global economy, bringing great benefits: the lives of millions of Chinese have been transformed, providing them with new opportunities for work, travel and personal development. But there are challenges that need to be addressed if China is to continue on this growth path. They include increasing inequality in income distribution; regional disparities; population ageing; environmental degradation and impediments to innovation. Yet, by overcoming those, the Chinese economy will provide the foundation to future prosperity and wellbeing of its population.

In recent years, OECD has worked ever more closely with China to examine issues such as these, sharing insights we have gained from our member countries and learning from the extraordinary experience of this country. Our analysis has focused on issues such as governance, the economy, agriculture, innovation and environmental performance, as well as its growing economic relationships with countries in Africa and South America.

Now, as this book – the 2nd edition of *Chinese Economic Performance in the Long Run* – goes to press, OECD is beginning a new phase of our relationship, a process we call "enhanced engagement". A deepening of our ties with China is indeed essential if OECD is to continue to play its role in developing responses to global policy challenges. To prepare for where we are going, of course, we must first understand from where we have come. Thanks to Angus Maddison, we have never been better equipped to do so.

Angel Gurría
Secretary–General of the OECD

September 2007

ISBN: 978-92-64-03762-5 © OECD 2007

Acknowledgements

I was very fortunate to have Chinese friends — Gai Jianling, Meng Xin, Ren Ruoen, Wang Ziaolu, Harry X. Wu, Xu Xianchun and Yue Ximing who were willing to help in interpreting Chinese language material. I am grateful to Michèle Fleury–Brousse, Remco Kouwenhoven, Boon Lee, Peter van Mulligen, Aparna Rao and Ly Na Tang Dollon for help in statistical processing, to Sheila Lionet for her skill and patience in typesetting a very difficult manuscript and Michèle Girard for bibliographical help. The Food and Agriculture Organization was kind enough to provide access to its data files on Chinese agricultural output. Graeme Snooks and Prasada Rao were very generous in providing comments and hospitality when I visited their universities. I received useful comments from Derek Blades, Pierre van der Eng, David Henderson, Peter Nolan, Eddy Szirmai, Victor Urquidi, Donald Wagner and from participants in seminars in the Australian National University, CEPII, Griffith University, the Hong Kong University of Science and Technology, Melbourne Business School, the University of New England, Peking University, the Reserve Bank of Australia, the School of Oriental and African Studies, the Oxford Centre for Chinese Studies, the European Historical Economics meeting in Montecatini Terme, an SSB–OECD Workshop on National Accounts and a seminar in Beijing organised by the OECD Development Centre and the Institute of Industry and Techno–economics of the Chinese State Planning Commission. My biggest debt is to my wife, Penelope Maddison, for continuous encouragement, sustained moral and material support.

The second edition of this book was made possible by a generous financial contribution from the Government of the Czech Republic to which the Development Centre expresses its gratitude.

ISBN: 978-92-64-03762-5 © OECD 2007

Table of Contents

List of Chapter Tables, Figures and Box

ISBN: 978-92-64-03762-5 © OECD 2007

Appendix Tables and Maps

ISBN: 978-92-64-03762-5 © OECD 2007

This book has...

StatLinks

A service that delivers Excel® files from the printed page!

Look for the StatLinks at the bottom right-hand corner of the tables or graphs in this book.
To download the matching Excel® spreadsheet, just type the link into your Internet browser,
starting with the *http://dx.doi.org* prefix.
If you're reading the PDF e-book edition, and your PC is connected to the Internet, simply
click on the link. You'll find StatLinks appearing in more OECD books.

Preface

It is news to no-one that China's influence in the world economy and in international affairs has been growing very rapidly over the past few decades. To some this is a threat, to others a promise, but for most, it is a mystery.

In this new edition of an already remarkable book published by the Development Centre in 1998, Angus Maddison provides a detailed analysis of the development of the Chinese economy over the past millennium and the prospects for the next quarter century. He demonstrates that Chinese per capita income was higher than that of Europe from the tenth to the early fifteenth century and it was the world's biggest economy for several centuries thereafter, before falling into decline. Its extraordinary progress in the reform period since 1978 has been a resurrection, not a miracle and it is likely to resume its normal position as the world's number one economy by 2015. He applies standard OECD measurement techniques to estimate the pace of Chinese progress and finds somewhat slower growth, nearly 8 per cent a year rather than the 9.6 per cent of Chinese Bureau of Statistics. Instead of using the exchange rate to measure the *level* of Chinese performance, which greatly understates China's role in the world economy, Maddison uses purchasing power parity to convert yuan into US dollars and finds that China accounted for 5 per cent of world GDP in 1978, 15 per cent in 2003 and that this is likely to rise to 23 per cent in 2030.

These conclusions are important, as the Development Centre must assess the impact of Chinese growth on the world economy and, in particular on the economies of Africa, Asia and Latin America. This new edition comes precisely when the Centre has published its own related work, richly nourished by the data and conclusions included in this book. We have drawn attention to the need for developing and emerging economies throughout the world to recognise potential weaknesses in their own performance related to growth in China, while reinforcing sectors that can benefit from it. Development Centre research, much of it related to the analyses of Angus Maddison, draws lessons from Chinese experience for other countries. At the same time, we recommend that developing countries should not simply shift their dependence from one part of the world to another but should diversify their economic partners as well as the structures of their economies in order best to benefit from the re-emergence of China.

Angus Maddison has been associated with the OECD for more than half a century. The author of twenty books on economic growth and development, nine of them published by or for the Development Centre, including the monumental 2006 book, *The World Economy*. This new edition of *Chinese Economic Performance in the Long Run* is thus but the latest in his contribution to our ambition to enhance understanding of the rise and decline of economies in order to develop policies to encourage growth and spread prosperity.

Javier Santiso
Acting Director
OECD Development Centre

September 2007

ISBN: 978-92-64-03762-5 © OECD 2007

Author's Prelude to the Second Edition

This study analyses the performance of the Chinese economy over the past millennium and assesses its prospects for the next quarter century. This is done in comparative perspective, analysing China's standing in the ranking of nations and its interaction with the rest of the world economy via technology, trade, investment and geopolitical leverage. There have been six transformations in Chinese development which I managed to quantify:

i) Intensive and extensive growth in the Sung dynasty, 960-1280, when per capita income rose by a third and population almost doubled. In the eighth century three-quarters of the population lived in north China growing dry-land crops of wheat and millet. By the end of the thirteenth, three–quarters of the population lived south of the Yangtse, with a massive development of wet rice cultivation. There was also a significant opening to the world economy, which ended abruptly in the early Ming dynasty (1368–1644). China turned its back on the world economy, when its maritime technology was superior to that of Europe.

ii) After a long period of mediocre progress and episodic setbacks, population rose more than three–fold between 1700 and 1840 (much faster than in Europe and Japan), with no fall in per capita income. This extensive growth was possible because of accelerated use of dry-land crops from the Americas (maize, sweet potatoes, potatoes and peanuts), which could be grown in hilly, sandy and mountainous areas. There was a big expansion of the national territory and closer control of docile tributary states, but China remained isolated from the outside world and repudiated British efforts to establish diplomatic and commercial relations at the end of the eighteenth century.

iii) Because of technological backwardness and weakness of governance, China suffered from internal conflict and collusive foreign intrusions on its territory and sovereignty from 1840 to 1950. The economic results were disastrous. GDP fell from a third to a twentieth of the world total and per capita income fell in a period when it rose three-fold in Japan, four–fold in Europe and eight–fold in the United States.

iv) The Maoist period (1950-78), saw a significant recovery of per capita income, but growth was interrupted by disastrous economic and social experiments, wars with Korea, India and Vietnam and long years of almost complete autarchy.

v) From 1978, China reversed Maoist policies and pursued pragmatic reformism which was successful in sparking off growth much faster than in all other parts of the world economy. There were large, once-for-all, gains in efficiency in agriculture, an explosive expansion of foreign trade and accelerated absorption of foreign technology through large-scale foreign direct investment. The opening to the world economy was a major driving force for economic growth. If Hong Kong is included, China is now the world's biggest exporter.

 ISBN: 978-92-64-03762-5 © OECD 2007

vi)   Catch-up will continue, but the pace of progress will slacken as China gets nearer to the technological frontier. Nevertheless, by 2030, the per capita GDP level should reach that of western Europe and Japan around 1990.

A substantial part of this study is a scrutiny of China's official statistics and a reassessment of performance since 1952, using the same measurement techniques as OECD countries (see Appendices B, C, D and E). The official GDP measure exaggerates growth. For 1978-2003, I found average annual GDP growth of 7.9 per cent compared with the official 9.6 per cent. On the other hand, the size of the Chinese economy is greatly understated, if exchange rates are used to compare performance. With a purchasing power parity converter, China's GDP in 2003 was 74 per cent of that in the United States and more than twice as big as Japan. By 2015, on rather conservative assumptions, China should have resumed its position as the number one economy. By 2030, it will represent 23 per cent of the world economy, compared with less than 5 per cent in 1978.

Except for Appendix A, this edition has been revised and updated and Chapter 4 is completely new. I am indebted to Professor Harry X. Wu for revision of Appendix B and for help in revising Appendix C.

Angus Maddison

September 2007

Summary and Conclusions

This study is mainly concerned with Chinese economic policy and performance in the second half of the twentieth century in which there was major institutional change and the trajectory of growth accelerated sharply. China now plays a much bigger role in the world economy and its importance is likely to increase further. I have tried to assess why and how this acceleration occurred and to throw light on future potential. I have also made a considerable effort to recast the estimates of Chinese GDP growth to make them conform to international norms.

Reasons for Taking a Long View

In order to understand contemporary China it is useful to take a long comparative perspective. In many respects China is exceptional. It is and has been a larger political unit than any other. Already in the tenth century, it was the world's leading economy in terms of per capita income and this leadership lasted until the fifteenth century. It outperformed Europe in levels of technology, the intensity with which it used its natural resources and its capacity for administering a huge territorial empire. In the following three centuries, Europe gradually overtook China in real income, technological and scientific capacity. In the nineteenth and first half of the twentieth century, China's performance actually declined in a world where economic progress greatly accelerated.

A comparative analysis of Chinese performance can provide new perspectives on the nature and causes of economic growth. It can help illuminate developments in the West as well as in China. In the past, analysis of economic progress and its determinants has had a heavy Eurocentric emphasis. Assessment of the Chinese historical record has been highly Sinocentric. A more integrated view can illuminate both exceptionalism and normality and provide a better understanding of the reasons for the rise and decline of nations.

Adoption of more distant horizons can clarify causal processes. Growth analysis has concentrated on the past two centuries of capitalist development in which rapid technical change, structural transformation and rising per capita incomes were the norm. Earlier situations where per capita income was fairly static are usually neglected because it is assumed there was no technical change. But extensive growth — maintaining income levels whilst accommodating substantial rises in population — may also require major changes in the organisation of production. Technological progress needs to be interpreted broadly. It should not be restricted to advances in machinofacture, but should encompass innovations in administration, organisation and agricultural practice.

A long view can also help understand China's contemporary policies and institutions. Echoes from the past are still important.

China was a pioneer in bureaucratic modes of governance. In the tenth century, it was already recruiting professionally trained public servants on a meritocratic basis. The bureaucracy was the main instrument for imposing social and political order in a unitary state over a huge area.

ISBN: 978-92-64-03762-5 © OECD 2007

The economic impact of the bureaucracy was very positive for agriculture. It was the key sector from which they could squeeze a surplus in the form of taxes and compulsory levies. They nurtured it with hydraulic works. Thanks to the precocious development of printing they were able to diffuse best practice techniques by widespread distribution of illustrated agricultural handbooks. They settled farmers in promising new regions. They developed a public granary system to mitigate famines. They fostered innovation by introducing early ripening seeds which eventually permitted double or triple cropping. They promoted the introduction of new crops — tea in the T'ang dynasty, cotton in the Sung, sorghum in the Yuan, and new world crops such as maize, potatoes, sweet potatoes, peanuts and tobacco in the Ming.

Agricultural practice compensated for land shortage by intensive use of labour, irrigation and natural fertilisers. Land was under continuous cultivation, without fallow. The need for fodder crops and grazing land was minimal. Livestock was concentrated on scavengers (pigs and poultry). Beef, milk and wool consumption were rare. The protein supply was augmented by widespread practice of small–scale aquaculture.

Agriculture operated in an institutional order, which was efficient in its allocation of resources and was able to respond to population pressure by raising land productivity. Landlords were largely non–managerial rentiers. Production and managerial decisions were made by tenants and peasant proprietors who could buy and sell land freely and sell their products in local markets.

Chinese Performance from the Ninth to the Eighteenth Century

Between the ninth and the thirteenth centuries there was a major shift in the centre of gravity of the Chinese economy. In the eighth century three–quarters of the population lived in North China, where the main crops were wheat and millet. By the end of the thirteenth, three–quarters of the population lived and produced rice south of the Yangtse river. This had been a swampy lightly–settled area, but with irrigation and early ripening seeds, it provided an ideal opportunity for massive development of rice cultivation.

Higher land productivity permitted denser settlement, reduced the cost of transport, raised the proportion of farm output which could be marketed and released labour for expanded handicraft production, particularly the spinning and weaving of cotton, which provided more comfortable, more easily washable and healthier clothing.

While there is widespread agreement that this change in the locus of production and product–mix increased Chinese living standards, there has hitherto been no quantification of how big a rise occurred. My assessment is that it was relatively modest — a rise in per capita income of about a third. The rise in income was accompanied by a more intensive use of labour, so labour productivity did not rise as much as per capita income.

China's economic advance in the Sung dynasty relied heavily on exploitation of once–for–all opportunities for switching to intensive rice agriculture and there is little convincing evidence for believing that China was on the brink of developing a mechanised industry.

From the thirteenth to the eighteenth century, China was able to accommodate a four–fold increase in population whilst maintaining the average level of per capita income more or less stable over the long run. However, the pace of growth was far from smooth. In the fourteenth and seventeenth centuries, population dropped by more than 30 million. These crises were due largely to devastation that accompanied changes in regime and to epidemic disease (bubonic plague and smallpox). In the eighteenth century the demographic expansion was particularly large. It was in this century that China's extensive growth was most impressive.

ISBN: 978-92-64-03762-5 © OECD 2007

Institutional Differences between Europe and China

Outside agriculture, China's bureaucratic system hindered the emergence of an independent commercial and industrial bourgeoisie on the European pattern. The bureaucracy and gentry of imperial China were quintessential rent–seekers. Their legal and customary privileges defined their status, lifestyle and attitudes. They were the group that dominated urban life. They had a strong regulatory bias. Entrepreneurial activity was insecure in a framework where legal protection for private activity was exiguous. Any activity which promised to be lucrative was subject to bureaucratic squeeze. Larger undertakings were limited to state or publicly licensed monopolies. China's merchants, bankers and traders did not have the city charters and legal protection which merchants had in European cities. International trade and intellectual contacts were severely restricted. This self–imposed isolation was also a barrier to growth.

Between the fifteenth and eighteenth centuries economic leadership passed from China to Western Europe. This was not due to specially unfavourable conditions in China but to Western exceptionalism. There were several reasons why Europe was better placed to promote the emergence of modern capitalism.

The most fundamental was the recognition of human capacity to transform the forces of nature by rational investigation and experiment. Thanks to the Renaissance and the Enlightenment, Western elites gradually abandoned superstition, magic and submission to religious authority. The Western scientific tradition that underlies the modern approach to technical change and innovation had clearly emerged by the seventeenth century and begun to impregnate the educational system. China's education system was steeped in the ancient classics and bureaucratic orthodoxy. It was not able to develop the fundamental bases of modern science.

Europe had a system of nation–states in close propinquity. They were outward looking, had significant trading relations and relatively easy intellectual interchange. This stimulated competition and innovation.

The Adverse Impact of Internal Disorder and Imperialist Intrusions

Between 1820 and 1952, the world economy made enormous progress by any previous yardstick. World product rose more than eight–fold and world per capita income three–fold. US per capita income rose nearly nine-fold, European income four–fold and Japanese more than three–fold. In other Asian countries except Japan, economic progress was very modest but in China per capita product actually fell. China's share of world GDP fell from a third to one twentieth. Its real per capita income fell from 90 per cent to less than a quarter of the world average. Most Asian countries had problems similar to those of China, i.e. indigenous institutions which hindered modernisation and foreign colonial intrusion. But these problems were worse in China and help to explain why its performance was exceptionally disappointing.

China was plagued by internal disorder which took a heavy toll on population and economic welfare. The Taiping rebellion (1850–64) affected more than half of China's provinces and did extensive damage to its richest areas. There were Muslim rebellions in Shensi, Kansu and Sinkiang. In the Republican era there were three decades of civil war.

The colonial intrusions led to cession of extraterritorial rights and privileges to nineteen foreign powers in a welter of colonial enclaves. There were three wars with Japan and two with France and the United Kingdom. The Boxer rebellion involved a simultaneous armed struggle with all the foreign powers. Russia took 10 per cent of Chinese territory in the 1850s in what is now Eastern Siberia and in the first years of the Chinese republic, it helped detach Outer Mongolia. After all these foreign wars, the victorious powers added to China's humiliation by exacting large financial indemnities.

 ISBN: 978-92-64-03762-5 © OECD 2007

The Imperial regime and the Kuomintang were both incapable of creative response to these problems. They did not react positively or effectively to the Western technical challenge. The Ch'ing authorities were incapable of reactive nationalism because they themselves were Manchus not Chinese. After the imperial collapse the warlord regimes pursued regional rather than national objectives. The KMT was not effective in asserting China's national interests. It achieved very little in regaining Chinese territorial integrity and did not respond effectively to Japanese aggression. The Ch'ing and the KMT were fiscally weak and failed to mobilise resources for effective defence and development.

The Maoist Transformation and its Impact

The establishment of the People's Republic in 1949 marked a sharp break with the past. It provided a new mode of governance, a new kind of elite and a marked improvement on past economic performance. It was the Chinese equivalent to the 1868 Meiji revolution in Japan. However, China set out to create a socialist command economy inspired in substantial degree by the Soviet model, whereas Japan embraced a dirigiste variant of capitalist institutions. Both countries executed their development strategy without intending to provide any role for foreign capitalist interests.

The new Chinese regime was successful in the areas in which the Ch'ing and the KMT had failed. It was able to impose internal order, its ideology was a brand of reactive nationalism and it was able to mobilise resources for defence and development. The commitment to communist ideology and techniques of governance was strongly influenced by China's peculiar history. The colonial intrusion in China had involved all the major capitalist countries and the failure to end it after the Treaty of Versailles in 1919 gave an anti–Western bias to Chinese nationalism. In the 1920s the USSR provided military and organisational support to the KMT and in the aftermath of the Second World War helped the Communist forces to take military and political control in Manchuria. The outbreak of the Korean war in 1950 created an unusual degree of international economic and political isolation for China and meant that the USSR was its only source of technical and financial assistance.

Although the ideological commitment to a socialist economy and rejection of capitalism was very strong in China, the alliance with the USSR was in substantial degree opportunistic. Russia had been one of the major colonial intruders in the past. The USSR had at times supported the KMT against the interests of the Chinese communist party. After the Second World War it treated East European countries as puppet states. The Chinese situation was very different. The new government was not created as a Soviet dependency. It had developed substantial intellectual and political autonomy in two decades of armed struggle.

The new regime had three major objectives: a) to change the sociopolitical order; b) to accelerate economic growth; c) to improve China's geopolitical standing and restore its national dignity.

There have been two very distinct phases of policy and performance since the creation of the People's Republic. The first of these, the Maoist phase lasted until 1978 and the Reform period from 1978 onwards.

From 1952 to 1978 there was a major acceleration in the pace of growth, with GDP rising three–fold and per capita income by 80 per cent. The economic structure was transformed. The industrial share of GDP rose from 8 to 30 per cent. The acceleration in performance was due to a massive increase in inputs of physical and human capital. The capital stock grew by 7.7 per cent a year, labour input rose faster than population. Human capital was improved by significant advances in education and health. However, the productivity picture was dismal. This was a boom period in many parts of the world economy, particularly in Europe and Japan. In spite of its growth acceleration, China grew somewhat less than the world economy as a whole (per capita growth was 2.3 per cent a year compared with a world average of 2.6 per cent). There were several reasons for these disappointing results.

Economic development was interrupted by major political upheavals. There were changes in property rights, the Korean war, the disruption caused by the Sino–Soviet split, the self–inflicted wounds of the Great Leap Forward and the Cultural Revolution. All these had adverse effects on efficiency and productivity by making the growth path unstable.

Production units were too large. This was particularly evident in agriculture. The 130 million family farms of 1957 were transformed into 26 000 people's communes in 1958 with an average size of 6 700 workers. This was a disastrous move. Within three years, farm management reverted to 6 million production teams with an average size of 30 workers. In industry and services there was also an overemphasis on bigness. By 1978 the average industrial firm in China had eleven times as many workers as in Japan.

China was isolated from the booming world economy. Its share of world trade fell and it was cut off from foreign investment. Resources were allocated by government directives and regulation. Market forces played a negligible role. Hence there were inefficiencies in the production process (as witnessed by the massive investment in inventories) and neglect of consumer welfare.

In the reform period from 1978 onwards major changes in policy were successful in generating substantially higher growth in per capita income. There was a rapid increase in the capital stock, but the major reason for the improvement was better use of resources and substantial growth of total factor productivity.

Reformist Policies since 1978 Produced Three Decades of Dynamic Growth

There were several forces which contributed to the greater efficiency and faster productivity growth after 1978.

Peasants regained control and management of their land. The average production unit became the farm household employing 1.4 persons on less than half a hectare. There were better prices for farmers and greater access to markets. The result was a big improvement in incentives and productivity.

There was a huge expansion of small–scale industry, particularly in rural areas. The average size of state enterprise did not change, but in the non-state sector it fell from an average of 112 to 8 employees per firm by 1995. Productivity growth was much faster in the non–state sector, which had lower labour costs, virtually no social charges, much smaller and more efficient use of capital.

China made massive strides to integrate into the world economy. The state monopoly of foreign trade and the policy of autarkic self–reliance were abandoned after 1978. Foreign trade decisions were decentralised. Between 1980 and 1997 there was a five–fold devaluation of the yuan. Special enterprise zones were created as free trade areas. In response to the greater role for market forces, competition emerged, resource allocation was improved and consumer satisfaction increased. The volume of exports rose by 15 per cent a year from 1978 to 2006 and China's share of world exports rose from 0.8 to 8 per cent. If Hong Kong exports are included, China was the world's biggest exporter ($1 286 billion, 10.7 per cent of the total) in 2006, Germany was second with $1 126 billion, the United States third with $1 036 billion, Japan fourth with $650 billion and Russia seventh with $305 billion. Its integration in the world economy has been furthered by reduction of its own trade barriers and the greater security of its access to foreign markets thanks to its membership in the World Trade Organization.

In 1978 China had no foreign debt and received virtually no foreign investment. The annual inflow of direct foreign investment rose slowly to $3.5 billion in 1990, but by 2005. it had risen to $60 billion. The total inflow from 1979 to 2005 was more than $620 billion. Chinese foreign borrowing has been relatively modest, a total of $147 billion between 1979 and 2005, most of it long or medium term. The debt structure presents negligible exposure to sudden changes in foreign confidence, the

ISBN: 978-92-64-03762-5 © OECD 2007

Peoples' Republic has never been in arrears on foreign debt and had accumulated huge foreign exchange reserves of $1.2 trillion early in 2007. It has become a significant investor and supplier of foreign aid to countries which supply it with oil and raw materials. China's opening to the world economy has been remarkably trouble free by comparison with the situation in some other Asian and Latin American countries and the successor states of the USSR.

As a consequence of successful policy in the reform period, Chinese per capita income rose by 6.6 per cent a year from 1978 to 2003, faster than any other Asian country, very much better than the 1.8 per cent a year in western Europe and the United States and four times as fast as the world average. Per capita GDP rose from 22 to 74 per cent of the world level. Its share of world GDP rose from 5 to 15 per cent and it became the world's second biggest economy, after the United States. The big question is how long this catch–up process can last and how far it can go?

The Outlook for the Next Quarter Century

China is still a relatively poor country. In 2003 its per capita income was only 17 per cent of that in the United States, 23 per cent of that in Japan, 28 per cent of that in Taiwan and 31 per cent of that in Korea. Countries in this situation of relative backwardness and distance from the technological frontier have a capacity for fast growth if they mobilise and allocate physical and human capital effectively, adapt foreign technology to their factor proportions and utilise the opportunities for specialisation which come from integration into the world economy. China demonstrated a capacity to do this in the reform period and there is no good reason to suppose that this capacity will evaporate.

It is likely that the catch-up process will continue in the next quarter century, but it would be unrealistic to assume that the future growth trajectory will be as fast as in 1978-2003. In that period there were large, once-for-all, gains in efficiency of resource allocation in agriculture, an explosive expansion of foreign trade and accelerated absorption of foreign technology through large-scale foreign direct investment. The pace of Chinese progress will slacken as it gets nearer to the technological frontier. I have assumed that per capita income will grow at an average rate of 4.5 per cent a year between 2003 and 2030, but that the rate of advance will taper off over the period. Specifically, I assume a rate of 5.6 per cent a year to 2010, 4.6 per cent between 2010 and 2020 and a little more than 3.6 per cent a year from 2020 to 2030. By then, in our scenario, it will have reached the same per capita level as western Europe and Japan around 1990, when their catch-up process had ceased. As it approaches this level, technical advance will be more costly as imitation is replaced by innovation. However, by 2030 the technical frontier will have moved forward, so there will still be some scope for catch-up thereafter.

With such a performance, China should overtake the United States as the world's biggest economy before 2015 and by 2030 account for about a quarter of world GDP. It would have a per capita income like that of western Europe in 1990. Its per capita income would be only one third of that in the United States, but its role in the world economy and its geopolitical leverage would certainly be much greater.

The Policy Problems of Rapid Growth are Changing

In the projections I made in 1998, I cited three major problems, which might impede China's prospects of high economic growth. One was the difficulty in reducing the role of inefficient state enterprises. A large proportion were making substantial losses. They were kept in operation by government subsidies and failure to service loans which the state banks were constrained to give them.

Their importance has fallen very significantly. In 1993, state employment in manufacturing was more than 35 million; by 2005 it was less than 6 million. In the economy as a whole, state employment fell from 19 to 9 per cent of the occupied population. Hence this problem is no longer likely to be a significant obstacle to rapid economic growth.

A related problem was the weakness of the financial system. In the reform period there was an explosive growth of household savings and rapid monetisation of the economy. Savings were captured by the state banking system and the government had large seigniorage gains from the monetisation process. These new funds offset the disappearance of the operational surplus of state enterprise and the decline in tax revenue.

Although these developments were helpful to the authorities in maintaining financial stability, there were clear dangers in a banking system which operated with a large proportion of non-performing assets due to diversion of private saving to prop up state enterprises which by any normal standard would be regarded as bankrupt. Here again there has been considerable progress. There have been major improvements in the solvability and efficiency of the banking system. Most of the bad debts have been written off and China has attracted foreign participation in state banks by the sale of shares on the Hong Kong and Shanghai stock markets. In the two years since June 2005, more than $60 billion was raised this way and some foreign banks have been allowed to operate in China.

The third related problem was the weak fiscal position of central government. Total government revenue fell from 31 per cent of GDP in 1978 to 10 per cent in 1995. The tax base was seriously eroded by the large range of tax concessions granted by provincial and local governments, as well as by the dramatic fall in revenue from state enterprise. Tax revenue rose to 17 per cent of GDP by 2005, but needs to rise further to extend social protection and strengthen health and education facilities. These social benefits have been eroded by the decline in benefits formerly provided by state enterprises.

Energy supply and the Environment: The problem of energy supply and the environment has emerged as a significant new challenge to China's future development. Electricity supply rose ten–fold between 1978 and 2005 and its availability at rather low prices transformed living conditions in many urban households. Car ownership has also risen and is likely to become the most dynamic element in private consumption. In 2006 there were about 19 million passenger cars in circulation, (one for every 70 persons). This compared with 140 million and one for every 2 persons in the United States. Judging by the average west European relationship of car ownership to per capita income, it seems likely there will be 300 million passenger cars in China (one for every 5 persons) in 2030.

There has been a surprisingly large improvement in the efficiency with which energy is used. In 1973, 0.64 tons of oil equivalent were used per thousand dollars of GDP, by 2003, this had fallen to 0.22 tons. The International Energy Agency (IEA) projects a further fall to 0.11 tons in 2030 in a scenario which takes account of energy efficiency policies the government can reasonably be expected to adopt. Energy efficiency was better in China than in the United States in 2003 and the IEA expects this to be true in 2030.

However, the environmental impact of energy use in China is particularly adverse because its dependence on coal is unusually large and carbon emissions are proportionately much bigger from coal than those from oil or gas. In 2003, 60 per cent of energy consumption came from coal, compared to 23 per cent in the United States, 17 per cent in Russia and 5 per cent in France. Eighty per cent of its electricity is generated by coal powered plants. This means that the ratio of carbon emissions to energy consumption is higher in China than in most countries. In the IEA "A" scenario, China is expected to emit 0.8 tons of carbon per ton of energy used in 2030, compared with 0.63 in the United States and a world average of 0.60.

ISBN: 978-92-64-03762-5 © OECD 2007

Chinese coal is particularly dirty, sulfur dioxide and sooty particles released by coal combustion have polluted the air in its major cities and created acid rain which falls on 30 per cent of its land mass. There are more than 20 000 coal mines and nearly six million miners with low productivity and dangerous working conditions. Several thousand are killed every year in mining accidents. In north China there are some coal seams near the surface which burn continuously in unstoppable fires. These environmental problems are likely to be bigger in China than in the rest of the world, as it is more difficult and more costly to reduce the proportionate role of coal.

The other major problems facing China are social rather than economic.

The Legal System and Private Property Rights: China has made giant strides in moving towards a market economy and its legal system allows private enterprise to flourish. Property rights have recently been strengthened, but are a good deal weaker and more ambiguous than they would be in a capitalist economy. Land is still state or "collective" property. Peasants can get 30–year leases for their farms and urban householders can get 70–year leases on their houses; thereafter, their property reverts to the state. It is difficult to sell such properties or use them as collateral for loans. Paradoxically for a socialist country, property rights are weaker for ordinary citizens than they are for domestic or foreign capitalists. Urban developers find it easier than would be the case in a capitalist country to expropriate land of peasants or poor urban residents and demolish their homes without adequate compensation. Influential party officials are able to enrich themselves by conniving in such transactions. These problems have led to increased public protests and punishment of party officials for corruption. The equity and efficiency of the economy would benefit considerably if property rights were strengthened and the judiciary were less subject to official pressure.

Regional and Urban Rural Inequality: Regional inequality is extreme. There is a ten-to-one spread of average per capita income between persons living in China's 31 administrative regions and the gap has hardly changed since 1978. Shanghai has always been top and Guizhou bottom. The divergence could be narrowed by major investment in transport and other infrastructure, improved education opportunity in the low income areas, removal of barriers to migration between different areas and elimination of the tax advantages enjoyed by special enterprise zones in eastern China. However, the mitigation of inter-regional income divergence is likely to be a slow process.

Rural-urban inequality is bigger than in other Asian countries. The gap is biggest in the western provinces and lowest in the east. An important reason is the household registration system (*hukou*) established in the Maoist period to control population movement. It is reinforced by legislation to penalise immigrant workers who seek unregistered employment in urban areas. Despite some easing in the system, they are still denied public services such as health and education, they have difficulty in getting housing and employers who hire them may suffer financial penalties. Hence they are in a weak bargaining position and get low wages for long hours. Their wages are often in arrears and sometimes fail to be paid. These unregistered households are about a sixth of the urban population and their average income is 60 per cent lower than that of registered urban households. It is clear that this discriminatory registration system is a major source of social discontent which is in need of remedy. Removal of the system would certainly increase the urban inflow, but this is in any case inevitable in the long term.

ISBN: 978-92-64-03762-5 © OECD 2007

Chapter 1

Intensive and Extensive Growth in Imperial China

Analysis of economic growth generally concentrates on the nineteenth and twentieth centuries in which the pace of economic progress was unprecedented. Earlier performance has received much less attention because economic advance was at best very slow, quantification more difficult or non–existent.

However, there is a strong case for considering distant horizons in the case of China. From the eighth to the thirteenth century there was a major transformation of its economy, with a switch in the centre of gravity to the South. In the eighth century three–quarters of the population lived in north China, where the main crops were wheat and millet. By the end of the thirteenth, three–quarters of the population lived and produced rice below the Yangtse. This had been a swampy, lightly settled area, but with irrigation and early ripening seeds, it provided an ideal opportunity for massive development of rice cultivation.

Higher land productivity permitted denser settlement, reduced the cost of transport, raised the proportion of farm output which could be marketed, released labour for expanded handicraft production, particularly the spinning and weaving of cotton, which provided more comfortable, more easily washable and healthier clothing. There is widespread agreement that this change in the locus of production and product mix increased Chinese living standards. It also permitted a doubling of population.

China's economic advance in the Sung dynasty relied heavily on exploitation of once–for–all opportunities for switching to intensive rice agriculture. Some analysts have exaggerated the breadth of advance, believing that China was on the brink of developing a mechanised industry, but there is little convincing evidence of this.

From the thirteenth to the eighteenth century, the available evidence for agriculture and for the relative size of the urban population suggests that Chinese per capita income did not improve significantly. However, China was able to accommodate a four–fold increase in population whilst maintaining average per capita income more or less stable over the long run. The pace of growth was far from smooth. In the fourteenth and seventeenth centuries, population dropped by more than 30 million. These crises were due largely to devastation that accompanied changes in regime and to epidemic disease (bubonic plague and smallpox). In the eighteenth century the demographic expansion was particularly large. It was in this century that traditional China's capacity for extensive growth was most clearly demonstrated.

This chapter examines the evidence for believing that the Sung period was one of intensive growth and that the following five centuries were, with some interruptions, characterised by extensive growth. The section on agriculture illustrates the processes of technical adaptation which were necessary to sustain extensive growth.

The first section examines the system of governance in Imperial China and the nature of the bureaucracy which fostered advance in agriculture, but put a brake on progress in other parts of the economy, maintaining an institutional framework which inhibited the growth of capitalist enterprise and restricted opportunities for international trade and exchange of ideas. The second section deals in more detail with the evidence of intensive growth in the Sung. The third analyses the institutional and technical characteristics of Chinese agriculture and its capacity to accommodate big increases in population. The last two sections cover non–farm activity of rural households and performance in the urban sector.

 ISBN: 978-92-64-037625 © OECD 2007

Table 1.1. **Chinese Imperial Dynasties and Capital Cities**

Dates	Dynasty	Capital
221–206 BC	Ch'in	Hsien–yang
206 BC – 8 AD, 23–220 AD	early Han, and later Han	Ch'ang–an/Loyang
220–589 Empire disintegrated		
589–617	Sui	Ch'ang–an
618–906	T'ang	Ch'ang–an
906–960 Empire disintegrated		
960–1127	Sung	K'ai–feng
1127–1234	Jurchen (Chin) in North	Peking
1234–1279	Mongol (Yüan) in North	Karakorum
1127–1279	Southern Sung	Hangchow
1279–1368	Yüan (Mongol)	Peking
1368–1644	Ming	Nanking/Peking
1644–1911	Ch'ing (Manchu)	Peking

Source: Reischauer and Fairbank (1958), Hucker (1985), and *Cambridge History of China*.

http://dx.doi.org/10.1787/087333476804

Table 1.2. **Rough Comparative Estimates of the Population of China, Europe, India, Japan and World, 1–2003 AD**
(million)

	1	1000	1300	1500	1700	1820	2003
China	60	59	100	103	138	381	1 288
Europe[a]	30	32	52	71	100	170	516
India[b]	75	75	88	110	165	209	1 344
Japan	3	7.5	10.5	15.4	27	31	127
World	226	267	372	438	603	1 042	6 279

a) excluding Turkey and former USSR; b) India + Bangladesh + Pakistan.

Source: See Maddison website: www.ggdc.net/Maddison

http://dx.doi.org/10.1787/086071252700

Bureaucratic Governance and its Economic Consequences

For the last thirteen centuries of the Empire, Chinese rulers entrusted the administration of the country to a powerful bureaucracy. This educated elite, schooled in the Confucian classics, was the main instrument for imposing social and political order in a unitary state with twice the territory of Europe.

In the West, recruitment of professionally trained public servants on a meritocratic basis was initiated by Napoleon, more than a millennium later, but European bureaucrats have never had the social status and power of the Chinese literati. Within each country power was fragmented between a much greater variety of countervailing forces.

From the earliest days, Chinese Emperors aspired to enlist meritorious officials rather than territorial vassals. In the Han dynasty, they were recruited on a recommendatory basis, as a supplement to military and aristocratic minions. Thereafter there was a relapse into predominantly feudal regimes in a multistate polity which lasted for nearly 370 years. Bureaucratic enrolment by examination was initiated at the beginning of the seventh century. The role of bureaucracy expanded under the T'ang when the political power of the hereditary aristocracy was gradually broken (Ho, 1962, p. 259). Under the Sung, procedures for examination were improved to ensure anonymity of candidates. In the examinations the names of candidates were no longer revealed to examiners and clerks copied the responses to avoid recognition of the calligraphy. The meritocratic basis of selection was widened by improved provision for public education. The number of graduates grew substantially. Criteria for recruitment, advancement and evaluation were clarified. All important officials were recruited on the basis of academic performance.

Bureaucratic control was temporarily interrupted by the Mongol military occupation in the thirteenth century, but they came to recognise the usefulness of a bureaucratic mechanism for tax collection and restored civil service recruitment in 1315.

After the collapse of Mongol rule in 1368, a meritocratic bureaucracy again became the main instrument of imperial power. The Ming and Ch'ing kept titled nobility in check, without territorial fiefs, independent military or political jurisdictions. At a very early stage, the primogeniture system of inheritance was abolished. The aristocracy became a costly fossil, with its income derived mainly from imperial sinecures, dropping in rank with each successive generation. Landed aristocracy had already disappeared as a significant political force in the course of the Sung dynasty. Eunuchs and bondservants within the Imperial household influenced policies but posed no real threat to bureaucratic control.

The bureaucratic elite was always small in relation to the size of the country. In the sixteenth century and the first half of the seventeenth there were ten to fifteen thousand officials (Gernet, 1982, p. 393) for the whole of the empire. They staffed the Grand Council and Secretariat, the six ministries and the specialised departments in Peking and serviced the provincial, prefectural and district administration. At the lowest level (the district — *hsien*), the magistrate was tax collector, judge, record keeper, administrator of public works and regularly present at ceremonial observances, sacrifices to Heaven, other supernatural forces and local temple gods. There was necessarily a good deal of local discretion because of the size of the country. From Canton to Peking, the normal courrier service (by foot) took 56 days each way, urgent mail 18 days and super urgent mail 9 or 10 days each way. At the district level the magistrate operated his headquarters (*yamen*) with a staff of locally recruited clerks, policemen, jailers and guards. He levied taxes and maintained law and order for a district population rising from about 80 000 in the Sung to 300 000 in the Ch'ing dynasty. Below the district level, control was exercised by derogation and delegation. The local gentry played an important role in settling disputes and acting as informal agents of officialdom. Neighbourhood associations were collectively responsible for local policing and tax collection. Selected commoner household heads took their turn on a rotating basis as unpaid conscript administrators to ensure that taxes were paid.

The bureaucracy were a social elite. They and their families were exempt from many types of levies, punishments and duties to which commoners were exposed. They were entitled to wear robes, buttons, belts and other sartorial signs of elevated status. These perquisites were so attractive that vast numbers of aspirants who failed to become officials nevertheless obtained degrees. Many privileges of office holders were also accorded to these degree holders and their families. They were the second layer of the social elite (often referred to as the "gentry"). Degree holders derived substantial income from landownership, mercantile activities and teaching. They enjoyed favourable tax treatment, earned extra income by acting as agents for commoners in their dealings with office holders. Thus the competitive recruitment process for officials had two important side effects: *a)* it determined the nature and content of education; *b)* it greatly augmented the prestige attached to credentials and had a profound influence on social attitudes and social structure. Amongst the property–owning group, only the credentialled gentry had easy access to office holders.

There was no significant church hierarchy or doctrine to resist or counterbalance bureaucratic power after the important Buddhist properties were seized in the ninth century. There was continued toleration of a wide variety of religious practice, including Buddhism, Taoism, Islam in the central Asian borderlands, Lamaistic Buddhism in Tibet and Mongolia. But the official ideology was essentially secular — a set of pragmatic prescriptions for behaviour in this world, a Confucian unconcern with problems of immortality, the soul, the afterlife or God. It stressed virtue, decorum, social discipline and gentlemanly polish. It had no sacred law, no concept of sin or salvation, no social division into castes. It inculcated belief in providential harmony, promoted orthodoxy and obedience to the state. It attached little importance to personal liberty or salvation. It had no distinctive priesthood. It was a state cult whose local temples were maintained and whose rituals were carried out by the bureaucracy with an accommodatory rather than adversarial attitude towards other systems of belief.

ISBN: 978-92-64-037625 © OECD 2007

There were virtually no lawyers or litigation in China and very limited possibilities for challenging bureaucratic decisions. Citizens were supposedly protected by the Confucian virtue of the bureaucracy. To discourage corruption, officials could not be appointed to positions in their region of origin and were regularly rotated to avoid too great an identification with local interests.

Except in times of dynastic crisis, the military were usually subordinate to the civilian authorities. In the Ming and Ch'ing most soldiers came from hereditary military families. The qualifying examinations for military officials were less demanding and held in lower regard than the credentials of civil officials. The ministers in charge of the military were usually civilians.

The urban bourgeoisie (i.e. merchants, bankers, retailers, commodity brokers and shippers, entrepreneurs in industries such as textiles, clothing or food processing) were deferential to the bureaucracy and gentry and dependent on their good will. Although they had guilds and other associations to foster their interests, they did not have the city charters and legal protection which merchants had in European cities from the middle ages onwards (see Cooke Johnson, 1995 for an account of merchant activity in Shanghai from the eleventh to the nineteenth century).

Bureaucrats needed a lengthy literary education to ensure that the flow of paperwork was elegant in expression and calligraphically pleasing. Candidates for bureaucratic credentials had to learn the Confucian classics by heart. In Legge (1960) these classics with their English translation and exegetical notes take up nearly 2 800 large pages, or a total of more than 430 000 characters to be remembered (Miyazaki, 1976, p. 16). The main emphasis was on texts which were already 1 500 years old in the Sung dynasty. Thus the power of tradition and orthodoxy was reinforced and the intellectual authority of the official elite was difficult to challenge.

The institutions of such a far–flung bureaucracy reporting to and controlled by the central authority would not have been possible without the precocious development of paper and printing. Paper was officially adopted by the court early in the second century as a replacement for silk and bamboo (though the first Chinese paper appears to have been available 400 years earlier). The first complete printed book was a Buddhist Sutra of 868 and printing became fully developed in the Sung dynasty. This facilitated the functioning of the bureaucracy, greatly increased the reading matter available in cheap form to the education process and helped to diffuse technical know–how. Editions of the Confucian classics, encyclopedias, dictionaries, histories, medical and pharmaceutical books, works on farming and arithmetic were officially sponsored. Private firms and booksellers also promoted the spread of knowledge (Tsien, 1985).

The bureaucratic system was the major force maintaining China as a unitary state. The bureaucracy was a docile instrument of the Emperor (as long as he did not seriously breach the mandate of heaven), but exercised autocratic power over the population, with no challenge from a landed aristocracy, an established church, a judiciary, dissident intellectuals, the military or the urban bourgeoisie. They used a written language common to all of China and the official Confucian ideology was deeply ingrained in the education system. This system was relatively efficient and cheap to operate compared with the multilayered structure of governance in pre–modern Europe and Japan. It facilitated central control by maintaining an efficient communications network and flow of information which enabled the imperial power to monitor and react to events. It maintained order without massive use of military force. It created the logistics (the Grand Canal) for feeding a large imperial capital on the edge of the Empire. It raised and remitted taxes to maintain a lavish imperial household and the military establishment. It maintained the Great Wall as a defensive glacis against barbarian invaders. Maintenance of a single economic area did not ensure a single national market for goods because of high transport costs, but it had an important impact in facilitating the transmission of best–practice technology. New techniques which the bureaucracy sponsored or favoured could be readily spread by use of printed matter. Thus the gap between best–practice and average practice was probably narrower than it was in the polycentric state system of Europe.

The economic impact of bureaucracy was generally very positive in agriculture. Like eighteenth century French physiocrats, the Emperor and bureaucracy thought of it as the key sector from which they could "squeeze" a surplus in the form of taxes and compulsory levies. They nurtured agriculture through hydraulic works. They helped develop and diffuse new seeds and crops by technical advice. They settled farmers in promising new regions. They developed a public granary system to ensure imperial food supplies and mitigate famines. They commissioned and distributed agricultural handbooks, calendars etc.

Outside agriculture, the bureaucratic system had negative effects. The bureaucracy and gentry were quintessential rent–seekers. Their legal and customary privileges defined their status, lifestyle and attitudes. They were the group which dominated urban life. They prevented the emergence of an independent commercial and industrial bourgeoisie on the European pattern. Entrepreneurial activity was insecure in a framework where legal protection for private activity was exiguous. Any activity that promised to be lucrative was subject to bureaucratic squeeze. Larger undertakings were limited to the state or to publicly licensed monopolies. Potentially profitable activity in opening up world trade by exploiting China's sophisticated shipbuilding and navigational knowledge was simply forbidden.

The other feature of this bureaucratic civilisation, which had long–term repercussions on economic development, was the official Confucian ideology and education system. By comparison with the situation in Europe in the middle ages, its pragmatic bias gave it the advantage. The official orthodoxy was probably most benign during the Sung dynasty. Educational opportunity was widened by state schools which provided a broader curriculum than the bureaucratic academies in later dynasties. Taoism and Buddhism were in decline. Neo–Confucian thought was re–invigorated and at that time was free of the dogmatism it displayed in later centuries (see Kracke, 1953; Miyazaki, 1976). Needham (1969) argued that the Chinese bureaucracy was an enlightened despotism, more rational than European Christendom; more meritocratic in its concentration of the best minds in situations of power and hence more favourable to the progress of "natural knowledge" than the European system of military aristocratic power. After the European Renaissance and the development of Galileian and Newtonian science, the balance of advantage changed. Needham argues that China was never able "to develop the fundamental bases of modern science, such as the application of mathematical hypotheses to Nature, the full understanding and use of the experimental method, the distinction between primary and secondary qualities and the systematic accumulation of openly published scientific data" (Needham, 1981, p. 9). However, he adds that the European breakthrough was due to "special social, intellectual and economic conditions prevailing there at the Renaissance and can never be explained by any deficiencies either of the Chinese mind or of the Chinese intellectual and philosophical tradition".

China failed to react adequately to the Western challenge until the middle of the twentieth century, mainly because the ideology, mindset and education system of the bureaucracy promoted an ethnocentric outlook, which was indifferent to developments outside China. There were Jesuit scholars in Peking for nearly two centuries; some of them like Ricci, Schall and Verbiest had intimate contact with ruling circles, but there was little curiosity amongst the Chinese elite about intellectual or scientific development in the West. During large parts of the Ming and Ch'ing dynasties, China virtually cut itself off from foreign commerce. In 1792–93, Lord Macartney spent a year carting 600 cases of presents from George III. They included a planetarium, globes, mathematical instruments, chronometers, a telescope, measuring instruments, chemical instruments, plate glass, copperware and other miscellaneous items (Hsü, 1975, p. 207). After he presented them to the Ch'ien–lung Emperor in Jehol, the official response stated: "there is nothing we lack.... We have never set much store on strange or ingenious objects, nor do we need any more of your country's manufactures" (Teng and Fairbank et al., 1954). These deeply engrained mental attitudes helped prevent China from emulating the West's protocapitalist development from 1500 to 1800 and from participation in much more dynamic processes of economic growth thereafter.

ISBN: 978-92-64-037625 © OECD 2007

The Contours of Economic Development

In the first millennium of the Chinese imperial state, there was little if any net growth in population and probably not much change in average income levels. In the Sung Dynasty (960–1280) virtually all authorities agree that there was significant new momentum in the Chinese economy, with an acceleration of population growth, clear indications of progress in agriculture, increased specialisation and trade and a more flourishing urban economy. Many writers have stressed the dynamism of this period — Liu and Golas, 1961; Hartwell, 1962, 1966 and 1967; Hollingsworth, 1969; Shiba, 1970; Ma, 1971; Elvin, 1973; Jones, 1981 and 1988; Gernet, 1982; McNeill, 1982; Bray, 1984 and Mokyr, 1990.

The main grounds for accepting the fact of acceleration in the Sung are:

i)   Reasonable evidence of a substantial increase in population to levels not previously reached, probably a rise from around 55 million at the beginning of the dynasty to 100 million at its end. Ho (1959) suggests the latter figure, others have higher estimates for 1280 (Zhao and Xie, 108 million; Durand, 123 million; Elvin, 140 million);

ii)   A switch in the regional centre of gravity, with a substantial rise in the proportion of people in the rice growing area south of the Yangtse and a sharp drop in the proportionate importance of the dry farming area (millet and wheat) of north China. Balazs (1931, p. 20) estimates the population South of the Yangtse to have been 24 per cent of the total in the early T'ang (around 750). Durand (1974), p. 15, shows 60 per cent living there at the end of the 12th century. Elvin (1973, p. 204) suggests that more than 85 per cent lived in south China at the end of the 13th.

Large parts of south China had been relatively underdeveloped. Primitive slash and burn agriculture and moving cultivation had been practiced but the climate and accessibility of water gave great potential for intensive rice cultivation. Substantial moves were made by Sung rulers to develop this potential, notably by the introduction of new quick ripening strains of Champa rice.

The Sung had their capital in the new centres of population, first in K'ai–feng, which was further east than the ruined T'ang capital at Ch'ang–an. In 1127, when they lost north China to invaders from Manchuria (the Chin), they moved their capital below the Yangtse to Hangchow. This city was not designed in traditional ceremonial style (see Wright, p. 65, in Skinner, 1977), but was already a large commercial centre with access to the sea. With the big influx of refugees from the north it became an exciting boom town (see Gernet, 1982). The location of the capital in south China meant that its population could be fed more cheaply in a productive rice area with ready access to transport by water. Thus the Sung were relieved of the cost of maintaining the expensive Grand Canal route which previous and subsequent dynasties needed to provide a north China capital with grain;

iii)   Woodblock printing techniques had been developed in the T'ang period. This and the prior development of paper, made possible a fairly wide diffusion of illustrated books from the tenth century onwards though really large editions came only in Ming times. This was a key innovation in Chinese history. It strengthened the potential for bureaucratic education and governance and was used by the government to diffuse best–practice technology, particularly in agriculture;

iv)   In the Sung period, there was evidence that increased density of settlement gave a boost to internal trade, a rise in the proportion of farm output which was marketed, productivity gains from increased specialisation of agricultural production and an increase in handicraft production in response to higher living standards (see Bray, 1984; Liu and Golas, 1969; Ma, 1971; and Shiba, 1970). The introduction of paper money facilitated the growth of commerce and raised the proportion of state income in cash from negligible proportions to more than half;

v)   The Southern Sung initiated improvements in shipping and shipbuilding. They built a naval force of paddle wheel ships on the Yangtse to protect themselves against Chin and Mongol invasion. Capacity was greatly expanded in government shipyards and there was a significant growth of overseas trade. Nine official ports were opened to maritime commerce, though overseas trade was dominated by Canton and Ch'üan–chou (Ma, 1971, p. 37).

All of the above developments give reason to think that growth accelerated in the Sung. There was clearly an increase in the pace of population growth and it seems likely that there was an increase in per capita income as well. However, some authors who have stressed the dynamism of the Sung seem to exaggerate its achievements:

i)   Chao (1986, pp. 49–60) suggests that in the southern Sung the urban population rose to one fifth of the total and fell to a third of this proportion by 1820. The evidence for such dramatic changes is exceedingly flimsy. For the Sung he relies on dubious accounts of Marco Polo and Hollingsworth (1969) which do not deserve serious credence[1]. For 1820 he relies on Rozman (1973) without mentioning Rozman's totally different estimates for the Sung. Table 1.7 below shows Rozman's estimates which present a very different picture from those of Chao;

ii)   Hartwell claimed to have discovered an "early industrial revolution" in Sung China, generalising from evidence for the iron industry. He greatly exaggerates its dynamism by concentrating on its rapid ascension in eleventh century K'ai–feng. However, this local boom was caused primarily by the relocation of government — the major consumer of iron goods[2];

iii) Shiba (1970) suggests that in the Sung dynasty a "nationwide" market had emerged for rice. There was an increase in the proportion of commercial sales of standard items which started in the T'ang (Twitchett, 1968), but transport costs were too high to speak of "nationwide" markets. In fact, as Shiba (1977, p. 432) himself put it, China consisted of "semiclosed regional economies";

iv)   Elvin (1973, p. 123) attributes changes to the Sung which occurred over a longer period. He suggests that "in the far south double or triple cropping of rice was almost universal", whereas Perkins (1969, pp. 44–45) suggests that the proportion was small in 1400 and expanded gradually thereafter.

None of the authors who have dealt with the Sung period have tried to quantify the achievement in macroeconomic terms. This is understandable as hard evidence is scarce. Nevertheless, it seems useful to advance a quantitative guesstimate because one is otherwise left with qualitative and literary interpretations whose meaning is very elastic. In this situation it is difficult to know the degree to which judgements diverge. The advantage of quantification is that it helps to sharpen the focus of debate.

Table 1.3 compares the levels of economic performance in China and Europe from 1 to 1700 AD. At the beginning of the first century AD, Europe's per capita GDP was higher than that in China. By the year 1000, European income levels had dropped considerably after the collapse of the Roman Empire, whereas China had begun a period of expansion under the Sung dynasty when per capita income rose by about a third[3].

Table 1.3. **Levels of Chinese and European GDP Per Capita, 1–1700 AD**
(1990 $)

	1	960	1300	1700
China	450	450	600	600
Europe[a]	550	422	576	924

a. Excluding Turkey and former USSR
Source: see Maddison (2007).

http://dx.doi.org/10.1787/086106141246

ISBN: 978-92-64-037625 © OECD 2007

Chinese population fell by a third during Mongol rule of China. This was due a) to the initial savagery of the Mongol conquest and b) to the plague epidemic which struck in China at about the same time as the Black Death in Europe.

The Mongols took over north China in 1234. Their initial impact, under Ghengis Khan and his son Ogotai, was very destructive. North China had already suffered from hydraulic neglect (the Yellow River had burst its banks and the Grand Canal had ceased to function). Then the Mongols razed many cities, inflicted great damage on agriculture, enserfed or enslaved part of the rural population and began to pastoralise the economy to provide grazing for horses and other animals. Some north Chinese migrated south but many more were exterminated. Mongol policy changed by the time the Southern Sung Empire was defeated in 1280 (see Perkins, 1969, pp. 196–200). The first Yuan emperor Kubilai reversed the pastoralisation policy and began to sinicise his governmental apparatus. He established a military occupation which preserved the Southern Sung economy and many of its institutions.

McNeill (1977, pp. 141–44, 259–69) explains how Mongol horsemen spread bubonic plague in China just as they brought the Black Death to Europe. He suggests its heaviest incidence came in China after 1353 and that this source of mortality played at least as big a role as Mongol ferocity in reducing population. Durand (1960, p. 233) also argued that in the last phase of Mongol rule "the pandemic of bubonic plague raged no less fiercely in China than it did in Europe".

The population collapse at the end of the Yuan dynasty had its counterpart in the mid–seventeenth century transition between the Ming and the Ch'ing dynasties when savagery, smallpox and famine reduced the population by a fifth (see Figure 1.1).

Figure 1.1. **Chinese Population 1–2030 AD**

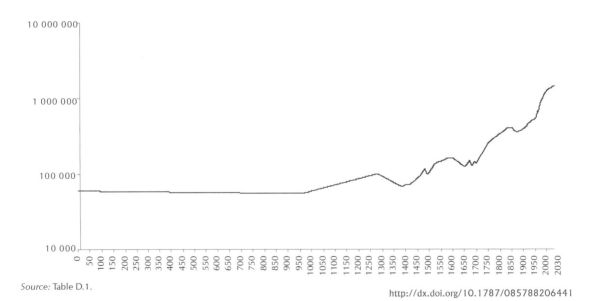

Source: Table D.1.

http://dx.doi.org/10.1787/085788206441

ISBN: 978-92-64-037625 © OECD 2007

There are two kinds of evidence which suggest more or less stable Chinese per capita performance in the Ming–Ch'ing. The first of these is Perkins' (1969) presumption of per capita stability in the agricultural economy (see Table 1.6 below). The second is Rozman's assessment that there was relatively little change in the proportionate size of the urban population from the T'ang to the early Ch'ing (see Table 1.7). Perkins maintains that grain output remained steady on a per capita basis and there is little indication of change in the nature of the livestock economy. The Perkins (1969) position is much more firmly documented than that of Chao (1986) who suggests a substantial decline in per capita grain output and consumption from the Sung to the early nineteenth century.

In the absence of direct indicators for developments in the urban economy, I assume that Rozman is right in his finding that there was only a slight rise in the urban proportion of the population. This contrasts with the much faster urban growth of Europe as shown by Jan de Vries (Table 1.8).

Agricultural Performance

In imperial China, agriculture was by far the biggest part of the economy. In 1890 it still represented over 68 per cent of gross domestic product and four–fifths of the labour force. These proportions must have been at least as high over the preceding two millenia. The economic and technological performance of the imperial system can therefore be judged in large part by what happened in this sector.

The Institutional Setting

In the first millennium of the Empire, people were scarce relative to the land available, so various forms of coercion were used to make farmers work harder. These included both serf and slave labour, particularly in areas where the imperial regime had to feed the sizeable urban centres it created for administrative or military needs. Until an effective bureaucratic system was created in the Sung period, the imperial authorities delegated administrative responsibility to various types of landowning aristocrat who used servile labour.

When population growth began its long term ascension, land became scarcer. This, together with the success of a better organised bureaucracy in ousting aristocratic remnants, made it easier to move towards a system of freer labour. In these circumstances the state could successfully levy land taxes first in kind, then in money. Private landlords remained important, but were generally cronies of the bureaucracy. Their desire for serf or corvee labour declined as the feasibility and profitability of collecting rental income increased. By the Ming dynasty, landordism had few feudal remnants. Landlords were largely non–managerial rentiers. The bureaucratic system provided the social discipline they needed and protected their assets.

Between the Sung and the Ming dynasty, China moved to a system where production and managerial decisions in agriculture were made by peasant proprietors and tenants, who could buy and sell land quite readily and sell their products on local markets (see Skinner, 1964–65, on the structure and functioning of these local markets). Chinese agriculture acquired an institutional order which was efficient in its allocation of resources and capacity to make technical changes as successive generations (in a system with partible male inheritance) had to make do with smaller family holdings.

 ISBN: 978-92-64-037625 © OECD 2007

Table 1.4. **Land Use and Population in China and Other Parts of the World, 1993**

	Total Land Area	Arable Land & Permanent Crop Area	Proportion Arable	Population	Arable Land per head of Population
	(000 ha.)		(per cent)	(000s)	(ha.)
China	959 696	95 975	10.0	1 178 440	.08
Europe[a]	487 696	135 705	27.8	506 910	.26
India	328 759	169 650	51.6	899 000	.19
United States	980 943	187 776	19.1	239 172	.73
Japan	37 780	4 463	11.8	124 753	.04
Former Soviet Union[b]	2 240 300	231 540	10.3	293 000	.79
Australia	771 336	46 486	6.0	17 769	2.62
Brazil	851 197	48 955	5.8	158 913	.31
Canada	997 614	45 500	4.6	28 386	1.58

a.   Excluding Turkey and former Soviet Union.
b.   1988.
Source: FAO, *Production Yearbook*, Rome, 1994, and Maddison (1995a) updated.   http://dx.doi.org/10.1787/087337724060

Land Shortage

Because of climate and topography (large areas of mountain and desert), the proportion of land suitable for crop production is unusually small by international standards. China is a country of ancient settlement, but at the end of the twentieth century, cultivated land was only 10 per cent of the total area, not very different from the situation in countries of recent settlement and in stark contrast to India which is able to cultivate more than half its total area, or Europe where the proportion is more than a quarter. Even the United States, where settled agriculture is much more recent, is able to cultivate twice the Chinese proportion (see Table 1.4). The Chinese man/land ratio is extreme. For every person engaged in farming, there is only one–third of a hectare of cultivated land, compared with 99 hectares in the United States.

In the past thousand years the population of China has risen nearly 22–fold, from 55 million to nearly 1.3 billion. The government and the farm population struggled to increase the cultivated area by draining lakes, swamps and jungles, reclaiming land from the sea, terracing hillsides and cutting forests. They moved the centre of gravity of the Empire. In the early years, the Imperial heartland was in the northwest loess area of dry–farming. The now very densely settled area in the lower Yangtse was then a "large territory sparsely populated, where people eat rice and drink fish soup; where land is tilled with fire –– the place is fertile and suffers no famine or hunger. Hence the people are lazy and poor and do not bother to accumulate wealth" (Chi, 1936, p. 98). The landscape has been completely transformed. Nevertheless, the cultivated area has probably expanded no more than four or five–fold since the Sung dynasty. To maintain living standards the Chinese were under great pressure to find new ways of extracting more food per hectare. The pressure of population on the land was always very marked by comparison with Europe. There was no common land, forests were destroyed and fallowing was abandoned eight centuries earlier than in Europe.

Double cropping, intercropping, seedbedding and transplantation were further methods for economising land. Shortage of land was also reflected in Chinese dietary habits.

Concentration on Crops not Livestock

For the past millenium, Chinese have eaten less meat than medieval or modern Europeans, milk is not consumed by adults and there has been an almost total absence of milk products. The concentration on crop products was influenced by land scarcity, for less land is required when proteins and calories come from grains rather than animals. The meat the Chinese eat comes mainly from pigs and chickens which rely on scavenging rather than pasture. Protein intake is supplemented by soybeans and the widespread practice of fish farming in small ponds. Chinese made very little use of wool. Ordinary clothing came largely from vegetable fibres (hemp, ramie and then cotton). Quilted clothing supplied the warmth which wool might have provided. The richer part of the population relied on the long established products of Chinese sericulture. Silk cocoons came from mulberry bushes often grown on hillsides which were not suitable for other crops.

Early advances in farm tools reduced the need for work animals. Bray (1984) gives elaborate detail of the precocity of Chinese ploughs, which had curved iron mouldboards from the Han dynasty onwards. She argues that until the eighteenth century, these were far superior to European ploughs which had straight wooden mouldboards and required powerful animal traction (teams of horses or oxen). In China a single ox could pull a better plough.

The emphasis on grain and textile fibres rather than livestock and livestock products was strengthened by official policy. The authorities preferred settled agriculturists to pastoralists because they were easier to control and tax.

The contrast between Chinese practice and that of their Mongol and Manchu neighbours was quite extreme. In these border regions, population was small and settled agriculture largely absent. Mongols were transhumant pastoralists living mainly from meat and milk products, moving their herds across the steppes when better pasture was needed; making extensive use of wool products for clothing and for covering their mobile homes — yurts which could be easily transported by horse traction. In the course of time, the Chinese enlarged their empire and absorbed these non–Han pastoralists, but the fringe areas were very thinly settled. In Manchuria, Chinese farmers were permitted to settle only in the nineteenth century, after Russia had grabbed large parts of the empty land in eastern Siberia.

Intensive Use of Manure

A third feature of Chinese agriculture has been heavy use of manure. Animal manure comes largely from pigs and chickens and there was very intensive use of human droppings, in contrast to practice in Europe and India. In Europe it was only in the Netherlands and Flanders that this was widespread. The Chinese designed a special privy–cum–pigsty to collect both human "nightsoil" and pig manure. Silage techniques were used to kill off noxious and harmful micro–organisms. Many kinds of manure were manhandled in mixing it with chaff, crop waste, dead leaves, ashes, household waste, or aquatic weeds. China was well endowed with rich silt deposits and river mud which were mixed with other fertiliser elements. Commercial bean cake and green leguminous plants were also important fertilisers. The intensive use of fertiliser was induced by the relative scarcity of land.

Heavy Use of Irrigation

Chinese agriculture is heavily dependent on irrigation and careful water management, which augment fertility, reduce the risk of floods and mitigate the impact of droughts. In the northwest loess region, the emphasis was mainly on canals. Further east, in the lower reaches of the Yellow River, the problem was mainly one of flood control. In the Yangtse and Pearl River valleys irrigation was necessary to secure regularity and manageability of water resources. In the south all farming involves detailed water management and maintenance to ensure high fertility on tiny rice paddies. China has two very large rivers. The Yellow river has a much smaller flow than the Yangtse, but carries huge quantities of silt from the west of the country, where the disappearance of forests has led to continuous soil erosion.

ISBN: 978-92-64-037625 © OECD 2007

Table 1.5a. **Dated Irrigation Works by Dynasty**
(average number of projects per century)

	Chi (includes repair projects)	Perkins (excludes repair projects)
Pre T'ang	16	10
T'ang	87	79
Sung	349	233
Yuan	351	492
Ming	822	723
Ch'ing	1 222	600

Source: Chi (1936), p. 36 and Perkins (1969), p. 334.

http://dx.doi.org/10.1787/087361583144

Table 1.5b. **Irrigated Area, 1400–1995**

	Irrigated Land	Total Cultivated Area (million ha.)	Proportion Irrigated (per cent)
1400	7.5	24.7	30.3
1820	21.7	73.7	29.4
1952	20.0	107.9	18.5
1995	49.3	94.9	51.9

Source: Irrigated area 1400 to early 1930s from Perkins (1969), p. 64. For 1400, Perkins suggests a possible range from 4.3 to 10.7 million hectares which I have averaged. 1820 estimated from pp. 61 and 64. 1952 and 1995 from Tables A.8 and A.10.

http://dx.doi.org/10.1787/087361583144

From time to time the course of the Yellow River has changed disastrously (e.g. in 1194 and in 1855) when dynastic decline led to neglect of river management (see Gernet, 1982, for a map of successive changes of course of the Yellow River in the past three millennia).

Official activity played a major role in large–scale irrigation projects, particularly in the north. South of the Yangtse where polders, levies, dikes and lake or swamp drainage were involved, the role of private associations or groups was bigger. The state has also had a major stake in hydraulic works for transport purposes. From the Sui period, the Grand Canal was developed to transport tribute grain to the imperial capital in the northwest, first Ch'ang–an, then Peking, where local farm conditions were not propitious for feeding a huge capital city.

Chi (1936) and Perkins (1969) have given a very rough quantitative picture of irrigation development by scrutinising official bureaucratic gazetteers for provinces and counties over several centuries. Perkins confined his listing to new projects whereas Chi included major repair work as well. Their sources give dates and dimensions for only a fraction of the total projects they describe. Perkins (1969), p. 338, shows that the average proportion of dated projects was less than a tenth of the total recorded. The proportion varied a good deal over time and between provinces. Nevertheless, one can reasonably conclude from Chi and Perkins: a) that the effort to expand irrigation was much more substantial in the thirteen centuries from the T'ang period than it had been in the first eight centuries of the empire; b) that the volume of construction increased in successive dynasties, except for the move from the Ming to the Ch'ing where Chi shows an increase and Perkins a decrease. Perkins' estimates are probably a better guide in this case; c) a third conclusion that seems reasonable is that the rate at which construction accelerated was most impressive in the T'ang–Sung period.

Table 1.5b shows that irrigated land was about 30 per cent of the cultivated area in 1400 and in 1820. Between 1820 and 1952 the irrigated proportion fell to less than a fifth, but it was very much higher than in India and Europe. In India only 3 million hectares were irrigated in 1850 (see Maddison, 1971, pp. 23–24) or about 3.5 per cent of the cultivated area. In Europe, aggregate figures are not available, but the average was probably much nearer to that in India than in China. In the United States about 10 per cent of cropland is irrigated compared with 52 per cent in China in 1995.

Chinese irrigation involved huge labour inputs, both in constructing major works and in constant maintenance. However, since the 1960s pumps and tubewells powered by electricity have reduced labour requirements significantly.

Official Encouragement of New Crops, Multicropping, Higher Yields and Diffusion of Best Practice Technology

Another feature of Chinese agriculture was its centrality in economic policy. Like the eighteenth century French Physiocrats, the Emperor and the bureaucracy thought of agriculture as the key economic sector. They helped develop and diffuse new seeds and crops by technical advice. They commissioned and distributed agricultural handbooks, calendars etc. They ensured that the advice they contained was adopted by selected farmers in different regions. Bray (1984) cites extensive bibliographies which show the existence of more than 500 (mostly official) works on Chinese agriculture (78 pre Sung, 105 Sung, 26 Yuan and 310 Ming–Ch'ing texts). From the tenth century they were available in printed form. The most remarkable was Wang Chen's *Nung Shu*. This exhaustive treatise on agricultural practice had many illustrations with the intention of diffusing knowledge of best practice north Chinese techniques to the South and vice versa. The original version (1313) of this oft cited work was lost and many of its illustrations were redrawn in subsequent editions (see Bray, p. 63). She used the edition of 1783. This official Chinese literature had only one counterpart elsewhere in Asia (in Tokugawa Japan) and, for a very long period, none in Europe. In the Roman period there were treatises by Columella and Varro, but European works in this field did not reappear until the fourteenth century. By 1700, according to Bray, the volume of European agricultural publications had caught up with the Chinese.

China's territory stretches over many climatic zones and its biodiversity is richer than Europe because glaciation was less severe and ancient botanical species were preserved in greater numbers. In the Imperial period, China adopted and diffused a number of new crops which became important. Tea spread widely and was subject to taxation in the T'ang dynasty. Cotton was introduced in the Sung period and began to be widely used for cloth in the Yuan dynasty — prior to this ordinary people wore less comfortable fibres such as hemp or ramie. Sorghum was disseminated widely after the Mongol conquest. Crops from the Americas were introduced in the mid–sixteenth century. Maize, peanuts, potatoes and sweet potatoes added significantly to China's output potential because of their heavy yields and the possibility of growing them on inferior land. Tobacco and sugar cane were widely diffused in the Ming period.

From early times Chinese farmers succeeded in getting higher yields from their seeds than Europeans. Seeds were planted in rows with drills in north China; seed beds and transplanting techniques were used in the southern rice growing areas. In China, wheat and barley yield/seed ratios were about 10:1 in the twelfth century (Bray, 1984, p. 287) and a good deal better for rice. Slicher van Bath (1963) suggests that the typical medieval European yield/seed ratio for wheat was 4:1. Duby (1988) cites even more miserable results and a 4:1 yield is not out of line with what Mayerson (1981) cites for Roman times. It was not until the eighteenth century that European agriculture began to show serious improvement in this respect.

With official encouragement, early ripening seeds were developed which eventually permitted double or even triple cropping of rice. Until the beginning of the eleventh century, the total time for rice to mature was at least 180 days (4 to 6 weeks in a nursery bed and 150 days to mature after transplanting). The Sung emperor Chen–Tsung (998–1022) introduced early ripening and drought resistant Champa rice from Vietnam. Over time, this made double cropping feasible and allowed extension of cultivation to higher land and hillier slopes. The original Champa rice matured 100 days after transplanting. By the fifteenth century there were 60–day varieties. In the sixteenth century 50–day

ISBN: 978-92-64-037625 © OECD 2007

varieties were developed, in the eighteenth a 40–day variety and in the early nineteenth a 30–day variety became available (see Ho, 1959, pp. 170–74). Government policy also encouraged intercropping in the north and promoted expansion of wheat as a second crop in the south.

Chao (1986, p. 199) suggests that the Chinese multiple cropping index was 0.6 in the Han dynasty in the first century (i.e. 40 per cent of land was left fallow on average), rose to 0.8 in the eighth century (T'ang dynasty) and to 1.0 under the Sung (i.e. on average there was no fallow at that time). Rice/wheat double cropping was stimulated in the south by policy incentives of the Sung dynasty, but double cropping of rice expanded rather slowly. He suggests that the double cropping ratio reached about 1.4 in the nineteenth century, then fell with the opening up of Manchuria from the 1860s when settlement by Han Chinese was permitted but where the climate did not allow double cropping. In the 1930s to 1950s the coefficient was about 1.3 and by 1995 had risen to nearly 1.6.

The figures quoted above are averages for the whole country, but the situation varies a lot by region. In the northeast and northwest the cropping index was about 1 in 1990 and slightly less in Heilungkiang and Inner Mongolia. In eastern China the average was nearly 2 with a high of 2.53 in Kiangsu. Further south it was 2.44 in Kiangsi and 2.25 in Kwangtung (see Colby, Crook and Webb, 1992, p. 24).

In Europe, widespread use of fallow was common in medieval times (see Slicher van Bath, 1963, pp. 243–54) and it was not until the development of crop rotation in eighteenth century England and the Netherlands that fallow began to disappear. For Europe as a whole the twelfth century Chinese situation was not achieved until the twentieth century.

Quantifying Agrarian Performance

A good deal of information about the nature of long–run changes in Chinese agrarian performance can be found in the work of Ping–ti Ho. His 1959 book contains a detailed survey of the development of new crops and changes in practice which he gleaned from Chinese bureaucratic records (local gazetteers — fang shih). Thousands of these have survived from the Ming (1368–1644) and Ch'ing (1644–1911) dynasties. They cover the 18 imperial provinces and many of the 1 300 or so county (hsien) jurisdictions. He explains the care which must be used in interpreting figures from such sources, as incentives to report or to evade registration varied over time and place and so did the precise meaning of traditional measures. Ho (1975) goes back further and uses archaeological and archaeobotanical evidence to examine the origins of agriculture over the five millennia before the Chinese empire was created.

He does not provide any aggregate quantitative estimates, but clearly believes that Chinese agriculture was "persistently self sustaining". Over the long run he considers that real levels of per capita consumption did not fall but were maintained by adaptive changes in technical practice. He also recognises that the process of increasing land productivity involved a gradual decline in labour productivity.

Perkins (1969) approached Chinese agrarian history in the same spirit as Ho, but made a big step forward. He presented a carefully modulated and scholarly assessment of the magnitude of movements in output and land productivity over six centuries. His basic assumption is not too different from that of Ho, that Chinese traditional agriculture was successful in sustaining living standards in face of a massive population increase. He felt that his conclusion was reasonably conservative and did not exclude the possibility that there may even have been a 20–30 per cent rise in food consumption per head in the six centuries he covered.

Table 1.6. **Major Magnitudes in Chinese Farming, 1400–1952**

	Population (millions)	Grain Output (thousand tons)	Cultivated Area (million ha.)		Grain Yield kg/ha.
			Grains	Total	
1400	72	20 520	19.8	24.7	1 038
1650	123	35 055	32.0	40.0	1 095
1750	260	74 100	48.0	60.0	1 544
1820	381	108 585	59.0	73.7	1 840
1952	569	162 139	86.3	107.9	1 879

Source: This is a simplified presentation of Perkins' basic argument in terms of grains. Here I use his assumption that grain output for consumption, feed and seed was approximately constant at 285 kg of unhusked grain per head of population throughout. Population from Table D.1. Cultivated area from Perkins (1969), midpoint of his range for 1400, 1650 and 1750 from Wang (1973). 1820 is an interpolation of Wang's estimates for 1770 and 1850. It was assumed, following Perkins, that 80 per cent of the cultivated area was devoted to grain. One can see in Table A.20 that my detailed estimate of grain output in 1952 was 154 560 tons – about 5 per cent lower than the stylised estimate shown above.

http://dx.doi.org/10.1787/087367124662

The main productivity ratio with which Perkins is concerned is yield per unit of arable land cultivated. Given his assumption of stable consumption levels, one can infer that yield increased very considerably over the period he covers. He assumes that arable land was in constant use with no fallowing and he ignores pasture land. His assumptions about land under cultivation and yields are backed by a good deal of evidence from provincial gazetteers.

Table 1.6 shows Perkins' (1969, pp. 16–17) simple long term assumptions converted into metric units. For 1650 and 1750 the figures of Wang (1973) were used for cultivated area. Wang was Perkins' main research assistant. His figures are consistent with the Perkins framework of analysis and come from the same sources.

Perkins states his argument entirely in terms of grains which occupied 80 per cent of the cultivated land. He assimilates potatoes and other tubers to the cereal group and assumes that output and consumption of other crop items and livestock products moved in the same proportion as cereal output. In his long run analysis he excludes forestry, fishing and hunting. His basic assumptions are that annual per capita use of grains for consumption, feed and seed remained more or less steady in a range about 10 per cent either side of 285 kg. (of unhusked grain). Traditional inputs were seed grain, a small amount of feed grain, manure, irrigation costs and the services of draft animals. One can assume that, for Perkins, inputs and value added moved parallel with gross output.

From Table 1.6 one can see total grain output rising by a factor of 5.3 from 1400 to 1820, in the same proportion as population. The cultivated area increased about three–fold, yields by about three–quarters. The increase in yields was partly due to: *a)* multiple cropping of rice, wheat and barley which was negligible in 1400 (see Perkins, 1969, pp. 44–47); *b)* introduction of maize and potatoes from the Americas whose yield was higher than that of indigenous crops; and *c)* increased input of manure per hectare as the population of humans and animals grew faster than the cultivated area.

Perkins is reluctant to characterise the improvements he describes as technical change. In fact (pp. 186–89) he describes the Ming–Ch'ing period as one of technical stagnation mainly because there was little change in farm tools. This is too narrow a view of technical change. In the period he covers there was an increase in the proportion of double cropped land, improvement in the speed with which early ripening seeds developed, an important assimilation and adaptation of new crops from the Americas, a move from hemp to cotton cultivation as clothing habits changed, widespread dissemination of sorghum, increased use of beancake as fertiliser and an extension of the irrigated area. Much of this involved wider diffusion of best practice procedures which were already known. There was certainly an improvement in average practice and a successful effort to absorb and adapt knowledge. This long term process of assimilation should be recognised as technical progress.

ISBN: 978-92-64-037625 © OECD 2007

Non–Farm Activity of Rural Households

Apart from their labour intensive activities in cropping, manuring and irrigation, Chinese rural households had a large range of other pursuits. These included vegetable gardens and orchards, raising fish in small ponds, sericulture, gathering grasses and other combustible material for fuel, feeding pigs and poultry. Important "industrial" activities were also centred in rural households. Textile spinning and weaving, making garments and leather goods were largely household activities. The same was true of oil and grain milling, drying and preparation of tea leaves; tobacco products; soybean sauce; candles and tung oil; wine and liqueurs; straw, rattan and bamboo products. Manufacture of bricks and tiles, carts and small boats and construction of rural housing were also significant village activities. It is clear from the work of Skinner (1964–1965) that Chinese farmers did not live in a subsistence economy, but were engaged in a web of commercial activity carried out in rural market areas to which virtually all villages had access. The relative importance of these rural activities grew in the Sung dynasty, together with the improvement in land productivity, rural living standards and the increased commercialisation which most analysts have discerned. Skinner (February 1965, p. 208) speaks of "intensification" of rural market activity over time due to demographic growth, but seems to doubt whether there was much change in the proportion of individual peasant activity going into such pursuits. However, a proportionate increase seems plausible because of the growing importance over the long term of cash crop items like cotton, sugar, tobacco and tea. In the nineteenth century (Table C.1) well over a quarter of GDP came from traditional handicrafts, transport, trade, construction and housing and most of these were carried out in rural areas. These activities had probably been more important for centuries in China than they ever were in Europe.

Performance in the Urban Sector

It is very difficult to assemble detailed evidence on urban economic activity, but one can use estimates of the proportionate size of the urban population as a proxy. Fortunately Rozman (1973) provides rough estimates of Chinese urban characteristics from the T'ang dynasty to 1820.

Rozman is mainly concerned with the structure of the urban "network" rather than its significance for the economy. His hierarchy describes the operational locus of the Chinese imperial administration. The top level is the national capital with a population of around a million (similar to Beloch's estimate of the size of imperial Rome at the death of Augustus and to Constantinople when it was at its peak as the capital of the Byzantine Empire). His next category covers secondary capitals such as Nanking. The third refers to provincial capitals and other "elevated" provincial cities; the fourth to prefectural capitals or major regional ports. The fifth refers to the lowest level of officialdom — the county (*hsien*); in the whole period he covers, their number remained in a narrow range from 1 235 in the T'ang to 1 360 in the Ch'ing (Skinner, 1977, p. 19) despite the huge increase in population. The supervisory function of officialdom was spread more thinly over time. The bottom of Rozman's hierarchy is more rural than urban and refers to local agricultural marketing areas; at that level bureaucratic control operated "only in a very attenuated form" (Skinner, 1964, p. 31).

Rozman (1973) got his basic information from regional gazetteers (pp. 341–346). His search was most systematic for the province of Chihli where the imperial capital was situated. Here he consulted 246 gazetteers of which 2 were from the sixteenth century, 40 from the seventeenth century and 60 from the eighteenth century. For the other seventeen provinces he cites 272 gazetteers (an average of 16 per province). Of these, 4 were from the seventeenth century, 55 from the eighteenth century. The rest were at various dates up to 1936. For many towns he had no exact population figure but felt he had

Table 1.7. **Rozman's Urban Ratios for China from T'ang to Later Ch'ing**

Dynasty	Reference Year	Rozman's Urban Ratio (% of total population)	Ratio of Cities with 10 000 inhabitants or over	No. of Cities with 10 000 inhabitants and above	Average size of Col. 4 Cities (000s)	Rozman's Population Total for China (million)	My Estimates of Total Chinese Population
mid T'ang	762	4.7	3.0	50	60	100	52
mid Sung	1120	5.2	3.1	91	41	120	78
mid Ming	1506	6.5	3.8	112	44	130	124
early Ching	1650	6.8	4.0	136	44	150	123
later Ching	(c.1820)	5.9	3.8	310	48	400	408

Source: Rozman (1973), pp. 279, 280, 282, and 102 for the T'ang to later Ch'ing respectively. The reference year is my assessment of what he means by his somewhat vague descriptions. Rozman's hierarchy of urban places is described analytically on p. 14, and on p. 60 he gives statistical cut off points. He does not actually treat his lowest category as urban as it refers to a "standard marketing settlement, differing from an ordinary village because of the presence of a periodic market". He simply lists the assumed number of such settlements without estimating their population. His second lowest level consists of "intermediate market" settlements. He includes half of these as urban, but their average population is only about 1 000. His reason for treating the two lowest levels as part of an "urban" network presumably derives from Skinner (1964, 1965, 1966) who developed the idea that there was a systematic standardised framework of such rural markets in China. Rozman's third lowest level consists of places with 3 000 to 9 999 inhabitants; these are assumed to have an average of 4 000 to 5 000 inhabitants

http://dx.doi.org/10.1787/087376838667

enough information to allocate them to one of his seven hierarchical levels (p. 5). In most provinces (p. 146) he had only a 20 per cent sample of counties (*hsien*) and prefectures (*chou*) which he extrapolated to get provincial totals. His estimates for China are an aggregation of these provincial estimates. In some cases his figures for total Chinese population deviate a good deal from the source used (compare the last two columns of Table 1.7). I have not adjusted his urban ratios for this as I am not sure to what extent his numerators and denominators are independent. It is clear, however, that his estimates are very rough.

Table 1.7 gives Rozman's estimates of "urban" population as well as the ratio one can derive for towns with 10 000 inhabitants or more. He shows an increase in the urban proportion from the T'ang to mid–Ming but no rise from mid–Ming to later Ch'ing.

Fortunately, it is possible to compare Rozman's findings for China with the situation in Europe, thanks to the work of de Vries (1984) whose results are shown in Table 1.8. He defines European urban population as those in towns with inhabitants of 10 000 or more and his ratios can be compared with those for China in Table 1.7.

De Vries' statistical procedures are much more systematic, transparent and better documented than those of Rozman. He estimates urban population at fifty year intervals from 1500 to 1800, using a database for 379 specified cities which he subdivides into six size categories. These differ in their cut–off points from those of Rozman, but the database can be reordered in the Rozman categories, for towns over 10 000 inhabitants. The de Vries estimates cover 16 countries or regions. Most of these are west European or Mediterranean. In eastern Europe he covers only Austria–Bohemia and Poland. His urban ratios would probably have been somewhat lower if he had covered more of eastern Europe.

If one compares the de Vries estimates with those of Rozman, it is clear that there was a very different situation in China and Europe. In the T'ang period China had an urban civilisation and Europe had none. By 1820 the Chinese degree of urbanisation was not much greater than it had been a thousand years earlier, whereas European urbanisation made a great leap forward from 1000 to 1500 and by the latter date was more urbanised than mid–Ming China. By 1800 the European urban proportion had almost doubled from the 1500 level, whereas China in 1820 had the same proportion as in 1500.

ISBN: 978-92-64-037625 © OECD 2007

Table 1.8. **De Vries' Estimates of the Urban Population of Europe, 1000 to 1800 AD**

Year	Ratio of Towns with 10 000 inhabitants or more to total population	Number of Cities with 10 000 or more inhabitants	Average Size of Towns (000s)	Total Population of De Vries "Europe" (million)	Total Population (million)
1000	0.0	(4)	n.a.	n.a.	45.0
1500	5.6	154	22	61.6	72.3
1650	8.3	197	31	74.6	90.9
1800	10.0	364	34	122.7	149.6

Source: De Vries (1984), Tables 2.2, 3.1, 3.2, 3.5, 3.6 and Appendix 1. De Vries constructed a data base for 379 potentially urban places and made an intensive literature search to identify their population at a date near to each of his seven benchmark years of which three 1500, 1650 and 1800, are shown above. He had six city size categories. For 1500 he identified 96 cities with 10 000 population or more with a total population of 2 494 thousand. In that year he could not identify the population of 87 places, but from other evidence he inferred that 58 of these fell into one or other of his six categories, bringing his urban total to 3 441 thousand. For 1650, he identified 156 cities with a population of 10 000 or over and inferred the population of 41 of the 73 places where he lacked direct evidence of population size. For 1800 he lacked direct evidence for only three places all of which he inferred to have had 10 000 population or more. For the year 1000 he made no estimates but suggests on p. 41 that there were no cities with 10 000 or more inhabitants outside Italy and that the overall urban average was zero in that year. For the year 1000 I believe there were probably four Italian cities in the urban category. The fourth column shows the total population of the 16 countries or areas in the De Vries sample. The last column shows my estimates of total European population (excluding the 1990 area of USSR and Turkey) which I derived from the same sources as in Table 1.2.

http://dx.doi.org/10.1787/087385862416

Although China had much slower urban growth, the average size of Chinese towns was bigger than in Europe. Over the period covered by Rozman those with 10 000 or more inhabitants varied between 41 000 and 60 000, whereas in Europe the range was from 22 000 to 34 000. The imperial capitals are estimated by Rozman to have had around a million people in all the dynasties and there were usually some other cities with more than 300 000 (1 in the T'ang and mid–Ming, 3 in early Ch'ing and 9 in the later Ch'ing). In Europe, the four largest cities in 1500 were Milan, Paris and Venice (around 100 000) and Naples (150 000); in 1650 they were Amsterdam and Naples (175 000 and 176 000 respectively), London (400 000) and Paris (430 000); in 1800 Vienna (231 000), Naples (427 000), Paris (581 000) and London (865 000).

Imperial officialdom was of great importance in Chinese cities, not only as a proportion of population, but also in terms of power. Officialdom had a powerful role in dictating the layout of cities, it controlled communications and was not challenged by a countervailing judicial, military, aristocratic or ecclesiastical power. Their clerks and runners were locally recruited and responsible for detailed fiscal demands, for economic regulation and exaction of penalties for crimes and misdemeanours. They had considerable power to vary these and to augment their income by dispensing favours, so the rest of the populace was in a state of dependency. The Chinese non–bureaucratic elite tended to mimic the habits and education of officialdom and were dependent on official favours to lighten their tax burdens and get other legal privileges like immunity from corporal punishment for criminal offences. They were also eager to purchase official degree status on those occasions in imperial history when fiscal need led the government to raise money this way.

European cities were more autonomous. Most of them had charters and codes of civil law which protected the legal rights of citizens and commercial influence was very much stronger.

Max Weber's work on China (see the 1964 translation) stressed the differences between the constraining role of officialdom in Chinese cities and the greater opportunities for capitalist development in Europe. Balazs' (1964) writings are also in the Weberian tradition. He emphasises the predatory fiscal approach of the bureaucracy, the potentially arbitrary character of the justice they dispensed which put constraints on capitalist development and inhibited risk taking. In bigger industrial enterprises, the state usually played a leading role (e.g in state iron works, imperial porcelain works, in licensing the salt trade, in control of land for urban real estate, control of communications and trade on the Grand Canal).

The striking difference between Chinese state enterprise and European commercial interests can be seen in the field of international trade. In the early Ming, the Yung–lo Emperor built up a fleet of large ships for ocean voyages and sent his eunuch admiral, Cheng Ho, on major expeditions between 1405 and 1433 (Levathes, 1994). Thereafter the shipbuilding industry was neglected and foreign trade more or less prohibited. This decision cut China out of the huge expansion of overseas trade which was a key element in the development of capitalist enterprise in Europe from the end of the fifteenth century onwards.

Notes

1. Chao's exaggeration of Sung urban development derives partly from Hollingsworth's (1969, p. 246) implausible estimates of the population of Hangchow. He suggests that it was at least 5 million and probably 6–7 million; he makes no attempt to explain how it would be possible to feed such a huge agglomeration. Hollingsworth relies heavily on Marco Polo. Polo claimed that Hangchow consumed 4 338 kg. of pepper a day. Hollingsworth figures that this would require at least 5 million people to digest it. To illustrate the size of the city he quotes Polo's statement that there were 12 000 bridges. By contrast, Needham, vol. IV.3 (1971, p. 148), states that the city contained only 347 bridges in Polo's time. Gernet and Balazs, who have scrutinised the sources more seriously, suggest a population of around one million.

2. Hartwell suggested that iron production in the Northern Sung increased nine–fold from 806 to 1078 and per capita output about six–fold. He regards this as an "early industrial revolution". Extrapolating from what he found for iron, he infers that there was an "impressive expansion of mining and manufacturing in eleventh–century China" (Hartwell, 1966, p. 29). Hartwell inferred iron output in 1078 from various tax returns. Assuming a 10 per cent rate of tax he estimated total taxed output to be 75 000 short tons (68 000 metric tons). He doubled this figure to take account of illegal or unrecorded production (Hartwell, 1962, p. 155). This estimate seems plausible and fairly modest in the light of his own comparative figures. It implies a per capita consumption of 1.4 kg in 1078, compared to 3 kg in England and Wales in 1540, 6.4 in 1640 and 15.4 kg in 1796. The most implausible aspect of Hartwell's estimate is his suggestion that per capita consumption rose six–fold from 806 to 1078. He does not explain what changes in demand patterns would warrant this and his 806 estimate is not properly documented. He deals mainly with the supply of iron to the early Sung capital K'ai–feng. A large part of demand for iron came from the central government which needed it for weapons and iron coinage. He shows (1967, p. 152) the population of K'ai–feng rising sixfold from 742 to 1078 and falling more than ten–fold from 1078 to 1330. In the light of this there is nothing surprising in the rapid growth and subsequent decline of iron output in this region. Needham (1958, pp. 18–19) says that "regular industrial production of cast iron must have existed in China from the 4th century BC". Use of iron for military purposes, agriculture, building, various trades and household use had been widespread for centuries before Hartwell's period. I am therefore extremely sceptical of the representativity of Hartwell's evidence of "industrial revolution". Nevertheless, it influenced the interpretation of Sung performance by McNeill (1983) and Jones (1981, 1988).

3. Joseph Needham's view of the contours of Chinese development is different from that suggested in Table 1.3. His views deserve serious consideration in view of the encyclopaedic exploration of Chinese science and technology which he directed. *Science and Civilisation in China* was inaugurated in 1954 and at the time of his death in 1995 about 6 000 pages of the still unfinished work had been published. The Needham

ISBN: 978-92-64-037625 © OECD 2007

associates generally provide a comparative view of technology in China and the West, particularly in matters of chronological precedence, but they do not usually assess the economic impact of technical change. The volumes of Francesca Bray (1984) on agriculture and Dieter Kuhn (1988) on textile technology are probably the most enlightening in this respect.

Needham's views on the contours of Chinese development are stated most clearly in *The Great Titration* (1969), which is a collection of essays published between 1946 and 1966. He perceived no great leap forward in the Sung, but stressed China's thousand year lead in siderurgy and paper production, its 700 year lead in printing etc. He suggests (p. 40) in a 1961 essay, that Chinese evolution could be "represented by a slowly rising curve, noticeably running at a higher level, sometimes at a much higher level, than European parallels, between say, the second and fifteenth centuries AD". In a 1964 essay (p. 117), he suggests that Chinese leadership originated seven centuries earlier: "it is clear that between the fifth century BC and the fifteenth century AD Chinese bureaucratic feudalism was much more effective in the useful application of natural knowledge than the slave owning classical cultures or the serf–based military aristocratic feudal system of Europe." A second 1964 essay (p. 190) gives yet another alternative "between the first century BC and the fifteenth AD, Chinese civilisation was much *more* efficient than occidental in applying human natural knowledge to practical human needs".

It is clear that his conclusions were not based on a careful analysis of the economic significance of Chinese technology and inventive activity. His general position on East–West levels of performance was developed well before his *magnum opus* was conceived. In his early days, he was greatly influenced by Wittfogel (1931). As a Marxist, Needham believed that the West was locked into inferior modes of production (slavery and then serfdom) from which China had escaped by installing an enlightened meritocratic bureaucracy (see Needham 1969, pp. 193–217, on the Asiatic mode of production).

I think Needham's assessment of the merits and ultimate limitations of bureaucratic power in China is reasonably valid, but meritocratic selection did not emerge before the T'ang dynasty and it is questionable whether China in the Han dynasty had a technology and level of economic performance superior to its European contemporary, the Roman empire. Roman organisational and military skills were at least as good as Chinese. Yields in Chinese agriculture were better than in Roman Italy (see Bray, 1984 and Mayerson, 1981) but lower than in Egypt. Roman civil engineering and architecture were better in terms of capacity to build roads, cities, aqueducts and walls made of masonry. Many of these are still visible in Europe, the Middle East and North Africa, whereas Chinese cities were made of wood and their walls were made of tamped earth until the Ming period. The Roman road transport network was more than twice as big as that of Han China, although it served a smaller population (see Needham, 1971, vol. IV 3, p. 29).

For these reasons, it seems likely that Chinese aggregate economic performance was inferior to that of Europe from the first century BC until the collapse of the Roman Empire in the West, in the fifth century AD (see Chapter 1 of Maddison, 2007, which presents new estimates of the economic performance of the Roman Empire).

Chapter 2

Economic Decline and External Humiliation, 1820–1949

The Ch'ing dynasty performed extremely well in terms of its own objectives from the end of the seventeenth to the beginning of the nineteenth century. From 1700 to 1820 population rose from 138 to 381 million — nearly eight times as fast as in Japan and nearly twice as fast as in Europe. This population growth was accommodated without a fall in living standards. Chinese GDP grew faster than that of Europe in the eighteenth century even though European per capita income rose by a quarter.

The second achievement was the feeling of security derived from the huge expansion in the area of imperial control. In 1820, China's national territory was 12 million square kilometres, about twice what it had been in 1680. The expansion was in very sparsely populated regions, which in 1820 accounted for only 2 per cent of total population. They were not then intended for ethnic Chinese settlement, but to secure the Inner Asian frontiers in great depth to prevent barbarian intrusions of the type China had experienced in the past. Mongolia was conquered in 1696–97. Its tribal structure was modified to make it more docile. The boundary of the Manchu dynasty's own homelands was fixed deep into Siberia in the 1689 Treaty of Nerchinsk with Russia. Taiwan was conquered in 1683, Tibet in 1720 and a huge area of central Asia (Chinese Turkestan, later Sinkiang) in 1756–57. There was an outer perimeter of docile tributaries in Burma, Nepal, Siam, Annam, Korea and the Ryukus which were felt to provide an extra layer of security.

China's nineteenth century was a dismal contrast. There were a whole series of internal rebellions which were difficult and costly to suppress. The biggest, the Taiping rebellion, lasted 14 years and incurred enormous damage to China's central provinces. The traditional military forces failed to suppress it and fiscal resources were under great strain in developing a new military response. The authorities ceased to be able to maintain major hydraulic works. The Yellow River dikes were not maintained. There was a disastrous change in the course of the river in 1852–55 and a silting up of the Grand Canal. By the end of the century it could no longer be used to provide grain supplies to Peking. As a result of these disasters, China's population was no higher in 1890 than in 1820 and its per capita income was almost certainly lower. China had been the world's biggest economy for nearly two millennia, but in the 1890s this position was taken by the United States. The record under the various Republican regimes (1912–49) was also dismal. Chinese GDP per capita was lower in 1952 than in 1820, in stark contrast with experience elsewhere in the world economy. China's share of world GDP fell from a third to one–twentieth. Its real per capita income fell from parity to a quarter of the world average.

ISBN: 978-92-64-03762-5 © OECD 2007

Table 2.1. Comparative Levels of Economic Performance, China and Other Major Parts of the World Economy, 1700–2003

	China	Japan	Europe	United States	USSR	India	World
	GDP (billion 1990 "international" dollars)						
1700	82.8	15.4	92.6	0.5	16.2	90.8	371.4
1820	228.6	20.7	184.8	12.5	37.7	111.4	694.5
1952	305.9	202.0	1 730.7	1 625.2	545.8	234.1	5 912.8
1978	935.1	1 446.2	5 268.2	4 089.5	1 715.2	625.7	18 969.0
2003	6 188.0	2 699.3	8 643.8	8 430.8	1 552.2	2 267.1	40 913.4
	Population (million)						
1700	138	27	100.3	1	26.6	165	603.2
1820	381	31	169.5	10	54.8	209	1 041.7
1952	569	86.5	398.6	157.6	185.9	372	2 616.0
1978	956	114.9	480.1	222.6	261.5	648	4.279.7
2003	1 288.4	127.2	516.0	290.3	287.6	1 050	6 278.6
	GDP per capita (1990 "international" dollars)						
1700	600	570	923	527	610	550	615
1820	600	669	1 090	1 257	688	533	667
1952	538	2 336	4 342	10 316	2 937	629	2 260
1978	978	12 585	10 972	18 373	6 559	966	4 432
2003	4 803	21 218	16 750	29 037	5 397	2 160	6 516

Source: Maddison (2001 and 2003) updated, see www.ggdc.net/Maddison. Europe includes 29 west and 10 east European countries (Turkey is not included). The figures for India exclude Bangladesh and Pakistan from 1952. The figures for the United States include the indigenous population.

http://dx.doi.org/10.1787/086121023387

Table 2.2a. Shares of World GDP, 1700-2003
(per cent)

	1700	1820	1952	1978	2003
China	22.3	32.9	5.2	4.9	15.1
India	24.4	16.0	4.0	3.3	5.5
Japan	4.1	3.0	3.4	7.6	6.6
Europe	24.9	26.6	29.3	27.8	21.1
United States	0.1	1.8	27.5	21.6	20.6
USSR	4.4	5.4	9.2	9.0	3.8

Source: Derived from Table 2.1 and www.ggdc.net/Maddison.

http://dx.doi.org/10.1787/086178556753

Table 2.2b. Rates of Growth of World GDP, 1700-2003
(annual average compound growth rates)

	1700-1820	1820-1952	1952-78	1978-2003
China	0.85	0.22	4.39	7.85
India	0.17	0.56	3.85	5.28
Japan	0.25	1.74	7.86	2.53
Europe	0.58	1.71	4.37	2.00
United States	2.72	3.76	3.61	2.94
USSR	0.69	2.05	4.50	-0.40
World	0.52	1.64	4.59	3.12

Source: Derived from Table 2.1 and www.ggdc.net/Maddison.

http://dx.doi.org/10.1787/086178556753

Table 2.2c. Rates of Growth of World Per Capita GDP, 1700–2003
(annual average compound growth rates)

	1700-1820	1820-1952	1952-78	1978-2003
China	0.00	-0.10	2.33	6.57
India	-0.03	0.13	1.66	3.27
Japan	0.13	0.95	6.69	2.11
Europe	0.14	1.05	3.63	1.79
United States	0.72	1.61	2.24	1.85
USSR	0.10	1.11	3.55	-0.78
World	0.07	0.93	2.62	1.55

Source: Derived from Table 2.1 and www.ggdc.net/Maddison.

http://dx.doi.org/10.1787/086178556753

The Disintegration of the Imperial Regime

Domestic difficulties were worsened by a whole series of foreign challenges to Chinese sovereignty from the 1840s onwards. China was totally unprepared to meet intrusions from the sea. Her coastal defenses had been completely neglected. There were virtually no naval forces or modern artillery to stand up to foreign intruders. For a century China made humiliating concessions frittering away her sovereignty and losing large territories.

Psychologically and intellectually China was unable to respond or even to comprehend these new challenges. There was no foreign office and the capital city was far inland. The authorities had little interest in foreign trade. The only places where it was permitted were Macao (open only to Portuguese), Canton (for other Westerners), Amoy (for trade with the Philippines), Ningpo (for trade with Japan and Korea) and Kiakhta (for trade with Russia). There was almost no knowledge of Western geography and technology, even less knowledge of Western languages, an education system that concentrated its full attention on the Chinese classics and a power elite of gentry–bureaucrats who had no notion of changing the system of governance.

The First Foreign Intrusion 1840–42 and the Opening of Treaty Ports

Canton was the port the British had used for a century to buy tea. By the 1840s, they were buying 14 000 tons a year. Over several decades they built up a Chinese market for opium to pay for tea and other imports. By the 1840s the Chinese had to export silver to meet a deficit, whereas they had earlier had a silver inflow. Between 1820 and 1839 the annual opium shipments rose from 4 000 to 40 000 chests (Greenberg, 1951, p. 221). These imports were illegal and occurred only because of the laxity of local officials. However, Chinese concern about the currency outflow and the arrival of a new and vigorous commissioner, led to official seizure and destruction of 20 000 cases of British opium in 1839. The British trading lobby succeeded in provoking a war over the issue.

The result was a major surrender by China. British naval forces seized Hong Kong Island, which was ceded in perpetuity by the Treaty of Nanking in 1842. Canton, Amoy, Foochow, Ningpo and Shanghai were opened as "treaty ports" where extraterritorial rights were given to British traders and residents and consular jurisdiction prevailed. China agreed to end its previous import restrictions and to impose only moderate tariffs. It paid the British 6 million silver dollars to compensate for destruction of their opium and a further war "indemnity" of $21 million. In 1843, a supplementary agreement granted most–favoured–nation treatment, which meant that future Chinese concessions of rights to one foreign nation could then be claimed by other foreigners.

These treaties set the pattern for foreign commercial penetration of China. Within two years the French and Americans obtained similar concessions. Eventually 19 foreign nations acquired extraterritorial rights and privileges. By 1917, there were 92 treaty ports[1]. Some of them went deep into the heart of China, from Shanghai 1 400 kilometres up the Yangtse to Chungking.

The Taiping Rebellion 1850–64

The Taiping uprising lasted from 1850 to 1864, affected 16 provinces and involved occupation of China's most prosperous areas. It was a major ideological challenge to Ch'ing imperial authority and to the Confucian gentry–bureaucrats.

ISBN: 978-92-64-03762-5 © OECD 2007

The rebellion originated in the deep south in Kwangsi province. The imperial authority was weakened there by defeat in the opium war and there was very longstanding hostility between Hakka immigrants and local natives who had different dialects and habits.

The ideology of the rebellion originated with Hung Hsiu–Ch'üan, a Hakka from near Canton, who had studied for and failed the civil service examinations. After an encounter with Protestant missionaries, he had millenarian visions of a new social order, a kingdom of Heavenly Peace (Tai–p'ing). He thought he was the son of God, a younger brother of Jesus, destined to be the emperor of the new heavenly kingdom. Over a period of a decade he built up a large following of Hakkas, nominating leading associates as junior sons of God, or kings. As a demonstration of anti–Manchu fervour they gave up shaved foreheads and pigtails. They attacked official corruption, were against opium, alcohol, prostitution and polygamy. They also favoured abolition of private land ownership, to be replaced with government land allocations varying according to family size and land fertility, though they did not in fact implement this idea. They integrated their military and civil administration, abolished the Confucian educational curriculum, and desecrated temples and shrines. They built up a disciplined army of zealots, considerate to the ordinary populace, but hostile to the old bureaucrats and gentry.

The new movement had extraordinary success. In 1851 the Taipings started to move North, captured a huge arsenal of munitions and more than 5 000 vessels at Yochow in Hunan in 1852, then captured and looted the triple cities (Wuchang, Hankow and Hangyang) at the junction of the Yangtse and Han rivers in Hupei province. With their newly acquired grain, ammunition and ships, they took Nanking in Kiangsu province in 1853 where they established their Heavenly Capital and maintained their occupation for eleven years. The regular Imperial troops (the Manchu banner forces and green standard garrisons) had been swept aside in their northward path and the major camps which they had established on either side of Nanking were destroyed by the Taiping forces in 1856. In the same year there were major quarrels within the leadership, which ended with large scale slaughter of those who challenged the Heavenly King. In spite of this, the Taipings had renewed success in 1860, enlarging their domain eastwards by capturing Soochow, as well as Ningpo and Hangchow in Chekiang province.

The Taiping movement was not anti–foreign and the Western occupants of the treaty ports were initially neutral towards the movement. They regarded its version of Christianity as blasphemous and found the Taipings condescending, but were not convinced that the rebellion was against their own interests until the rebels started harassing their trade. In 1861–62 the merchant and business interest in Shanghai hired a foreign legion to keep them at bay.

However, the defeat of the rebellion was primarily the work of new professional armies created to defend the interests of the Ch'ing dynasty and the gentry. As the traditional military force was undisciplined, incompetent and badly generalled, the government called on a scholar–official, Tseng Kuo–fan, to raise a new kind of professional force with better training, discipline and tactics. Tseng created a new Hunan army and navy of 120 000 men and attracted other brilliant Chinese officials who became successful generals. Tseng's associate, Li Hung–chang, organised another new army. These forces took some time to develop their fighting strength but eventually surrounded and destroyed the Taiping in Nanking in 1864.

The emergence of a new kind of military force made a lasting change in the nature of the Ch'ing regime. It meant a significant devolution of central power to the provincial authorities and it ended the previous strict separation of bureaucrats and the military. There was increasing reliance on Chinese rather than Manchu officials as governors and governors general of provinces. The Ch'ing regime would have liked to disband the new forces and indeed started to do so, but they were needed to liquidate the Nien rebellion in North China and the Muslim revolts in Shensi and Kansu. During the Taiping rebellion Tseng had been in charge of four major provinces. Li became governor general of the province of Chihli and virtual prime minister from 1870–95, Tso T'sung–t'ang was governor general of

Chekiang and Fukien and later of Shensi and Kansu where he put down the Muslim rebellion and later reconquered Sinkiang. The new generals remained an important pressure group for the post–Taiping programme of self–strengthening but their bureaucratic–gentry interests kept them loyal to the dynasty. Their moves for modernisation were to a substantial degree frustrated, limited by shortage of fiscal resources and the conservative policies of the Imperial house, dominated between 1861 and 1908 by the Dowager Empress Tz'u–hsi.

British, French and Russian Aggression

There were two major foreign actions against China during the Taiping rebellion — a joint attack by the British and French to expand their shipping and trading privileges and Russian seizure of eastern Siberia.

The war of 1858–60 was a joint undertaking by the British and French. A provisional Tientsin settlement of 1858 created eleven new treaty ports, added Kowloon to the territory of Hong Kong, opened coastal traffic and the Yangtse river network to foreign shipping, allowed foreigners to travel and trade in the interior and explicitly legalised the opium trade. To monitor the Chinese commitment to low tariffs, a Maritime Customs Inspectorate was created (with Sir Robert Hart as Inspector General from 1861 to 1908) to collect tariff revenue for the Chinese government. Part of this was earmarked to pay a 16 million silver dollar "indemnity" to defray the costs of the invaders. When the Chinese resisted ratification of the treaty in 1860, a Franco–British force destroyed the naval defences of Tientsin, occupied Peking and destroyed the Imperial Summer Palace. The Emperor fled to Jehol. As part of the peace settlement, China agreed to have foreign representatives in Peking and in 1861 opened a small foreign office. However, it did not establish legations abroad until 1877–79 (when they were opened in London, Paris, Washington, Tokyo and St. Petersburg) and the Ch'ing dynasty never developed the semblance of a foreign policy.

In 1858–60, Muraviev, the governor of Siberia took the opportunity to infiltrate Chinese territory North of the Amur river and East of the Issuri river down to the Korean border. China ceded this virtually uninhabited area in the Treaty of Peking, 1860 and thus lost the whole Pacific coast of Manchuria. Russia added more than 82 million hectares to eastern Siberia where the new port of Vladivostok was created. In the 1860s, Russia also expanded its central Asian empire by taking over the Khanates of Tashkent, Bokhara, Samarkand, Khiva and Khokand and later occupied Chinese territory on the Ili river, south of Lake Balkash. The Chinese eventually got part of this back in 1881 after paying a $5 million indemnity.

In the decade 1885–95 there were other blows which made a mockery of Chinese attempts at self strengthening. France had been gradually taking over Chinese tributary territory in Vietnam since 1859. In 1884–85 there was open war in Tongking. In 1885 the French destroyed the new naval yard at Foochow and blockaded Taiwan, leading to Chinese cession of suzerainty over Indo–China in 1885. Following the French lead, the British took Burma, where Chinese suzerainty was surrendered in 1886.

The War with Japan 1894–95 and Its Aftermath

There was a gradual buildup of Japanese pressure from the 1870s when they asserted their suzerainty over the Ryuku Islands (now Okinawa) and sent a punitive expedition to Taiwan to chastise aborigines for killing shipwrecked sailors. In 1876 Japan sent a military and naval force to Korea and opened the ports of Pusan, Inchon and Wonsan to Japanese consular jurisdiction. In 1894 Japan

ISBN: 978-92-64-03762-5 © OECD 2007

intervened militarily in Korea and sparked off a war. The Chinese navy was defeated off the Yalu river. The Japanese crossed the Yalu into China and took Port Arthur (Lushun) and Dairen (Talien) in the Liaotung peninsula. In the Treaty of Shimonoseki, 1895, China was forced to recognise that its suzerainty over Korea had lapsed. Taiwan, the Pescadores and the Liaotung peninsula were ceded to Japan. Chungking, Soochow, Hangchow and Shasi were opened to Japan with treaty port status. Japanese citizens (and hence other foreigners) were now permitted to open factories and manufacture in China. Japan received an indemnity of 200 million taels, raised to 230 million when it agreed (under French, German and Russian pressure) to withdraw from Liaotung. This was the biggest indemnity China had ever paid. It amounted to a third of Japanese GDP and China had to finance it by foreign borrowing.

The Chinese defeat led to an avalanche of other foreign claims. In 1896, Russia got a wide strip of land in Manchuria to build a new "Chinese Eastern Railway" from Chita to Vladivostok; in 1897 it occupied Port Arthur and Dairen and obtained the right to build a Southern Manchurian railway. In 1897 Germany seized a naval base at Kiachow and railway concessions in Shantung. In 1898 the British extorted a lease on the port of Weihaiwei in Shantung, obtained a 99 year lease on the "new territories" to provide a bigger base in Hong Kong and demanded Chinese acknowledgement of their sphere of influence in the Yangtse area. The French got a long lease on the southern port of Kwangchow (opposite Hainan island) and acknowledgement of a sphere of influence in the southern provinces of Kwangtung, Kwangsi and Yunnan. The Japanese were granted a sphere of influence in Fukien opposite Taiwan. The only demand which China rejected was Italy's attempt to secure a base at Sanmen bay in Chekiang province.

The defeat by an Asian country so much smaller than China and the subsequent dismemberment of Chinese sovereignty entailed major loss of face and political eclipse for the bureaucrats behind the self–strengthening movement. A younger generation of scholars started to press the regime for more fundamental institutional reform and persuaded the Kuang–hsü emperor to issue a stream of decrees in the 100 days reform of 1898 to change the educational curriculum, examination and school system, to simplify and modernise the administration and to promote railway and industrial development. These propositions were overturned by the coup d'état of the Dowager Empress in 1898, supported by the vested interest of bureaucratic office holders who did not want change in the system of governance and Confucian education. The Emperor became her prisoner and she reinforced the role of Manchus in the administration.

The Boxer War and the Collapse of the Ch'ing Dynasty

In 1900, the Empress organised her own atavistic response to foreign intervention by patronage of the "Boxers", a popular movement which began to attack Chinese christians and foreign missionaries. She prevented retribution for such actions, which made the Boxers more aggressive. They cut the telegraph lines, burned the British Summer Legation, killed the Chancellor of the Japanese Legation and the German Minister, burned churches and foreign residences in Peking and were allowed to take over in Tientsin. On 21 June 1900 the Empress declared war on the foreign powers, put the Boxers under Imperial command and encouraged them to attack the legations, which were grouped in the centre of Peking.

The provincial authorities at Canton, Wuhan and Shantung refused to accept the orders of the Empress, urged her to suppress the Boxers and protect the foreigners. Her generals were not eager for combat. An international force of 18 000 took Tientsin and relieved the Peking legations on 14 August. The Dowager's war had lasted less than two months and was an ignominious defeat. The court retreated to Sian in the north west province of Shensi. The allied powers were afraid of a complete Chinese collapse and war between themselves, so they were fairly lenient to the Empress. The peace settlement required the execution and exile of guilty ministers, permanent strengthening of the legation guards in

Peking, destruction of forts between Peking and the sea, the right to station foreign troops in this region and an indemnity of 450 million taels. During the crisis, the Russians had occupied the whole of Manchuria. They agreed to leave, but dragged their feet and were forced out in the Russo–Japanese war of 1905, when Japan took over Southern Manchuria and half of the island of Sakhalin (Karafuto). Korea became a Japanese protectorate and in 1910 a Japanese colony.

The Dowager Empress returned to Peking in 1902 and reluctantly introduced reforms on lines similar to the 100 days programme which she had overturned in 1898. They included restructuring the military, winding down the Green Standard forces and modernised training for the Manchu Banner forces. The predominant role in the military was allotted to General Yuan Shih–k'ai who had earlier helped her 1898 coup d'état. A Foreign Ministry was created and there were also educational reforms. The Confucian style civil service examinations were abandoned after 1905 with profound adverse repercussions for the status of the gentry. The Dowager Empress procrastinated over constitutional reform and died in 1908, the day after the death (probably by poison) of her nephew, the Emperor. Imperial responsibility fell on the regent for the new child emperor. The regent put Yuan Shih–k'ai into retirement, ordered the creation of provincial assemblies in 1909, but rejected demands for early convening of a parliament.

This refusal plus a clumsy government proposal to nationalise private railway companies sparked revolutionary action in Wuchang followed by secession of 15 provincial assemblies from the Ch'ing dynasty in October–November 1911. Since the 1880s, Sun Yat–sen had been the main activist promoting a nationalist republican movement. This he did largely outside China, appealing to Chinese students in Japan, the United States and Europe to join the revolutionary alliance he set up in Tokyo in 1905. On 25 December 1911 the provincial delegates in Shanghai elected Sun to be provisional president of the Republic of China, scheduled to emerge on 1 January 1912.

Meanwhile the Regent withdrew and recalled Yuan as premier. Instead of defending the Manchu dynasty, he persuaded the new Dowager Empress to abdicate (though the Imperial family and their retainers were allowed to live in the Forbidden City until 1924). Sun Yat–sen had always thought the revolution would start with military rule so he voluntarily stepped down as provisional president on 13 February, in favour of Yuan who was then elected by the same group which less than two months earlier had elected Sun.

The Republican Regimes

Military and Warlord Government 1911–28

Thus the dynasty was overthrown by the military, which had been increasing its power within the old system for the previous half century. Power was to remain in their hands and those of provincial warlords until 1928. The new republican president had no intention of implementing Sun's principles of democracy and people's livelihood. He had the leader of the KMT parliamentary party assassinated, dissolved the new parliament and created a lifetime position for himself as president with the right to name his successor. In fact he contemplated making himself emperor. Yuan continued to make concessions to foreigners. In 1915 he recognised Russian suzerainty over Outer Mongolia, British suzerainty in Tibet and accepted new demands from Japan for expanded power in Shantung, Manchuria, Inner Mongolia and the Yangtse valley.

In 1916 Yuan died in a situation in which several provinces were already in revolt against his rule. This was followed by 12 years of civil war in which central government disappeared and the country was run by regional warlords.

ISBN: 978-92-64-03762-5 © OECD 2007

The Rise of the Kuomintang

The period of decentralised warlord government was brought to an end in 1928 when Ch'iang Kai–shek set up a KMT (Kuomintang) government in Nanking.

The new republican government stemmed from the nationalist activism of Sun Yat–sen. He had fled to Japan in 1913, returned in 1916 and shuttled between Shanghai and Canton from then until his death in 1925, trying to build up a regional power base and rather opportunistically trying to get foreign finance for his movement. In 1923 he began to get financial and organisational support from the USSR which urged him to ally with the new Chinese Communist Party (created in 1921). Sun managed to set up a regional military government in Canton. He received Soviet financial support and organisational help from his Soviet political advisor, Michael Borodin. He also got rifles, machine guns, artillery, ammunition and a Soviet military advisor, Vasili Blyukher. The KMT party organisation was strengthened and Sun's disciple Chiang Kai–shek became head of the Whampoa military academy near Canton, after several months of training in Moscow. Following Sun's death in 1925, Chiang consolidated his leading role in the KMT and moved north with a new National Revolutionary Army of 85 000. By the end of 1926 he had captured Wuhan and Foochow and controlled seven provinces. In 1927 Chiang entered Shanghai where communist activists had organised a general strike in support of his approach. Chiang provided some temporary reassurance to the business and foreign interests in Shanghai by betraying his communist allies and arranging to have union activists murdered. Soon after he used blackmail and terror to raise substantial funds from the Shanghai capitalists. In 1928, after a serious clash with Japanese troops in Shantung, he managed to make deals with the remaining warlord interests in support of a new KMT government in Nanking. He maintained his position as effective head of this government until 1949.

The important warlords were allowed to operate in semi–independent regional territories in return for recognition of the new central government. However, it did not manage to liquidate the communist movement. The pro–Soviet elements in the CP were unsuccessful in establishing city Soviets, but Mao built up peasant support in rural areas outside the official party jurisdiction. He achieved broad rural support by redistribution of land to poor peasants, small landlords and richer peasants and fighting the KMT troops with guerilla tactics. He consolidated his leadership in the party by successfully leading the Long March from his south China base in Kiangsi in 1934 to a new, much more secure, base in Yenan in northwest Shensi in 1936.

The Japanese initiated hostilities in Manchuria in September 1931 and overran the whole of it within five months. Chiang's government offered little substantive resistance and appealed ineffectively to the League of Nations. In 1932, the Japanese opened a second front by attacking Shanghai and the KMT government had to retreat temporarily from Nanking. In 1933 Japan created a new state of Manchukuo which incorporated China's three Manchurian provinces and Jehol (which included parts of Inner Mongolia, Hopei and Liaoning). China was obliged to turn the area around Peking and Tientsin into a demilitarised zone, which left the north defenceless.

War and Civil War 1937–49

In July 1937, the Japanese attacked again in north China, near Peking. It is not altogether clear what their war aims were, but they presumably wanted to take over the whole of north China after a short campaign and thereafter to dominate a compliant KMT government in the south as part of their new order in East Asia. This time the KMT reacted strongly, inflicted heavy casualties on Japanese forces in their second front near Shanghai. They also rejected German attempts to arrange a peace settlement and the war lasted for eight years.

ISBN: 978-92-64-03762-5 © OECD 2007

The war went badly for the Nanking government. Peking and Tientsin were lost in July. The Japanese took Nanking in December 1937 and massacred about 100 000 civilians. The KMT government moved to the deep southwest in Chungking. They transferred equipment from factories in zones likely to be occupied by Japan and destroyed what was left in areas they had to evacuate. In 1938, the Japanese took Canton and the key junction of Wuhan on the Yangtse. Thus, after 18 months they had occupied most of east China with the biggest cities and the most advanced parts of the economy. In 1937–38 they set up three puppet Chinese administrations. In 1940 these were consolidated in Nanking under Wang Ching–wei, a prominent KMT politician who had broken away from the government in Chungking.

After 1938 Chiang avoided major engagements with the Japanese. The communists in Yenan also managed to survive, successfully resisting Japanese pressure by guerilla tactics. There was an uneasy truce between the KMT and the Chinese communist forces during the war, but nothing that resembled reconciliation. Both sides expected conflict once the war with Japan was over. After 1941, when the war between Japan and the United States started, the Japanese took over the treaty ports and diverted their main energies to other theatres of war. Eventually, Japan was defeated by US action, Japanese forces left China in 1945 and the civil war between the KMT and the communists started in 1946.

At the end of the war, the communists were much stronger than they had been in 1937. They had a million well disciplined regular forces and a substantial militia. However, the KMT had nearly three times as many troops and diplomatic recognition from both the United States and the Soviet Union. The United States ordered the Japanese army to surrender only to KMT forces, which acquired large stocks of weapons. The corrupt and autocratic KMT government created a bad impression in reoccupied areas where its officers and officials enriched themselves at the expense of the populace, who were suffering from hyperinflation. In the communist areas, the troops were more austere and better disciplined and made successful attempts to win peasant support by action to impose land reform.

Table 2.3. **Population by Province, China 1819-1953**
(million)

	1819	1893	1953
Five provinces most affected by Taiping Rebellion[a]	153.9	101.8	145.3
Three provinces affected by Muslim Rebellions[b]	41.3	26.8	43.1
Ten other provinces of China proper[c]	175.6	240.9	338.6
Three Manchurian provinces[d]	2.0	5.4	41.7
Sinkiang, Mongolia, Tibet, etc.	6.4	11.8	14.0
Total	379.4	386.7	582.7

a.   Anhwei, Chekiang, Hupei, Kiangsi, Kiangsu.
b.   Kansu, Shensi, Shansi.
c.   Fukien, Honan, Hopei, Hunan, Kwangsi, Kwangtung, Kweichow, Shantung, Szechwan, Yunnan.
d.   Heilungkiang, Kirin, Liaoning.

Source: Perkins (1969), p. 212. For 1819, Perkins provides no figure for the last group (except for Tibet). I assumed that their 1819-73 growth was at the same rate as between 1873 (for which he gives figures) and 1893. There were ultimately 23 provinces in the Ch'ing Empire, i.e. the 21 listed above plus Sinkiang and Taiwan which became provinces in 1885. Prior to that Taiwan had been part of Fukien. Taiwan is not included in this table; in 1893 its population was 2.5 million. Outer Mongolia, (with a population of about 1 million) seceded in 1911. The population of the large Siberian territory ceded to Russia in 1860 was only 15 000.

http://dx.doi.org/10.1787/087408307627

The Soviet Union declared war on Japan in the last week of the war and occupied Manchuria, as had been agreed at the Yalta Conference. However, they stayed for almost a year and Stalin started to back the Chinese communists rather than the KMT. Under Soviet protection, the Communist forces took over Japanese arms and equipment in Manchuria. By the time the Soviets left in mid–1946, they had effective military and political control of that area.

After three years of fierce fighting, the communist forces eventually defeated the KMT. Mao proclaimed the establishment of the People's Republic on 1 October 1949 and the KMT government fled to Taiwan in December 1949.

  ISBN: 978-92-64-03762-5 © OECD 2007

Economic Decline, 1820–1949

In the five provinces most affected by the Taiping rebellion, population in the early 1890s was 50 million lower than it had been 70 years earlier (see Table 2.3). The Taiping war is generally considered to have led directly to 20 million deaths, but it obviously also had important indirect effects in reducing birth rates and increasing death rates. Parts of the same area bore the main brunt of the Yellow River floods in 1855. Due to governmental neglect of irrigation works it burst its banks and caused widespread devastation in Anhwei and Kiangsu. It had previously flowed to the sea through the lower course of the Huai River, but after 1855 it flowed from Kaifeng to the north of the Shantung peninsula, reaching the sea more than 400 kilometres north of its previous channel.

Population also fell by more than 14 million in the three northern provinces (Kansu, Shensi and Shansi) which were affected by the northern Muslim rebellions and their brutal repression in the 1860s and 1870s and by very severe drought and famine in 1877–78.

In the rest of China, population grew by 74 million from 1819 to 1893 — a growth rate of 0.46 per cent a year. This was a good deal slower than in the eighteenth century, but big enough to offset the population loss in the provinces worst hit by the nineteenth century rebellions.

It seems clear that the large–scale nineteenth century rebellions caused a serious fall in living standards in the areas affected whilst they were under way. I have assumed that full recovery had not been attained by 1890. It is highly probable that there was a fall in per capita income from 1820 to 1890.

In 1890, modern manufacturing and transport represented only one half a per cent of GDP (see Table 2.5). China had virtually no railways, the main innovation in transport was the arrival of foreign steamers operating on the Yangtse and coastal routes. A telegraphy network was started in the 1880s. The modest self–strengthening programme involved creation of some government industrial undertakings — arsenals at Shanghai and Nanking and a dockyard in Foochow in the 1860s, inauguration of the China Merchants' Steam Navigation Company which bought out an American shipping company in Shanghai in 1877, creation of the Kaiping coal mines in Tientsin, a couple of textile mills in the 1870s, a few more factories in the 1880s and the Hanyang ironworks in 1890. The governmental effort at modernisation might have been bigger if the Dowager Empress had not diverted substantial funds to rebuilding the Imperial Summer Palace.

The urban proportion of the total population of China was probably not much bigger at the end of the nineteenth century than it had been in 1820 (see Perkins, 1969, pp. 292–95 for 1900–10 and Table 1.7 above for 1820). The character of most Chinese cities had not changed much except for those which had suffered extensive damage in the Taiping era (such as Nanking and the Wuhan cities). However, the Treaty ports, particularly Shanghai and Hong Kong, were islands of modernity. Foreigners were the main beneficiaries of the extraterritorial privileges, but they interacted with Chinese intermediaries (compradores) who were gradually becoming familiar with western banking, shipping and technology. By 1890, Chinese entrepreneurs were still a small group in the Treaty ports, but they were later to be the nucleus of Chinese capitalism.

In 1890 Chinese exports were about 0.6 per cent of GDP (see Table 3.25). There were virtually no imports of machinery or other modern inputs. Opium still represented more than a quarter of the total; cotton goods 41 per cent; food items about 15 per cent; and woollen goods about 3 per cent. The biggest export item was tea, with 27 per cent of the total; raw silk represented about a quarter; silk products 6 per cent; and raw cotton 3 per cent (see Hsiao, 1974, for the composition of trade).

From 1890 to 1933 per capita GDP rose by about 7 per cent (an average of about 0.16 per cent a year). This was a very poor performance by the standards of Western countries, but there were some changes in the structure of the economy (see Table 2.5). By 1933, the modern sector (manufacturing, mining, electricity production, transport and communications) had risen to 5.3 per cent of GDP, compared with 0.7 per cent in 1890. From 1937 to 1949 China endured eight years of war with Japan and three and a half years of civil war. As a result, per capita GDP in 1952 had fallen back to the 1890 level. Nevertheless, the share of the modern sector rose and by 1952 reached 10.4 per cent of GDP.

Ch'ing economic policy was hardly a prime mover in Chinese modernisation. Because of the huge indemnities associated with the Japanese war and the Boxer rebellion, it faced great financial strains. These together with the decline in world silver prices led to substantial inflation. Between 1890 and 1911, the value of the silver tael against the US dollar fell by half.

The continued expansion in treaty port facilities, the freedom which foreigners obtained in 1895 to open production facilities in China, and the Russian and Japanese interest in developing Manchuria contributed substantially to the growth of the modern sector, including railways, banking, commerce, industrial production and mining. There was also an associated growth of Chinese capitalist activity, which had its origins mainly in the *compradore* middlemen in the Treaty ports. There was an inflow of capital from overseas Chinese who had emigrated in substantial numbers to other parts of Asia. They maintained their cultural links with southeast China and those who became prosperous invested in their homeland[2].

The warlord governments which ran China from 1911 to 1928 did very little to stimulate industry and the continuance of local warfare and arbitrary levies on business was not particularly propitious to capitalist development. However, the ending of the civil service examinations and the switch of power from bureaucrats to the military, led to a crumbling of the social structure and mental attitudes of the old regime. Capitalists became a more respectable and less fettered part of the social order. For young educated people, it became more attractive to emulate their behaviour.

The advent of the First World War weakened the competitive strength of Western capitalists in the Treaty ports, but provided opportunities for Chinese capitalists to expand their role in industrial, mining, shipping, banking and railway ventures.

The KMT government made some institutional changes in economic policy from 1928 to 1937. Tariff autonomy was recovered in 1929. This permitted a large rise in duties on foreign goods which augmented government revenue and gave some protection to Chinese industry. In 1931, the *likin*, the internal tax on goods in transit, was abolished. This had been introduced as a desperate remedy for fiscal needs in the 1860s but it had hindered Chinese development in a discriminatory way, as foreigners had been able to purchase exemption from it. There was no attempt to reform land taxes, which had once been the mainstay of imperial finance, but had fallen into the hands of provincial governments in the 1920s. The government managed to increase revenues in the early 1930s, but Young (1971), p. 146, suggests that the ratio of revenue at all levels of government to GNP was only 5.4 per cent at its peak in 1936. There was always a sizeable budget deficit because of the large military expenditure. The government reduced its foreign debt burden in a prolonged cat–and–mouse game with creditors, which involved writing down and rollovers of debt, sweetened by occasional repayments of principal and interest. A substantial part of the debt arose from the "indemnities" following the war with Japan and the Boxer rebellion. The Western powers were more acquiescent on debt default than they might have been if the original loans had been raised for commercial purposes.

A central bank was created in 1928 in Shanghai with the finance minister as governor. The government was in effective control of the other big banks and one observer said "it would be difficult to know where the government ends and the banks begin" (Young, 1971, p. 264). There was a large expansion of branches of modern–style banks which led to a sharp decline in native banks, but the new banks did not engage significantly in rural lending or finance of new industrial enterprises. The monetary reform of 1935 created a new paper currency to replace silver. Thereafter, the government was much better placed to follow the inflationary policy which in the end drained its political credibility. The KMT had little success

ISBN: 978-92-64-03762-5 © OECD 2007

Table 2.4. **Exports per Capita, China, India and Japan, 1850-2003**

($)

	China	India	Japan	China	India	Japan
	(at current prices & exchange rates)			(at 1990 prices & exchange rates)		
1850	0.12	0.36	0.00	n.a.	n.a.	n.a.
1870	0.28	1.01	0.44	3.90	13.70	1.5.
1913	0.70	2.49	6.10	9.60	31.22	32.59
1929	1.36	3.39	15.32	12.90	24.64	68.67
1950	1.01	3.18	9.95	11.60	15.29	42.21
1973	6.60	5.00	341.00	13.24	16.69	874.87
2003	339.96	54.40	3 278.9	352.17	82.02	3 166.80

Source: China from Appendix E. India and Japan from W.A. Lewis in Grassman and Lundberg (1981), p. 49, Maddison (1995a), pp. 235 and 237, and IMF, *International Financial Statistics.*

http://dx.doi.org/10.1787/086217020318

Table 2.5. **Structure of Chinese GDP in 1933 Prices, 1890-1952**

(percentages of total GDP)

	1890	1913	1933	1952
Farming, Fishery & Forestry	68.5	67.0	64.0	55.7
Handicrafts	7.7	7.7	7.4	7.4
Modern Manufacturing	0.1	0.6	2.5	4.3
Mining	0.2	0.3	0.8	2.1
Electricity	0.0	0.0	0.5	1.2
Construction	1.7	1.7	1.6	3.0
Traditional Transport & Comm.	5.1	4.6	4.0	3.8
Modern Transport & Comm.	0.4	0.8	1.5	2.8
Trade	8.2	9.0	9.4	9.3
Government	2.8	2.8	2.8	
Finance	0.3	0.5	0.7	{ 10.4
Personal Services	1.1	1.2	1.2	
Residential Services	3.9	3.8	3.6	
GDP	100.0	100.0	100.0	100.0

Source: Table C.1.

http://dx.doi.org/10.1787/087487077184

in reducing the treaty port privileges[3] of foreign powers or their control of some of the organs of government. The Western powers had refused to end extraterritoriality at the 1919 Peace Conference in Paris and although most of them professed a willingness to surrender these at some time in the future, the system was only terminated by treaties with Britain and the United States in 1943. Foreign control of the customs service suffered only gradual attrition. In 1937 only one–third of the commissioners were Chinese and the Sino–foreign salt administration did not disintegrate until after 1938.

The government did nothing effective to help the peasantry with land reform or rural credit. It enacted a land law in 1930 intended to promote owner occupation and to put limits on rents. Young, the government's economic advisor commented as follows: "Unhappily the law of 1930 remained largely a dead letter. The government was too preoccupied with internal and external emergencies to promote large–scale progress in basic reform and improvement of rural conditions. Furthermore, most of the leaders had an urban background and were not oriented toward rural affairs and they had an empathy with landowning and financial interests" (Young, 1971, p. 302). Landlords probably became more predatory after they had lost their privileged gentry status and the rural population was still exposed to warlord depredations.

The successive finance ministers, Soong from 1928 to 1933 and Kung thereafter, were both brothers–in–law of Chiang Kai–shek and enjoyed a cosy relationship with the banking community. The government tried to promote industrial development through the activity of government corporations. In this respect it was as paternalistic as the "self–strengthening" Ch'ing reformers in the 1870s and 1880s. Transport was one of the few areas where progress was made, with significant extensions of the road and railway network.

For 1933, Liu and Yeh (1965, pp. 143 and 428) estimated that 67 per cent of gross value added in factories was produced in Chinese–owned firms, 18.8 per cent in foreign firms in China proper and 14.2 per cent in Manchuria, most of which was Japanese–owned. In cotton textiles, 48 per cent of spindles and 56 per cent of looms were foreign–owned in 1936. The great bulk of these were Japanese (Chao, 1977, pp. 301–7). Traditional manufacturing in the handicraft sector was entirely in Chinese hands and gross value added there was three times as big as in modern manufacturing. In shipping, 1936 foreign–owned tonnage was about 55 per cent of the total (Hou, 1965, p. 60); in 1937, foreign–owned railway mileage was about a third of the total (Hou, 1965, pp. 65 and 244). In 1937 about half of coal output was produced in foreign–owned or Sino–foreign companies (Hou, 1965, p. 231). In 1933, foreign banks seem to have accounted for less than one–third of value added in the financial sector (Liu and Yeh, 1965, p. 604). In agriculture, foreign participation was virtually nil. Altogether, it seems likely that in 1933, about 2.5 per cent of Chinese GDP was produced by foreign–owned firms.

Table 2.7 presents estimates of the stock of foreign direct investment in China for 1902–36. It is clear that there was a substantial increase. Nevertheless in the 1930s, it represented only about $5 per head of population, i.e. half the level in India, a seventh of the level in Taiwan and one hundredth of that in Australia (see Maddison, 1989, p. 61). In the 1930s, about 46 per cent of foreign direct investment was in Shanghai, 36 per cent in Manchuria and 18 per cent in the rest of China. In 1936, 37 per cent of the investment was in foreign trade and banking, 30 per cent in transport and communications; and 21 per cent in industry. The rest was mainly in real estate.

Chinese exports reached a peak of about 2.3 per cent of GDP at the end of the 1920s. They fell in the world depression of the early 1930s and then recovered somewhat, but by 1937, when the war with Japan started, they were still about 10 per cent below the 1929 volume. In 1937 about 38 per cent of exports came from the Japanese puppet state of Manchukuo. About 46 per cent of those from China proper left from Shanghai, 15 per cent from Tientsin and 7 per cent from Canton (see Hsiao, 1974).

The commodity composition of trade in 1937 was much more varied than it had been in 1890. Tea exports had fallen to only 3.5 per cent of the total, due to competition from the plantations developed in India and Ceylon by British investors. The biggest export items in 1937 were wood oil, raw silk, eggs, wolfram, tin, embroidered articles, raw cotton, tea, bristles and wool (see Table 2.8). Import structure had also changed drastically. Opium imports had petered out after World War I. 1937 textile imports had dropped to less than 6 per cent of the total, there were some food imports, a significant share for industrial inputs and capital equipment.

In the twentieth century, China ran a significant trade deficit, quite unlike the situation in India and Indonesia which had large surpluses. For the 1930s, Remer (1933) estimated that there were about 9 million overseas Chinese. About 3 or 4 million of these were making remittances to their families in China. For 1929, he estimated the total flow to be 281 million Chinese dollars ($180 million). Ninety per cent of these flows came via Hong Kong, about 44 per cent originated in the United States and most of the rest came from Asian countries. Remer also suggested that customs returns understated Chinese exports, particularly those to Russia and Hong Kong, so the overall trade deficit may have been smaller than it appeared.

 ISBN: 978-92-64-03762-5 © OECD 2007

Table 2.6. **Length of Railway Lines in Service, 1870-1995**
(kilometres)

	China	India	Japan
1870	0	7 678	0
1890	10	26 400	2 349
1913	9 854	55 822	10 570
1930	13 441	68 045	21 593
1950	22 238	54 845[a]	27 401
1975	46 000	60 438	26 752
1995	54 000	63 000	27 258

a. Excludes 11 166 kilometres in Bangladesh and Pakistan.

Source: 1870-1950 for China and 1870-1975 for India and Japan from Mitchell (1982), pp.504-7. China 1975 and 1994 from SSB, *China Statistical Yearbook 1995*, p. 467. India 1995 from Press Information Bureau, Government of India. Japan 1995 from Ministry of Transport, Tokyo.

http://dx.doi.org/10.1787/087516174305

Table 2.7. **Stock of Foreign Direct Investment, China, 1902-36**
($ million)

	1902	1914	1931	1936
At current prices	503.2	1 067.0	2 493.2	2 681.7
In 1931 prices	922.5	1 784.0	2 493.2	2 681.7

Source: First row from Hou (1965), p. 13. These figures include Hong Kong and Manchuria. The stock of British investment in Hong Kong in 1931 was about $94 million. The adjustment to 1931 prices is made from the Nankai price indices cited by Hou on p. 14. He suggests on p. 13 that there was no change in price levels from 1931 to 1936.

http://dx.doi.org/10.1787/087516174305

Table 2.8. **Leading Items in Chinese Commodity Trade, 1937**
(000 yuan)

Exports		Imports	
Wood Oil	89 846	Paper	56 498
Raw Silk	56 598	Kerosene	47 860
Eggs	54 382	Rice	40 781
Wolfram	40 759	Woollen Goods	35 000
Tin	39 917	Gasoline	27 613
Embroidery	36 900	Timber	23 239
Raw Cotton	31 301	Cotton Goods	21 710
Tea	30 787	Sugar	21 471
Bristles	27 921	Textile Machinery	20 986
Wool	19 427	Automobiles, Trucks & Spare Parts	19 096
Silk Piece Goods	17 728	Leaf Tobacco	19 449
Ground Nut Oil	17 332	Liquid Fuel	14 968
Coal	13 044	Railway Equipment	13 946
Hides	12 602	Iron and Steel	17 096
Antimony	11 446	Fishery Products	13 823
		Electrical Machinery	4 681
Total Exports	880 010	Total Imports	953 386

Source: Hsiao (1974). These figures exclude imports and exports of Manchukuo.

http://dx.doi.org/10.1787/087560164431

In the 1930s, China was a major exporter of silver. This situation was unusual, as China over the long run had been a silver importer. Net silver imports were $74 million in 1928 and $68 million in 1929. In 1934 under pressure from domestic silver producers, the US government instituted an official silver purchase programme the purpose of which was to help raise the general price level and to benefit US silver producers. Between 1932 and 1935, silver prices more than doubled in New York and this sparked off a large outflow from China. The Chinese authorities took advantage of this situation to effectively demonetise silver and shift to a paper currency in 1935, which became a floating peg unattached to sterling, the dollar or gold. The character of the currency reform had to be cosmeticised for diplomatic reasons. Overt abandonment of silver would have underlined the absurd consequences of US policy in pushing the world's biggest silver user off the silver standard (see Maddison, 1985). Paper money greatly increased the potential for deficit finance.

Prices rose by about a fifth from 1926 to the first half of 1937, but a situation of hyperinflation developed during the war years. From 1937 to 1941 retail prices rose 15–fold in Shanghai and 37–fold in Chungking. At the end of the war prices were 2 500 times as high as in 1937 in Chungking (see Young, 1965, p. 139).

From the 1860s onwards, the most dynamic areas in the Chinese economy were Shanghai and Manchuria.

Shanghai rose to prominence because of its location at the mouth of a huge system of waterways. "The total of inland waterways navigable by junks in nearly all seasons is nearly 30 000 miles. To this must be added an estimated half million miles of canalised or artificial waterways in the delta area. It is not surprising therefore that between 1865 and 1936, Shanghai handled 45 to 65 per cent of China's foreign trade" (Eckstein, Galenson and Liu (1968, pp. 60–61). It was already an important coastal port in the Ch'ing dynasty with a population of 230 000 in the 1840s. By 1938 this had risen to 3.6 million and Shanghai was the biggest city in China (see Cooke Johnson, 1993, p. 180 and Perkins, 1969, p. 293).

Manchuria had been closed to Chinese settlement by the Manchu dynasty until the 1860s. The population rose from about 4.5 million in 1872–73 to 38.4 million in 1940; in the Japanese puppet state of Manchukuo there were 48.8 million in 1941 (including Jehol as well as the three Manchurian provinces). The Manchurian cultivated area rose from l.7 million hectares in 1872 to 15.3 million in 1940, i.e. from about 2 per cent to 15 per cent of the Chinese total. However, agriculture, forestry and fishery represented only about a third of Manchurian GDP in 1941. There was very substantial railway development, initially by Russia, then by Japan. Japan made major investments in Manchurian coal and metalliferous mining and in manufacturing in the 1930s. Value added in modern manufacturing more than quadrupled between 1929 and 1941; in mining it trebled. For 1933, Liu and Yeh (1965, p. 428), estimated that Manchukuo produced about 14 per cent of Chinese factory output. By 1941 this was likely to have risen to a third and by 1945 may well have been a half of modern manufacturing. GDP growth averaged 3.9 per cent a year from 1929 to 1941 and per capita GDP about 1.8 per cent (see Chao, 1982).

In 1940 there were 820 000 Japanese civilians in Manchukuo. By 1945 there were more than a million. This group consisted mainly of bureaucrats, technicians and administrative, managerial and supervisory personnel. Only 10 per cent were in agriculture, about 45 per cent in industry, commerce and transport and 26 per cent in public service. They were a privileged elite in a total population which was 85 per cent Chinese, 6 per cent Manchu, 3 per cent Korean and 2.5 per cent Mongol (Taeuber, 1958).

In 1945–46, during the Soviet occupation, the USSR dismantled most of the moveable equipment in Manchurian factories and shipped it back to Russia. Nevertheless, Manchuria remained an important industrial base in the communist period.

ISBN: 978-92-64-03762-5 © OECD 2007

The Ch'ing regime collapsed in 1911, after seven decades of major internal rebellion and humiliating foreign intrusions. The bureaucratic gentry elite were incapable of achieving serious reform or modernisation because of a deeply conservative attachment to a thousand year old polity on which their privileges and status depended. After its collapse there were nearly four decades in which political power was taken over by the military. They too were preoccupied with major civil wars and faced more serious foreign aggression than the Ch'ing. They did little to provide a new impetus for economic change and the five-tier political structure of the KMT government was far from democratic. The limited modernisation of the economy came mainly in the Treaty ports and in Manchuria, where foreign capitalist enterprise penetrated and the sprouts of Chinese capitalism burgeoned. The foreigners forced China to open its ports to international trade, but the size of the trade opportunities disappointed them.

Notes

1. Feuerwerker in the Cambridge History of China, vol. 12, pp. 128–29, explains that there was some dispute about the meaning of treaty port. The Chinese text of the Treaty of Nanking referred to "harbours" or "anchorages", whereas the English text referred to "cities" and towns. The five towns in the 1842 treaty were clearly sea ports. "By 1893, 28 additional places had been opened to foreign trade and, during 1894–1917, 59 more, making a total of 92 by the latter date. Some were inland cities or places on China's land frontiers; others were coastal ports or railway junctions in Manchuria; many were river ports on the Yangtze or West Rivers. Collectively they were commonly called in Chinese shang–pu or shang–fou, 'trading ports'. Juridically, the ports that were open to foreign trade fell into three categories: 'treaty ports' proper, that is, ports opened as a consequence of an international treaty or agreement; open ports voluntarily opened by the government of China though not obliged to by treaty and 'ports of call' at which foreign steamers were permitted to land or take on board passengers and under certain restrictions goods, but at which foreign residence was prohibited. Maritime customs stations were maintained at only 48 of these various places as of 1915". A list of 90 places can be found in Allen and Donnithorne (1954), pp. 265–68.

2. The overseas Chinese originally came almost exclusively from the southeastern provinces. There had been some migration during the Ming and a big wave at the beginning of the Manchu dynasty. The anti–Manchu pirate Koxinga occupied Taiwan and made incursions on the southeast coast. To cut off his supplies and "intimidate the population of these regions whose sympathies were anti–dynastic, the Manchus made the latter forsake a zone of country from about eight to thirty miles deep on the coasts of Kwangtung, Fukien and Chekiang. This region was denuded of its crops and its villages were burnt down" (Purcell, 1965, p. 24). As a result many emigrated. There was another wave after 1870 when the Ch'ing government recognised the right of Chinese to emigrate, under US pressure, in the Burlingame Treaty.

3. The *China Handbook 1937–1943*, Chinese Ministry of Information, 1943, pp. 178–79, gives details of the winding up of foreign concessions. Before the First World War, "19 countries enjoyed extraterritoriality and consular jurisdiction in China under the terms of unequal treaties". They were Austro–Hungary, Belgium, Brazil, Denmark, France, Germany, Great Britain, Italy, Japan, Mexico, the Netherlands, Norway, Peru, Portugal, Russia, Spain, Sweden, Switzerland and the United States. Austro–Hungary and Germany lost their rights in the First World War, Russian rights were suspended by the Chinese in 1920 and the USSR accepted this in 1924. The 1919 Versailles Peace Conference refused to consider abolition of extraterritoriality and when the Chinese tried to terminate the system in 1921 and 1929, most of the treaty powers dragged their feet. By the end of 1930 Mexican, Finnish, Persian, Greek, Bolivian, Czech and Polish nationals became amenable to Chinese jurisdiction. After the outbreak of war in 1937 China ended extraterritorial privileges for Italians, Japanese, Rumanian, Danish and Spanish nationals. In 1943, the United Kingdom and the United States gave up their extraterritorial privileges in a treaty with China and the system was thus ended. Specific ports were retroceded between 1927 and 1943.

Chapter 3

Dynamics of Development in the New China

The establishment of the People's Republic marked a sharp change in China's political elite and mode of governance. The degree of central control was much greater than under the Ch'ing dynasty or the KMT. It reached to the lowest levels of government, to the workplace, to farms and to households. The party was highly disciplined and maintained detailed oversight of the regular bureaucratic apparatus. The military were tightly integrated into the system. Propaganda for government policy and ideology was diffused through mass movements under party control. Landlords, national and foreign capitalist interests were eliminated by expropriation of private property. China became a command economy on the Soviet pattern. After a century of surrender or submission to foreign incursions and aggression, the new regime was a ferocious and successful defender of China's national integrity, willing to operate with minimal links to the world economy.

In the Maoist era, these political changes had substantial costs which reduced the returns on China's development effort. Its version of communism involved risky experimentation on a grand scale. Self–inflicted wounds brought the economic and political system close to collapse during the Great Leap Forward (1958–60) and again in the Cultural Revolution (1966–76) when education and the political system were deeply shaken. Nevertheless, economic performance was a great improvement over the past. GDP trebled, per capita real product rose 82 per cent and labour productivity by 58 per cent from 1952 to 1978. The economic structure was transformed. In 1952, industry's share of GDP was one seventh of that in agriculture. By 1978, it was nearly equal to the agricultural share. China achieved this in spite of its political and economic isolation, hostile relations with both the United States and the Soviet Unionas well as wars with Korea and India.

After 1978, there was a major political shift to a cautious pragmatic reformism which relaxed central political control and modified the economic system profoundly. These changes brought a more stable path of development and a great acceleration of economic growth. In the 25 years from 1978 to 2003 GDP rose nearly seven–fold, labour productivity rose four–fold, population growth decelerated sharply and per capita real income rose nearly five–fold. With per capita GDP rising 6.6 per cent a year, China enjoyed faster growth. in this period than any other country. The growth acceleration was mainly due to increased efficiency. Collective agriculture was abandoned and production decisions reverted to individual peasant households. Small–scale industrial and service activities were freed from government controls, the proportionate importance of state enterprise in industry and services was greatly reduced and there was a huge expansion of industrial production in urban areas financed by private domestic savings and a very large inflow of foreign capital ($620 billion). Exposure to foreign trade was greatly enhanced; the volume of exports rose 28–fold from 1978 to 2003, compared to the modest two–fold increase in 1952–78. This strengthened market forces, made it much easier to develop and absorb new technology and introduced consumers to a wide variety of new goods.

ISBN: 978-92-64-03762-5 © OECD 2007

Table 3.1. **Growth of GDP, by Sector, at Constant Prices, China 1890–2003**
(annual average compound growth rates)

	1890–1952	1952–2003	1952–78	1978–2003
Farming, Fishery & Forestry	0.3	3.3	2.2	4.5
Industry	1.7	10.0	10.1	9.8
Construction	1.6	8.5	7.8	9.8
Transport & Communication	0.9	8.3	6.0	10.8
Commerce & Restaurants	0.8	6.5	3.3	9.9
Other Services	1.1	4.9	4.2	5.6
GDP	0.6	6.1	4.4	7.9
Per Capita GDP	0.0	4.4	2.3	6.6
GDP Per Person Employed	0.0	3.8	1.8	5.8

Source: Appendices C and D.

http://dx.doi.org/10.1787/086224110085

Table 3.2. **Structure of Chinese GDP, 1890–2003**
(per cent of GDP at constant prices)

	1890	1952	1978	2003
Farming, Fishery & Forestry	68.5	59.7	34.4	15.7
Industry	8.1	8.3	33.5	51.8
Construction	1.7	1.7	3.4	5.3
Transport & Communications	5.5	2.4	3.6	7.0
Commerce & Restaurants	8.2	6.7	5.1	8.2
Other Services	8.0	21.2	20.1	11.9
GDP	100.0	100.0	100.0	100.0

Source: Appendices C and D.

http://dx.doi.org/10.1787/086302558636

Table 3.3. **China's Geopolitical Standing, 1820–2003**

	1820	1890	1913	1952	1978	2003
Share of World GDP	32.9	13.2	8.8	4.6	4.9	15.1
Share of World Population	36.6	26.2	24.4	22.5	22.3	20.5
Per Capita GDP % of world average	90.0	50.3	41.7	23.8	22.1	73.7
GDP Ranking	1	2	3	3	4	2
Share of World Exports	n.a.	1.7	1.6	1.0	0.8	5.9

Source: www.ggdc.net/Maddison and Table 3.26.

http://dx.doi.org/10.1787/086466572827

The new policies were indigenously generated and quite out of keeping with the prescriptions for "transition" which were proffered and pursued in the USSR. The contrast between Chinese and Soviet performance in the reform period is particularly striking. As China prospered, the Soviet economy and state system collapsed. In 1978 Chinese per capita income was 15 per cent of that of the former Soviet Union, in 2003 it was 76 per cent.

The reform period was one of much reduced international tension. China's geopolitical standing, stature and leverage were greatly increased. China became the world's second largest economy, overtaking Japan by a respectable margin and the former USSR by a very large margin. Its share of world income increased three–fold and its share of world trade more than seven–fold. China took back Hong Kong and Macao peacefully and inaugurated a "two systems" policy designed to attract Taiwan back into the national fold.

China is still a relatively low–income country, but this is a favourable position for a nation which wants to achieve rapid catch up. The very fact that its level of income is still much lower than that of Hong Kong, Japan, Malaysia, South Korea, Singapore and Taiwan means that it still has great scope to capture the advantages of backwardness, and its period of super–growth can last longer than theirs did.

Figure 3.1. **Comparative Levels of GDP in China and Four Other Big Countries, 1952-2003**

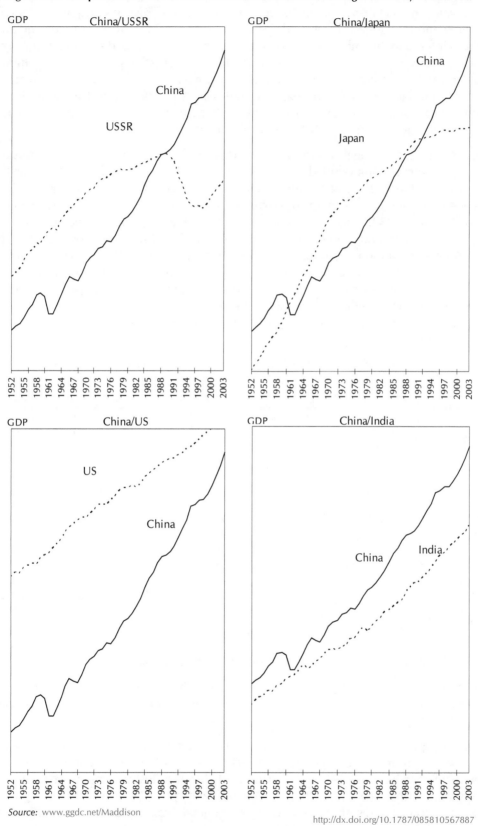

Source: www.ggdc.net/Maddison

http://dx.doi.org/10.1787/085810567887

ISBN: 978-92-64-03762-5 © OECD 2007

The postwar performance of most countries was buoyed by the rejuvenation of Western capitalism and the effects which this had in expanding the world economy. The Chinese situation was very different. In the 1950s its economy was tied closely to the Soviet bloc. In 1960 this tie was broken and until 1971 it operated in an international limbo, excluded from the United Nations and suffering from a complete US trade embargo from 1950–71. In the past quarter century its international status has been transformed. Foreign trade, travel, investment and transfer of technology have expanded rapidly. China has become an important foreign trade partner with many countries in Asia, Africa and Latin America and has embarked on a programme of aid and investment to strengthen their economies and guarantee its access to energy and raw materials for its own development.

Chinese experience has been fascinating, unpredictable and often difficult to understand. The difficulty in interpreting is compounded by the fact that the Chinese statistical system was based on Soviet concepts until the 1980s and there was a statistical blackout in the 1960s and 1970s, when information was very scarce and often distorted for political reasons. The statistical office was actually abolished from 1968 to 1972. Since 1978, the situation has improved greatly, the accounts are more transparent, while coverage and classification more or less conform to Western concepts. However, the reporting system and deflation procedures are still influenced by previous practice. Official statistics still exaggerate GDP growth and understate levels of performance. In view of these problems most observers simply use Chinese official statistics, as the task of adjusting them appears so complicated. However, it is possible to adjust the national accounts to improve the international and inter–temporal comparability of the GDP estimates (as I have done in Appendix C). My adjusted estimates are used throughout this chapter, in preference to the official figures.

Table 3.4. **Comparative Growth Performance, 14 Countries, 1913-2003**
(annual average compound growth rates)

	1913–52	1952–78	1978–2003	1913–52	1952–78	1978–2003
	GDP Per Capita			Population		
China	-0.1	2.3	6.6	0.7	2.0	1.2
Hong Kong	1.6	5.4	3.9	3.9	3.1	1.5
India	-0.2	1.7	3.3	1.0*	2.2	1.9
Indonesia	0.02	2.5	2.9	1.3	2.1	1.7
Japan	1.3	6.7	2.1	1.3	1.1	0.4
Singapore	1.5	4.8	4.2	3.3	2.9	2.4
South Korea	-0.1	6.3	5.6	1.8	2.2	1.1
Taiwan	0.9	6.6	4.7	2.3	2.7	1.1
Australia	0.9	2.4	2.1	1.5	1.9	1.3
France	1.3	3.7	1.6	0.1	0.9	0.5
Germany	0.6	4.3	1.4	0.2	0.5	0.2
Russia	1.8	3.1	-0.6*	0.4	1.0	0.2
United Kingdom	0.9	2.3	2.1	0.3	0.4	0.3
United States	1.7	2.2	1.8	1.2	1.3	1.1

*adjusted for boundary change
Source: www.ggdc.net/Maddison   http://dx.doi.org/10.1787/086472275717

In the Maoist period four major economic objectives were pursued:

i)   There was a fundamental change in property rights, with three main targets: landlords, the national bourgeoisie (capitalists, merchants, bankers) and foreign interests (mostly in Manchuria and in the former treaty ports).

ii)   There was a big increase in state revenue to finance expanded administrative mechanisms, maintain a high level of military preparedness and raise the rate of "accumulation". Investment was concentrated on industrial development, particularly heavy industry. Consumption was squeezed. Basic needs in terms of food, health and education were given priority, but clothing was drably conformist, housing and distributive services were minimal. From 1972 very strong official pressures were imposed to restrict family size.

Figure 3.2. **Total GDP and Labour Productivity, 1952-2003**
(Indices, 1952 = 1.00, Vertical Log Scale)

Source: Tables C.3 and D.3

http://dx.doi.org/10.1787/085847751830

iii) Market forces were replaced by regulatory devices for allocating investment funds and physical inputs, controlling movement of labour, fixing prices and wages. In the early years the authorities were particularly anxious to avoid inflation because of the major role it had played in discrediting the KMT regime. Rural consumption was contained by taxes and compulsory delivery quotas, which the state imposed in order to feed the urban population at low prices. This made it possible to keep urban wages low. A central planning mechanism was set up, but in such a large country with poor transport facilities, considerable emphasis was placed on "self–reliance" at national, provincial and enterprise levels. There was a distinct preference for large enterprises which were expected to be more vertically integrated than in a capitalist market economy. Urban social spending commitments were delegated to state enterprises, which were responsible for providing housing, education and health services to their employees, as well as canteens, clubs etc. Even more fundamental was the commitment to full employment. State enterprises could not dismiss workers who were redundant, lazy or inefficient.

iv) Foreign trade became a state monopoly whose goal was self–sufficiency. Imports were concentrated on essential producer goods and the domestic economy was isolated from international market forces. Foreign direct investment disappeared and foreign borrowing was restricted largely to interstate transactions with the Soviet Union and other communist countries. Chinese reliance on imports of capital equipment from communist countries was not merely an autarchic option but a political necessity dictated by trade embargoes, diplomatic isolation and the improbability of loans from capitalist countries.

ISBN: 978-92-64-03762-5 © OECD 2007

Table 3.5. **Comparative Levels of Economic Performance, 14 Countries, 2003–2006**

	2003 GDP per capita (in 1990 int. $)	2003 Population (million)	2003 Energy Consumption (million tons of oil equivalent)	2006 Exports ($ billion)
China	4 803	1 288.4	1 409	969
Hong Kong	24 098	6.8	17	317
India	2 160	1 049.7	553	120
Indonesia	3 555	214.5	162	99
Japan	21 218	127.2	517	650
Singapore	21 530	4.2	22	272
South Korea	15 732	48.2	205	326
Taiwan	17 284	22.6	99	224
Australia	23 287	19.7	113	123
France	21 861	60.2	271	485
Germany	19 144	82.4	347	1 126
Russia	6 323	144.6	640	305
United Kingdom	21 310	60.9	232	371*
United States	29 037	290.3	2 281	1 038

* 2005

Source: Per capita GDP and population from www.gdc.net/Madddison Energy from International Energy Agency, *Energy Balances of Non–OECD Countries, 2002-2003*, and *Energy Balances of OECD Countries, 2002-2003*, OECD, Paris 2005. Exports from IMF, *International Financial Statistics*, April 2007.

http://dx.doi.org/10.1787/086504075237

In the reform period, since 1978, policy has changed fundamentally in all four dimensions. There has been a sharp drop in the proportionate importance of the state. Fiscal revenue has fallen from 31 to 17 per cent of GDP, investment is now mainly financed (via the banking system) from private saving; market forces play a much bigger role in resource allocation; and the economy has been opened to foreign trade and investment. There has been no formal reversion to capitalist property rights through privatisation of state property, but capitalists have been admitted to membership of the communist party, peasants have substantially regained control of their land, private home ownership has grown rapidly and there is substantial scope for individual enrichment through private and quasi–private entrepreneurship. The average size of production units has been dramatically reduced. In 1978 farming was conducted by 6 million production teams; now there are 250 million family farms. In 1978, there were 384 000 industrial enterprises with an average employment of 175 persons. By 1996, there were 8 million enterprises with an average of 14 persons employed. In commerce and catering there were 1.6 million outlets in 1978, 18.6 million in 1996 with a drop in average size from 5.4 to 2.8 persons.

The Macroeconomic Record

Labour Input

Chinese labour input has risen faster than population as can be seen in Table 3.6. Official policy encouraged the fall in birth rates. This changed the age structure and raised the proportion of working age. Employment rose faster than the population of working age due to increasing participation of women. In the 1930s only 20 per cent of farm work was done by women, but by 1995 they were nearly half of the rural labour force.

In the Maoist period, China made inefficient use of its workers because of the inflexible way in which the labour market was segmented into rural and urban sectors. Rural residents were not allowed to migrate to urban areas. Under the household registration system they were forced to register with local authorities and were trapped in low income employment in agriculture, rural industry and services. They did not have the social benefits which urban dwellers enjoyed. They generally received subsistence in kind and accumulated work points which were paid in cash only at the end of the year.

Table 3.6. **Vital Statistics, Labour Input and Education Levels, 1952-2003**

	Crude Birth Rate per 1 000	Life Expectancy at birth (years)	Per cent of Population of Working Age	Per cent of Population Employed	Years of Education per person aged 15 and older
1952	37.0	38[*]	51.7	36.4	1.70
1978	18.3	64	53.6	41.9	5.33
2003	13.0	72	69.5	49.7	10.20

[*] 1950.

Source: NBS, *China Statistical Yearbooks*. Primary education is given a weight of 1, secondary 1.4 and higher 2, in line with international evidence on relative earnings associated with the different levels of education. http://dx.doi.org/10.1787/086561554774

Within the urban sector, state enterprises were not allowed to recruit or dismiss employees. They were assigned by Ministry of Labour offices according to a firm's employment quota. The Ministry also fixed the wage structure for workers, managers and technicians, using a grading schedule borrowed from the USSR. Virtually all registered urban residents of working age could expect to have a job which provided lifetime security and some degree of automatic advancement on a seniority basis. Job switches between enterprises were virtually impossible. As wages were low and there was no possibility of being fired, work incentives were dulled. Management in state enterprises tolerated shirking as they operated under soft budget constraints.

In the Reform period, allocation of labour has improved, particularly in rural areas, where the boom in small–scale industry and service employment absorbed surplus labour from farming. However, there are still important restrictions on rural–urban migration and large–scale overmanning is still characteristic of state enterprise in urban areas.

Quality of Labour

China's long–run record in human capital formation is quite impressive but progress has been far from smooth. The main emphasis was on expansion at the primary and secondary level (see Table 3.7). In 1949, about a third of children were enrolled in primary school and about 20 per cent of adults were literate. Now about four–fifths of adults are literate, but primary enrolment is not yet complete and drop–out rates are substantial in rural areas.

The record in higher education was disastrous in the 1960s. Enrolment fell from 962 000 in 1960 to 48 000 in 1970. It recovered thereafter, but was still below the 1960 level in 1978. During the cultural revolution virtually all higher education was closed, teachers were subjected to humiliating witch–hunts, students were encouraged to participate in Red Guard vandalism from 1966 to 1969 and thereafter many were deported to remote rural areas for several years. When the institutions reopened, preference was given to "correct" social background and political attitudes rather than to success in examinations. The picture was similar for specialised secondary (technical and teacher training) schools. Here enrolment fell from a peak of nearly two and a quarter million in 1960 to 38 000 in 1969 and recovery was very slow.

In the reform period, higher education enrolment has risen very fast, from less than a million in 1978 to nearly 16 million in 2005. There has also been a surge in the number of Chinese studying abroad, from virtually zero in the Maoist period to 118 500 in 2005 (and a cumulative total of more than a million since the 1970s).

From 1952 to 2003, the average level of education of the population aged 15 and over increased six–fold from 1.7 years to 10.2 years (see Tables 3.6 and 3.8). This increase in the quality of the labour force contributed importantly to China's production potential, which was further strengthened by

ISBN: 978-92-64-03762-5 © OECD 2007

Table 3.7. **Student Enrolment by Level of Education, China 1930s to 2005**
(000s)

	Higher	Secondary	Primary	Pre–school
1930s	31[a]	632[b]	12 670[b]	n.a.
1949	117	1 268	24 391	140[c]
1952	191	3 145	51 100	424
1957	441	7 081	64 283	1 088
1960	962	12 476	93 791	29 331
1970	48	26 483	105 280	0
1978	856	65 483	146 240	7 877
2005	15 618	85 809	108 641	21 790

a) 1937; b) 1939–40; c) 1950.
Source: 1930s from Ministry of Information, *China Handbook 1937–1943*, China News Service, New York, 1943. Other years from
NBS, *China Statistical Yearbooks*, 1984, pp.483–5, 1993, pp. 640–1; 2006, p. 800.
http://dx.doi.org/10.1787/086586755570

Table 3.8. **Years of Education Per Person Aged 15–64, Ten Countries, 1950–92**
(equivalent years of primary education)

	1950	1973	1992		1950	1973	1992
France	9.58	11.69	15.96	China	1.60	4.09	8.50
Germany	10.40	11.55	12.17	India	1.35	2.60	5.55
United Kingdom	10.84	11.66	14.09	Japan	9.11	12.09	14.86
United States	11.27	14.58	18.04	Korea	3.36	6.82	13.55
Spain	5.13	6.29	11.51	Taiwan	3.62	7.35	13.83

Source: Estimates for China from sources described in Table 3.6. Other countries from Maddison (1995a), p. 77. Primary education was given
a weight of 1, secondary 1.4 and higher 2, in line with international evidence on relative earnings associated with the different levels
of education.
http://dx.doi.org/10.1787/087817107017

improvements in health. Life expectancy at birth rose from 38 years in 1950 to 72 in 2003. Infant mortality is about an eighth of what it was in 1949. There continues to be a substantial reliance on traditional Chinese doctors and ancient remedies, but there has been a very large increase in the number of Western style doctors and in use of modern medicine. Improvements in sanitation, diet and wide availability of modern drugs have been the main contributors to increased life expectancy.

Investment Rates and Capital Inputs

There is no doubt about the success of the new regime in raising the rate of investment. The gross non–residential fixed investment rate rose from about 7 per cent of GDP in prewar years (see Table C.8 and its footnote) to an average of 11 per cent in the early 1950s, 18 per cent in the rest of the Maoist period and 22 per cent in the reform period. This is a very respectable performance and is now substantially higher than in the advanced capitalist countries (see Table 3.9).

China, like other communist countries, has had unusually large investment in inventories and work in progress. Chinese state enterprises kept large stocks of materials as a precaution against supply difficulties or inefficiency in the planning process. They are wasteful in their use of inputs such as steel and energy because of inefficiency in the price system and soft budgetary constraints. There was a large amount of unfinished building and firms often had big stocks of unsaleable goods whose quality or design is not to the taste of consumers. From 1978 to 2003, the increase in US inventories averaged only 0.45 per cent of GDP, but in China, in the same period, the ratio was 5.75 per cent. In the advanced capitalist countries, around two–thirds of GDP is now produced in the service sector where stocks are very low. In poorer countries where material product is a larger part of GDP, inventory formation plays a larger role, but even so China is an outlier, which suggests that the very high proportion of inventories was due to inefficient organisation of production, particularly in the state sector. However, the Chinese ratio of inventory change to GDP fell sharply in 2000–2003, when it averaged 1.55 per cent.

In order to construct estimates of the capital stock one has to cumulate assets of different vintages and this requires a long run of investment data at constant prices. Such estimates are not available for China and I had to use a proxy procedure using investment ratios in current prices in conjunction with estimates of GDP at constant prices (as explained in Appendix C and Tables C.7 and C.8). I used the perpetual inventory method and assumed an average asset life of 25 years. Using the limited information on pre–war capital formation, I made a rough estimate of the capital stock in 1952 and much firmer estimates for 1978 and 2003. I derived a capital/output ratio of 1.2 in 1952. This is a low coefficient by international standards, but pre–war rates of investment were very modest and there was extensive damage in the many years of war and civil war.

The capital stock rose much more quickly than output in the Maoist period with the capital/output ratio rising from 1.2 in 1952 to 2.7 in 1978. Since then, capital productivity has improved substantially and the capital/output ratio in 2003 was 2.6.

In the pre–reform period, the great bulk of investment was made by the state, which squeezed consumption and kept wages low in order to finance accumulation. In the reform period, a rapidly growing proportion of investment was financed from household savings and foreign investment. Although the state continues to have a significant role in the allocation of investment funds, the overall impact of greater non–state participation was to direct investment into areas where the yield is higher.

The impact of better resource allocation can be seen in the macroeconomic growth accounts in Table 3.9 which show large gains in total factor productivity from 1978 to 2003, compared with the negative record for 1952–78.

Total Factor Productivity

The top left–hand side of Table 3.9 provides a set of simplified growth accounts for the two major phases of Chinese growth: 1952–78 and 1978–2003.

The high level of resource mobilisation is most evident in the case of capital stock which rose very much faster than GDP in the Maoist period. Capital inputs rose faster in the first period even though the average rate of investment was lower because the initial stock was very low. Employment grew a good deal faster than population in both periods for reasons we have already analysed. In both periods there were substantial advances in educational levels which improved the quality of the labour force.

In the Maoist period there were modest gains in labour productivity, but capital productivity fell substantially. We can make a rough measure of the overall efficiency of the economy in allocating resources by combining the major factor inputs (labour, improvement in its quality due to education and fixed non–residential capital) and comparing their growth with that of GDP in order to measure "total factor productivity". It can be seen in Table 3.9 that this was negative, at a rate of –1.37 per cent a year, over the period 1952 to 1978.

After 1978 there was a sharp contrast. The rate of growth of labour input declined, the rate of growth of the education stock slowed and capital inputs increased at the same pace. Nevertheless GDP growth accelerated sharply, labour productivity grew much faster than before, capital productivity ceased being negative and total factor productivity increased by 2.95 per cent a year. The improvement in resource allocation in the reform period is dramatically illustrated in these simple macro–accounts. A more detailed understanding of why efficiency improved can be derived from the detailed analysis of policy and institutional changes in the subsequent sections of this chapter.

Table 3.9. **Basic Growth Accounts, China, Japan, South Korea and the United States 1952-2003**
(annual average compound growth rates)

	China		Japan	
	1952–78	1978–2003	1952–78	1978–2003
	Macroeconomic Performance			
Population	2.02	1.20	1.10	0.41
GDP	4.39	7.85	7.86	2.53
Per Capita GDP	2.33	6.57	6.69	2.11
Labour Input	2.57	1.89	1.12	0.07
Education	4.49	2.63	1.19	1.12
Quality Adjusted Labour Input	4.87	3.23	1.72	0.63
Non–Residential Capital	7.72	7.73	9.57	5.03
Labour Productivity	1.78	5.85	6.67	2.46
Capital Productivity	–3.09	0.11	–1.56	–2.39
Capital per Person Engaged	5.02	5.73	7.97	4.38
Total Factor Productivity	–1.37	2.95	3.32	0.36
Export Volume	2.6	14.42	13.17	4.09
	United States		South Korea	
	1952–78	1978–2003	1952–78	1978–2003
	Macroeconomic Performance			
Population	1.34	1.07	2.21	1.06
GDP	3.61	2.94	8.63	6.68
Per Capita GDP	2.24	1.85	6.28	5.56
Labour Input	1.12	1.10	3.40	1.75
Education	1.12	1.20	*3.13*	*3.13*
Quality Adjusted Labour Input	1.69	1.61	5.02	2.15
Non–Residential Capital	3.39	3.23	10.89	10.24
Labour Productivity	2.47	1.82	5.05	4.85
Capital Productivity	0.22	–0.38	–2.05	-3.22
Capital per Person Engaged	1.85	1.81	8.77	8.05
Total Factor Productivity	1.28	0.69	1.48	0.93
Export Volume	5.19	5.91	26.1	11.2

Source: Population and GDP for all countries from Maddison www.ggdc.net/Maddison. Hours, education and capital stock for Japan and United States mainly from Maddison (1995a pp. 253–4) updated in Maddison (2007). See also Maddison (1995b, pp. 50–156), for details of capital stock estimation for Japan and United States; for these two countries I assumed that nonresidential structures had a life of 29 years and machinery and equipment 14 years. Korean labour input and education 1952–78 from Maddison (1998, p. 66). Growth of Korean productive fixed capital stock 1952–78 from van Ark and Timmer (2002, pp. 239–240). Korean labour input 1978–2003 from Groningen Growth and Development Centre database; capital stock 1978–2003 from Pyo et al. (2006, p. 108). China employment, education and capital stock from Maddison (1998a) updated. I was unable to break down the Chinese capital stock between non–residential structures and machinery, and assumed an average asset life for the two assets combined of 25 years (see Table C.8). Labour input for Japan, Korea, and the United States refers to total hours worked, and to employment for China. Labour quality is improved by increases in the average level of education of the population of working age; it was assumed that the impact on the quality of labour input was half the rate of growth of education. In calculating total factor productivity growth, labour input was given a weight of 0.65, education .325 and capital 0.35.

http://dx.doi.org/10.1787/086618303411

It is useful to apply the simplified technique used in Table 3.9 to other countries to get a firmer view of the comparative significance of our findings on past growth and to provide a basis for the comparative analysis of future prospects in Chapter 4. Table 3.9 therefore includes estimates on the same basis for the world productivity leader, the United States; for Japan, the other giant of the Asian economy; and for South Korea, an economy which has demonstrated the possibility of rapid catch–up over four decades.

Japanese experience provides a striking contrast with that of China. Its period of super–growth took place in 1952–78 when GDP growth was virtually identical with that of China in the reform period. Since 1978, Japanese growth has slackened sharply and has been below that of China in the Maoist period. The inverse periodisation also holds good for the total factor productivity and foreign trade performance of the two countries.

However, one must beware of simple comparisons as the economic history of the two countries is very different. Japan's modernisation began in 1867 and for nearly eight decades it was directed in substantial degree to external aggression, particularly against China. By 1952 Japan had been completely demilitarised and was able to use its highly skilled labour force and prodigious capacity to mobilise savings entirely for non–military ends. It was also able to participate fully in the benefits of a rapidly expanding world economy. In 1952, Japan's population had an education level more or less comparable with that in west European countries and more than five times the proportion in China at that time. Its per capita income was then more than four times as high as China's. It had a long experience of independent indigenous capitalist development, with a sophisticated system of banks, trading companies and managerial experience. It was well equipped to achieve rapid catch–up to the productivity levels of the most advanced countries. It was able to make good on the backlog of opportunities squandered in prewar years on military pursuits. From 1952 to 1978 Japan raised its per capita income from less than a quarter to more than two–thirds of that in the United States. After that its growth was bound to slow down, as it had to operate nearer to the frontier of technology, where the pay–off on high levels of investment is much weaker.

Structural Change

There were massive structural changes in China between 1952 and 2003. Agricultural output and employment grew much more slowly than the rest of the economy. Agriculture's share of GDP fell from 60 to 16 per cent and its share of employment fell from 83 to 51 per cent. The most dynamic sector was industry whose share of GDP rose from 8 to 52 per cent. There was a small decline in the service share of GDP over the whole period, but its employment share grew substantially (see Table 3.2).

Structural changes generally reflect two basic forces which are operative in all countries as they reach successively higher levels of real income and productivity. The first of these is the elasticity of demand for particular products. These demand forces tend to reduce the share of agricultural products in consumption and raise demand for the products of industry and services as income rises. The second basic force has been the differential pace of technological advance between sectors. Both these forces have been operative in China, but the Chinese pattern of development has also been very strongly influenced by government policy.

Thus the poor performance of agriculture in the Maoist period was due to a government squeeze on peasant income by fiscal, price and procurement policies, constraints on rural–urban migration and the adverse effect of institutional change, as collectivist arrangements reduced efficiency and incentives. The relaxation of the price squeeze on agriculture and on labour movement to non–farm activity and the reversion to family farming in the reform period had an extremely favourable impact on productivity performance, which to some extent had a once–for–all character.

Similarly, the huge expansion of industrial–construction output in the pre–reform period was supported by government price incentives and a heavy concentration of investment resources, which helped to raise relative levels of labour productivity in this sector. In the reform period, industrial–construction growth continued at the same pace, but capital was used less wastefully, as the relative importance of state enterprise declined.

The service sector was also squeezed in the pre–reform period, particularly commercial and catering enterprise. These constraints were greatly relaxed in the reform period, when there was a big expansion of private entrepreneurial activity.

ISBN: 978-92-64-03762-5 © OECD 2007

Table 3.10. **Indicators of Sectoral Growth Performance, China 1952-2003**
(annual average compound growth rates)

	1952–78	1978–2003	Change in Growth Rate Between Periods
Agricultural GDP	2.20	4.52	2.32
Agricultural Employment	2.02	0.51	−1.51
Agricultural Labour Productivity	0.17	3.99	3.82
Industry & Construction GDP	9.76	9.76	0.00
Industry & Construction Employment	5.84	2.83	−3.01
Industry & Construction Productivity	3.70	6.74	3.04
Tertiary Sector GDP	4.18	7.60	3.42
Tertiary Employment	3.20	3.65	0.45
Tertiary Labour Productivity	0.96	3.81	2.85
Whole Economy GDP	4.39	7.85	3.46
Total Employment	2.57	1.89	-0.68
Aggregate Labour Productivity	1.78	5.85	4.07
Impact of Sectoral Employment Shift on Aggregate GDP Growth	0.88	2.01	1.13

Source: Appendices C and D.

http://dx.doi.org/10.1787/086224287020

The last line in Table 3.10 provides a crude measure of the impact of labour reallocation on GDP growth. In the pre–reform period, the annual average GDP growth rate would have been 0.88 per cent slower (i.e. 3.51 instead of 4.39 per cent), if no change in employment structure had occurred and if productivity growth within each sector had remained as actually experienced. In 1978–2003, annual GDP growth would have been 2.01 per cent lower (5.84 instead of 7.85 per cent) on the same assumptions. However, the structural shift effect should not be added as an explanatory component to the aggregative growth accounts shown in Table 3.9 because this would involve an important element of double counting. The large inter–sectoral differences in labour productivity levels and growth are due in substantial degree to differences in the sectoral distribution of physical capital and education. These elements of causality are already embodied in the aggregate growth accounts. A more sophisticated analysis of structural shift effects would require disaggregated information on the physical and human capital stock, which is not at present available.

Table 3.11. **Changes in Economic Structure, China 1952–2003**
(per cent of total)

	Agriculture, Forestry & Fishery	Industry & Construction	All Services	Total
		GDP		
1952	59.7	10.0	30.3	100.0
1978	34.4	36.8	28.8	100.0
2003	15.7	57.2	27.1	100.0
		Employment		
1952	82.5	7.0	10.5	100.0
1978	71.9	15.8	12.3	100.0
2003	51.1	19.9	29.0	100.0
		Relative Labour Productivity		
1952	72.7	142.9	288.6	100.0
1978	47.8	252.9	234.1	100.0
2003	41.2	287.4	93.4	100.0

Source: Appendices C and D.

http://dx.doi.org/10.1787/086262428768

ISBN: 978-92-64-03762-5 © OECD 2007

Performance in the Rural Sector

Agriculture

There were several reasons why the new regime gave priority to agrarian reform. The party was committed to the creation of a more equal society and to abolition of the propertied classes — particularly the last remnants of the Ch'ing landlord gentry. Appropriation of the agrarian "surplus" was a very important source of finance. In the areas where the Communist Party had already exercised political and military control, agrarian reform had proved an effective means of attracting mass support and further action was thought likely to consolidate and legitimate its ruling position.

It is important to get a realistic picture of the agrarian conditions which the new regime inherited. The rhetoric of the party was hardly accurate. Agriculture was described as "feudal" and landlord exploitation was regarded as extreme. In fact China had not been feudal for centuries. There were no large domains managed by a landed nobility and no serfdom. The bulk of the peasantry were working proprietors, tenants or wage labourers. Land could be bought and sold freely. Only 10 per cent of rural families were landless and, of those who were cultivators, 44 per cent were working proprietors, 23 per cent part–owner part–tenant and 33 per cent were tenants. These are Buck's (1937) estimates for 1929–33 and a government survey of 1931–6 showed similar proportions of 46, 24 and 30 per cent respectively (see Feuerwerker, 1977, p. 57). Rents averaged about 43 per cent of the crop on tenanted land (see sources cited by Feuerwerker, 1977, p. 59). Only 5 per cent of farm borrowing came via Western style banks or co–operatives, 14 per cent was supplied by pawnshops or native banks and 81 per cent by merchants, village shops, landlords or prosperous farmers (Feuerwerker, 1977, p. 64).

We have no surveys of the 1949 situation, but there is no reason to believe it was much different from that in the 1930s. According to Buck (1937, pp. 172–77) who conducted a huge survey of more than 38 000 farm families in 22 provinces in 1929–33, the average farm size in the early 1930s was about 1.7 hectares for an average farm family of 6.2 persons[1]. Holdings of more than 67 hectares were only 2 per cent of the land (Feuerwerker, 1977, p. 55) whereas the average US farm in 1930 had 63 hectares. There were no large plantations as in India, Indonesia and Ceylon. The average farm was split into 6 separate plots in different parts of a village. Fragmentation was due to long–standing population pressure in a country whose natural endowment permitted only a very limited area for cultivation. Partible male inheritance had led to fragmentation of holdings in successive generations. The splitting of holdings into separate parcels was intended to provide each inheritor with an equitable mix of different grades of land. Fragmentation was regarded as a form of insurance; Tawney (1932), p. 39, makes the point thus: "Land varies in quality from acre to acre; one man must not have all the best land and another the worst; a farmer needs both dry and wet land, hilly land for fuel and manure as well as level land for his crops; the dispersion of plots enables him to pool his risks of flood and drought."

About 90 per cent of land was used for crops, about 1.4 per cent for farm buildings, 1.9 per cent for ancestral graves, 2 per cent for paths and ponds and 3.1 per cent for pasture, fuel, forest and irrigation. Only 1.4 per cent was left uncultivated. Chinese farmers had not practiced fallow for centuries. There was no common land for grazing. The average multicropping ratio was 1.38, so that the average sown area per farm was 2.1 ha (2.45 ha. in the wheat region, 1.85 ha. in the rice region)[2]. Given this type of man/land situation and the nature of farm technology, it was not profitable to try to run large–scale managerial farms. The large estates which the Ch'ing dynasty had originally created for the Manchu nobles and military had long since been divided into small rental plots or sold (see Myers, 1970, pp. 217–20). In this rural world, the position of women was distinctly inferior. They did not inherit property, only 1.2 per cent were literate (compared with 30.3 per cent for males) and they were only 20 per cent of the farm labour force (see Buck (1937), pp. 291 and 373). Greater use of this female labour potential was a major element of communist development strategy. By 1995, 47 per cent of the rural labour force were women.

ISBN: 978-92-64-03762-5 © OECD 2007

Riskin (1975, pp. 68 and 75) estimated rural property income in 1933 to be about 26 per cent of net agricultural product as follows: rents 16.5 per cent, 5.2 per cent for profits of those who used hired labour and 4.3 per cent from money lending. In addition about 3.2 per cent was paid in land tax. Depreciation was about 2.2 per cent (see Liu and Yeh, 1965, p. 140). The Riskin estimates give some idea of the surplus which the communist government aimed to capture through transformation of property relations and expropriation of landlord, merchant and usurers' assets. Rents were replaced by a combination of state taxes, compulsory deliveries and a price scissors which kept farm prices low and industrial prices high. In the longer run the intention was also to keep farm consumption at a basic level, so that the appropriable surplus would increase proportionately over time.

After 1949, there were six major changes in policies affecting agricultural institutions. There were four successive steps deep into collectivism and two steps backward which nearly completed the circle. The 1949–50 agrarian reform confiscated about 43 per cent of cultivated land (45 million hectares) together with associated buildings and livestock and redistributed it to tenants and landless farmers. Temple lands and buildings were taken over. Merchants and moneylenders lost their function and their property. Stavis (1982) describes the process as follows: "Land was not redistributed through calm administrative procedures. Rather, meetings were held in villages to determine people's economic class and to denounce landlords. In some villages the meetings were violent. In the Chinese culture this loss of face was devastating. Landlords or other elite were beaten, humiliated to suicide and sometimes executed. In the emotion–charged environment of village meetings, excesses were frequent. At least one–half to one million were killed and another two million imprisoned." About 4 per cent of the population lost land. About 60 per cent of the peasantry had some gain from this process. The changes created a fairly egalitarian system for the 106 million peasant households who all became working proprietors, paying taxes (largely in kind) to the government in lieu of rent.

Soon after, in the second phase of reform, peasant households were encouraged to pool their labour, draft animals and farm implements in periods of seasonal shortage. At first these arrangements (typically amongst a handful of peasants) were called "mutual aid" teams. These were supplemented by elementary co–operatives where labour pooling was more ambitious and involved work on substantial capital projects related to irrigation and water control. By 1955 about two–thirds of peasants participated in mutual aid teams and "elementary co–operatives" on a "voluntary" basis. The average size was about 27 households (Lin, 1990).

These arrangements were not enough for the party leadership, as they perceived a danger that peasant land sales or leases would in time recreate the old patterns of ownership. They also wanted more power over rural decision making, convinced that they could achieve economies of scale and extract a bigger surplus by accelerating the socialisation process. In 1956–57, in a third phase, "advanced co–operatives" were created and virtually all peasants were compelled to join. The new arrangements involved pooling of land as well as labour. Thus peasants lost their individual property rights in land and became stakeholders in what were essentially collective enterprises on Soviet lines. As a consolation prize, they were allowed to raise vegetables and livestock on small private plots occupying about 5 per cent of the collective's land. The new collectives were about the same size in terms of labour as Soviet collectives at that time — about 160 households, but they were only a fifth of the size in terms of cultivated area. Production and management decisions were now taken over by party cadres and peasants were organised in work brigades with an average size of 20 households.

In the late summer of 1958, there was a fourth drastic change. 123 million peasant households in 753 000 "advanced co–operatives" were dragooned into 26 000 giant people's communes, each with an average of 4 600 peasant households and about 6 700 workers. These were thirty times as big as a Soviet collective in terms of labour and four times as big in average land area. Within the communes there were 500 000 brigades and over 3 million production teams. There were also state farms, but their importance was relatively small. Chinese state farms never covered much more than 4 per cent of land area, whereas Soviet state farms had 11 per cent of the cultivated area in 1950, 36 per cent in 1960 and 51 per cent in 1990.

Table 3.12. **Degree of Participation in Different Forms of Socialist Agriculture, 1950–58**
(per cent of peasant households)

	Mutual Aid Teams	Elementary Co–operatives	Advanced Co–operatives	Communes
1950	10.7	0.0		
195l	19.2	0.0		
1952	39.9	0.1		
1953	39.3	0.2		
1954	58.3	2.0		
1955	50.7	14.2		
1956	0.0	8.5	87.8	
1958 end–August				30.4
1958 late September				98.0
1958 end–December				99.1

Source: SSB, *Ten Great Years* (1960). This source gives no figures for 1957. http://dx.doi.org/10.1787/087583410182

Table 3.13. **Characteristics of Agricultural Performance, China 1933–2003**

	Gross Value Added in Farming, Forestry Fishery & Sidelines (million 1987 yuan)	Gross Value Added Per Head of Population 1987 yuan	Gross Value Added Per Person Engaged in FFFS 1987 yuan	Agriculture's Share of Total Employment	Agriculture's Share of GDP
1933	138 497	277	789	85	63
1952	127 891	225	748	83	60
1957	153 649	241	812	80	54
1958	154 538	237	889	68	49
1961	110 965	168	604	71	43
1978	225 079	235	781	72	34
2003	679 821	527	2 858	51	16

Source: Table A.3, updated from Appendices C and D. http://dx.doi.org/10.1787/086285537783

Communes were created at the time the so–called Great Leap Forward was launched in 1958–60. All private property disappeared — private plots, livestock, farm buildings and cash income. Rural markets were closed[3]. The state now controlled all marketing and credit arrangements. Families were required to eat in communal kitchens and mess halls. Work assignments were distributed as if peasants were soldiers. The new management made risky experiments in deep ploughing and dense planting? which usually proved to be costly failures. The communes took over responsibility for local administration, local tax collection, provision of health care and education, supervision of agricultural production, rural industrial construction and service activity in their area. Communes were expected to be virtually self–sufficient. The rationale for this was China's extreme isolation in international politics and the perceived need for an economic system which could survive a nuclear war. Statistical reporting became a political exercise feeding the fantasies of the political leadership, creating the impression that this millenarian transformation was achieving miracles which warranted a massive shift from the fields to backyard iron–smelting, cement making, construction and irrigation. Between 1959 and 1961 about 30 million people were diverted from farming to these other pursuits. As a result? agricultural output per capita in 1961 was 31 per cent lower than in 1957, priority in food allocation was given to urban areas and millions of rural dwellers died of famine. The famine deaths and the drop in births led to a fall of population of nearly 6 million in 1959–61, compared with a rise of over 28 million in 1957–59 (see Banister, 1987, for a more detailed analysis). A good deal of the increase in industrial output was worthless or unusable. As the evidence of this accumulated, industrialisation was put into reverse. Industrial employment had risen from under 23 million in 1957 to nearly 62 million in 1959, by 1963, it had fallen below the 1957 level (see Table D.3).

 ISBN: 978-92-64-03762-5 © OECD 2007

In 1962 there was a fifth major change in policy. Communes continued to the mid–1980s as organs of government, but farm management was switched to much smaller units — production teams of about 30 families. Private plots were restored, farm markets were reopened, communal eating was discontinued and major resources were allocated to provide modern inputs such as fertilisers, electrification and tractors. The remuneration of peasants was based on work points from the collective unit in which they operated, with allocation of subsistence items throughout the year and cash payments only at the end of the year. Party cadres had a considerable influence on allocation of points, so that rewards for effort and incentives to perform were a good deal weaker than under a system of household decision–making. The emphasis on self–sufficiency remained powerful and impeded specialisation between farms and regions.

After the death of Mao, and with a new political leadership, there was a sixth phase in agricultural policy. This time there was not a sudden dramatic shift of gear, but a series of pragmatic moves in a new direction which were more market–oriented and offered much better incentives. There were gradual moves after 1978 to relax agricultural controls, production targets and quotas. The ceiling on private plots was raised from 5 to 15 per cent of farmland and restrictions on sideline activities were relaxed. There was a major upward revision in prices paid for farm products. Between 1978 and 1983 the average prices received by farmers rose by 50 per cent, at a time when industrial prices rose much less. Quota prices were raised and a new 3 tier structure emerged with higher prices for above quota deliveries to the state and free market prices for the rest of output (see Table A.22c). Egalitarian payment systems were dropped in favour of household responsibility contracts. The reallocation of collective land to households started on an experimental basis in Anhwei province in 1978 and proved very successful. In 1980, 14 per cent of production teams had shifted to the household responsibility system, 45 per cent in 1981, 80 per cent in 1982 and 99 per cent by 1984 (Lin, 1992).

In the process of decollectivisation, fragmentation of household plots reappeared. Wu and Meng (1995) show that the average peasant household had 6.5 separate plots in the five provinces they surveyed for 1993–34. This is similar to what Buck (1937) found for the 1930s, when the average holding consisted of 6 separate plots.

After 1984/85, the relative price incentives for farm deliveries to the state were reduced. One reason was the improved supply situation following the rapid growth in output from 1978 and 1984 (a 53 per cent increase in farm GDP). Another was the need to ease the budgetary strain which arose from paying farmers more, whilst keeping prices low for urban consumers.

In 1984 commune and brigade enterprises became township and village enterprises. Townships and villages reappeared as administrative units. The old commune administration was replaced by separate township governments, township party committees and economic association committees. The government also sanctioned the development of private rural enterprise. These new opportunities for industrial and service activity decreased the attractions of farming as did the relaxation on control of movement from rural areas to cities.

There have been several other attempts to measure total factor productivity in agriculture using growth accounting or econometric techniques to assess the efficiency of different phases of Chinese policy. Wen (1993) was one of the most comprehensive and transparent and included a survey of other work in the field. He used the official measure of gross agricultural product (in farming, forestry, fishery and sidelines) in "comparable prices" as his output indicator and "explained" this by the movement of: *a)* current inputs (feed, seed, traditional and modern fertiliser and electricity); *b)* labour; *c)* land adjusted for multiple cropping and irrigation; and *d)* the stock of animals and machinery which he called "capital". He preferred the weights of Wiens (1982), i.e. 20 per cent for current inputs, 35 per cent for labour, 36 per cent for land and 9 per cent for "capital", but he also used four other sets of weights to test the sensitivity of his results. All five sets of results showed small or negative total factor productivity growth for 1952–57, substantially negative growth for 1957–78 and large productivity gains for 1978–87 (see Table 3.15). Wen's growth accounting like Lin's (1992) econometric approach attributed most of the productivity improvement after 1978 to the liberalisation of agricultural policy.

Figure 3.3. **Gross Value Added and Labour Productivity in Agriculture,**
1952-2003
(Indices, 1952 = 1.00, Vertical Log Scale)

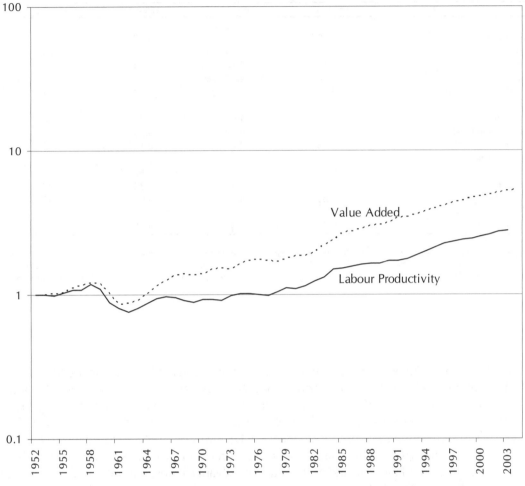

Source: Tables C.3 and D.3.

http://dx.doi.org/10.1787/085835777428

Table 3.14 provides a detailed account of changes in the pace of farm performance in four periods from 1952 to 1994. Between 1952 and 1957 when peasants were still nominal proprietors, labour productivity grew by 1.7 per cent a year and total factor productivity by 0.63 per cent. Between 1957 and 1978 labour productivity fell by 0.2 per cent a year and total factor productivity decelerated. These were two decades in which reckless experiments in collectivism created deep distortions in resource allocation and work incentives, which were not removed until after 1978. From 1978 to 1987 labour productivity rose by 5 per cent a year in response to more liberal policies and better prices for farmers and total factor productivity also accelerated to 4.6 per cent a year. There were obvious recovery elements in this phase. The rate of growth slackened somewhat in 1987–94 when labour productivity grew by 3 per cent a year and total factor productivity by 2.7 per cent.

 ISBN: 978-92-64-03762-5 © OECD 2007

Table 3.14. **Rates of Change in Farm Output, Inputs and Total Factor Productivity:**
Four Phases, China 1952–94

(annual average compound growth rates)

	1952–57	1957–78	1978–87	1987–94
Farm Gross Output	3.70	2.32	5.77	4.28
Farm Inputs	6.36	2.54	4.35	4.83
Non Farm Inputs	12.12	8.98	8.43	6.67
Total Current Inputs	7.36	4.57	6.42	5.86
Farm Gross Value Added	3.05	1.72	5.52	3.62
Farm Employment	1.35	1.92	0.49	0.58
Farm Labour Productivity	1.66	–0.19	4.99	3.05
Irrigated Area Cultivated	6.46	2.41	–0.16	1.32
Non–irrigated Area				
Cultivated	–0.79	–2.08	–0.60	–1.49
Augmented Land	1.70	0.18	–0.32	0.34
Other Capital	7.81	4.43	5.00	3.48
Total Factor Productivity	0.63	0.57	4.56	2.67

Source: Appendix A, Tables A.3, A.4, A.8, A.9 and A.10. "Augmented" land gives a weight of 2 to irrigated and 1 to non–irrigated land. "Other capital" consists of the stock of farm animals and agricultural machinery, giving animals a 1987 weight of 51 per cent and machinery 49 per cent as indicated in Wen (1993), p. 13. Total factor productivity gives a weight of 0.55 to employment, 0.30 to augmented land, and 0.15 to other capital.

http://dx.doi.org/10.1787/087621507276

Although Chinese farm performance since 1978 has improved greatly on that in the Maoist period, it should be remembered that Chinese labour productivity is very low by international standards. Table 3.16 presents comparisons of levels of farm performance in China and three other big countries for 1933–94, with value added expressed in 1987 US prices, as described in Appendix A. Labour productivity in Chinese farming was only 1.6 per cent of US levels in 1994 and its relative standing had fallen somewhat from the 1978 level. China's natural resource endowment is very much smaller than that of the United States (see Table 1.4) and its comparative advantage position suggests that the potential for significant catch–up on the United States lies outside farming. The Japanese case is also illuminating. Japan has even smaller natural resources in relation to population, but has followed very high–cost policies to ensure self–sufficiency, particularly in grains. Its farm labour productivity was only one–twentieth of that in the United States in 1994. Its real income would have been higher if it had pursued more liberal policies towards grain imports. This is certainly a point which Chinese policy makers should keep in mind in the future. Continuance of collectivist and state farming policies in the USSR (and Russia) have produced disastrously low productivity results in spite of a huge natural resource endowment. They demonstrate the wisdom of the change which has already occurred in China.

Rural Activity Outside Agriculture

In Imperial China there was always a significant amount of activity in rural handicrafts, commerce and transport. During the Great Leap Forward in 1958–60 there was a massive diversion of rural labour into non–agricultural activity with such disastrous consequences that it was put into even steeper reverse. Non–agricultural pursuits were 6.6 per cent of rural employment in 1957, jumped to 28 per cent by end 1958, were reduced to 2 per cent in 1962 and were still below the 1957 proportion in 1977 (see Table 3.17).

Table 3.15. **Wen's Measures of Rate of Change in Agricultural Output, Inputs and Total Factor Productivity: Three Phases, China 1952–87**
(annual average compound growth rates)

	1952–57	1957–78	1978–87
Gross Agricultural Output	4.56	2.33	6.93
Current Inputs	11.20	7.63	−0.53
Agricultural Employment	1.36	2.20	1.29
Augmented Land	1.92	−0.43	−0.63
"Capital"	6.03	4.32	4.48
Total Factor Productivity	0.08	−1.53	6.00

Source: Wen (1993). Total factor productivity is the average of his results with five different sets of weights. Wen's growth accounts are constructed using the Jorgenson approach, i.e. he tries to explain movements in real gross output, whereas my approach is like that of Denison, and I explain the movement in value added (see Maddison, 1987, for an analysis of the two approaches). Another difference is that my accounts refer to farming, whereas his cover forestry, fishing and sidelines as well. He uses the old official output measure. I use my own estimates as described in Appendix A. His estimate of inputs of manure and traditional fertiliser is much bigger than mine (see the note to Table A.8 for details).

http://dx.doi.org/10.1787/087638781464

Table 3.16. **Comparative Performance Levels in Chinese, Japanese, Soviet and US Farming, 1933–94**

	China	Japan	USSR/Russia	United States	China	Japan	USSR/Russia	United States
	Gross Farm Value Added (1987 $ million)				Employment (000s)			
1933	56 846	7 316	25 273	41 466	166 545	14 078	42 244	8 722
1952	52 071	7 482	33 913	37 522	161 097	16 450	35 318	5 946
1957	60 501	6 400	45 598	38 432	172 301	15 210	34 326	5 295
1978	86 732	6 925	70 337	41 972	256 726	6 330	29 740	2 723
1990	159 435	7 631	69 303	70 623	287 134	4 510	27 239	1 999
1994	180 517	7 665	26 274	83 337	279 487	3 740	10 350	2 114
	Gross Value Added per Person Engaged (1987 $)				Labour Productivity as per cent of US (US = 100.0 in each year)			
1933	341	520	598	4 754	7.1	10.9	12.6	100.0
1952	323	455	960	6 310	5.1	7.2	15.2	100.0
1957	351	420	1 328	7 258	4.8	5.8	18.3	100.0
1978	338	1 094	2 365	15 414	2.2	7.1	15.3	100.0
1990	555	1 692	2 544	35 329	1.6	4.8	7.2	100.0
1994	646	2 050	2 539	39 421	1.6	5.2	6.4	100.0
	Farm Employment as per cent of Total Employment							
1933	80.4	45.9	60.0	21.1				
1952	77.7	42.5	42.1	8.8				
1978	63.5	19.0	23.2	2.8				
1990	50.3	7.2	20.6	1.7				
1994	45.2	5.7	14.9	1.7				

Source: China and the United States from Table A.14. USSR 1933–90 gross value added from Kouwenhoven (1996). Kouwenhoven established his 1987 benchmark USSR/US comparison in exactly the same way as I did for China/US; he merged this with a time series mainly from CIA sources. Soviet employment 1952–90 from *Narodnoe Khoziastvo*, various issues as described in Maddison (1998), Table 2, 1933 is an interpolation from Maddison (1998). 1990–94 movement of value added and employment in Russia, and Russian 1990 shares of Soviet value added and employment from World Bank (1995). The Russian share of 1990 Soviet farm value added was 50.9 per cent, its share of Soviet farm employment was 36.6 per cent, and its farm labour productivity level was 39.1 per cent higher than the Soviet average. Its share of Soviet population in 1990 was 51.2 per cent. Japan gross value added relative to US for 1975 from Maddison and van Ooststroom (1993), 1933–90 time series of gross value added at constant prices from Pilat (1994), pp. 276 and 278 updated to 1994 from OECD, *National Accounts 1982–94*, p. 93; employment 1952–94 from OECD, *Labour Force Statistics*, various issues, 1933–52 movement from Pilat (1994), p. 277.

http://dx.doi.org/10.1787/087642861678

 ISBN: 978-92-64-03762-5 © OECD 2007

After 1978 there was a huge expansion of small–scale enterprise in rural areas, but this time it was much more successful and solidly based than in the Great Leap Forward. In 1977 there were 17 million people in small–scale industry, construction, trade, transport and other services in rural areas (see Table 3.17). By 2005 the number had risen to 166 million.

The number of township and village enterprises did not grow much after 1978 but their average size in terms of employment rose substantially, with total employment rising from 28 million in 1978 to 59 million in 1996. Worker productivity rose seven–fold in township and nearly 11–fold in village enterprise. The most dynamic growth was in individually owned firms. There were none of these in 1978, 4 million in 1984 and over 23 million in 1996. Employment in these firms rose from zero in 1978 to 76 million in 1996. They were generally quite small with an average of three persons per firm in 1996, compared with 73 in township and 26 in village enterprises.

Table 3.17. **Rural/Urban Distribution of Population and Employment, China 1952–2005**
(000s at end year)

	Rural Population	Urban Population	Agricultural Employment	Rural Non– Agricultural Employment	Urban Employment	Total Employment
1952	503 190	71 630	173 170	9 500	24 620	207 290
1957	547 040	99 490	193 090	13 690	30 930	237 710
1958	552 730	107 210	154 900	60 040	51 060	266 000
1959	548 360	123 710	162 710	48 030	51 000	261 740
1960	531 340	130 710	170 160	31 690	56 960	258 810
1962	556 360	116 590	212 760	4 550	41 790	259 100
1970	685 680	144 240	278 110	8 750	57 460	344 320
1977	783 050	166 690	293 400	17 320	83 050	393 770
1978	790 140	172 450	283 730	31 510	86 280	401 520
1987	816 260	276 740	308 700	81 304	137 826	527 830
2005	745 440	562 120	318 560	166 300	273 310	758 250

Source: Rural/urban population from SSB *China Statistical Yearbooks*, 1988 ed., p. 75, 1995 ed., p. 59, and 2006 ed., p. 99. In general the population is categorised by place of permanent residence. Urban population refers to residents of cities and towns. The above figures appear to refer to the 1964 definition of a town, i.e. a place with 3 000 or more inhabitants, of whom 75 per cent or more were working outside agriculture, or 2 000 and more inhabitants of whom 85 per cent were non agricultural. Total employment 1952–77 *from China Statistical Yearbook 1993*, p. 78, 1978–87 from 1996 *Yearbook*, p. 92 and 2005 from 2006 *Yearbook*, p. 99. Agricultural employment and rural non–agricultural employment 1952–78 from Wu (1992), 1987 from *China Statistical Yearbook 1996*, p. 354 and 2005 from 2006 *Yearbook*, p. 125. It should be noted that there are some small differences between the totals in this table and Table D.3 for years before 2005, and the 2005 figure is subject to the incongruity problem described in Appendix D.

http://dx.doi.org/10.1787/086286638653

There were several reasons for this. The large increase in modern inputs (fertilisers, power irrigation, use of small tractors, trucks etc.) in the 1960s and 1970s, and the better use of resources which came with household responsibility, produced a bigger reserve of rural labour, which had little opportunity for productive employment on family farms whose average size was less than half a hectare. Under the strict household registration system, it was not possible for most of these people to move into urban employment. There was thus a huge supply of people willing to work in rural enterprise at low wages.

The considerable rise in real farm income meant that peasants wanted a changing basket of agricultural products with heavier emphasis on meat and fish, but they also had a pent–up demand for manufactured consumer goods and better housing. Institutional changes favoured a productive interaction of these propitious elements of supply and demand. Rural markets were freed, bank loans became available and in 1981 tax holidays were introduced. Firms in rural areas did not have the onerous welfare responsiblities of the big state enterprises in urban areas. Even more fundamental was the ideological switch from planning by bureaucratic fiat to a situation where profit was no longer taboo. The local officials and party elite who had been running non–agricultural commune activities became directors and managers of township and village industries. Although these were publicly owned, they could now be run in practice almost as if they were capitalist enterprises. These enterprises produced extra–budgetary sources of revenue for local authorities and gave bureaucrats and former bureaucrats legal opportunities for greatly increasing their income if they ran the enterprise successfully.

Table 3.18. **Characteristics of Small–scale Enterprise by Type of Ownership, China 1978–96**

	Township	Village	Individual	Total	Township	Village	Individual	Total
	Number of Enterprises (000s)				Employment (000s)			
1978	320	1 205	0	1 525	12 576	15 689	0	28 265
1984	402	1 462	4 201	6 065	18 792	21 030	12 259	52 081
1987	420	1 163	15 919	17 502	23 975	23 208	40 869	88 052
1994	423	1 228	23 294	24 945	29 607	29 381	61 194	120 182
1995	417	1 201	20 409	22 027	30 294	30 311	68 016	128 621
1996	406	1 143	21 814	23 363	29 588	29 940	75 555	135 083
	Average Employment Per Enterprise (persons engaged, end year)				Gross Value of Output (billion current yuan)			
1978	39	13	0	19	28.11	21.19	0.00	49.30
1984	47	14	3	9	81.75	64.84	24.40	170.99
1987	57	20	3	5	182.59	141.16	152.68	476.43
1994	71	24	3	5	1 504.09	1 382.51	1 372.25	4 258.85
1995	73	25	3	6	2 140.09	2 031.04	2 720.39	6 891.52
1996	73	26	3	6				
	Gross Value Added (billion current yuan)				Gross Value Added (billion 1987 yuan)			
1978	6.18	4.86	0.00	11.03	8.86	6.97	0.00	15.84
1984	17.96	14.87	4.70	37.52	21.90	18.13	5.73	45.77
1987	40.11	32.37	29.39	101.87	40.11	32.37	29.39	101.87
1994	330.43	317.02	264.14	911.59	144.52	138.65	115.53	398.70
1995	470.15	465.73	523.64	1 459.52				
	Gross Value Added Per Person Engaged (1987 yuan)							
1978	705	444	0	560				
1984	1 166	862	467	879				
1987	1 673	1 395	719	1 157				
1994	4 881	4 719	1 887	3 317				

Source: The top four panels are from SSB, *China Statistical Yearbook*, 1995 ed., pp. 363–5, 1996 ed., pp. 387–90 and 1997 ed., pp. 399. Before 1995, values were only available for gross output, but the 1996 *Yearbook*, p. 390, also showed gross value added for the year 1995. From this it appeared that the 1995 ratio of value added to gross output was .2197 for township, .2293 for village and .1925 for individual enterprises. In panel 5, these ratios were applied to all the years to get a rough measure of value added in current prices. None of the SSB estimates are in constant prices, so I applied the implicit price deflator of Wu (1997) for industrial products (derived from the fourth column of Table B.4 and the third column of Table B.1) to get the estimates in the sixth panel. Panel 7 is derived from panels 6 and 2.

http://dx.doi.org/10.1787/087702305204

Table 3.19. **Sector Breakdown of Small–scale Enterprise, China 1995**

	Per cent of Small Scale Value Added (per cent of total)	Average Employment per Enterprise (persons)	Gross Value Added per Person Engaged (1995 yuan)
Industry	74.0	10.5	14 282
Construction	8.8	18.1	6 631
Transport	5.5	1.9	8 447
Services	9.8	2.5	6 791
Agriculture–Related	1.9	11.3	8 771

Source: *China Statistical Yearbook 1996*, pp. 387–90.

http://dx.doi.org/10.1787/087713647088

ISBN: 978-92-64-03762-5 © OECD 2007

Industrial Policy and Performance

Rapid industrialisation was the top priority for the new China. It was expected to provide the flow of materials and machinery essential to raise the rate of investment and provide the hardware which would guarantee military security. To obtain the structural shift, the new regime was prepared to squeeze the agriculture and service sectors and to keep consumption at modest levels to free resources for investment.

Table 3.20. **Comparative Performance in Agriculture, Industry and Services, China 1952–2003**

	Growth of Real Value Added, Employment and Labour Productivity (annual average compound growth rates)							
	Industry & Construction		Agriculture		Services		Whole Economy	
	1952-78	1978-2003	1952-78	1978-2003	1952-78	1978-2003	1952-78	1978-2003
Value Added	9.8	9.8	2.2	4.5	4.2	7.3	4.4	7.9
Employment	5.8	2.8	2.0	0.5	3.2	6.5	2.6	1.9
Productivity of Labour	3.7	6.5	0.2	4.0	2.0	2.0	1.8	5.8
	Levels of Labour Productivity (1987 yuan per person employed)							
	Industry & Construction		Agriculture, Forestry and Fisheries		Services			
1952	1 482		748		2 292			
1978	3 128		781		3 831			
2003	19 454		2 858		6 345			

Source: Tables C.3 and D.3.

http://dx.doi.org/10.1787/086330013871

The strategy was successful. Industrial value added was 126 times as high in real terms in 2003 as in 1952. In agriculture, by contrast, progress was modest, with 2003 output about five times that in 1952. As a result, industry now accounts for 52 per cent of GDP compared with less than 8 per cent in 1952 (see Table 3.2). Proportionately, China is now one of the most industrialised countries in terms of output. Its 52 per cent of GDP compares with 17 per cent in the United States, 18 per cent in the United Kingdom, 23 per cent in Japan and Germany. However, industry's employment share in China is relatively modest (14 per cent in 2002) because this sector has been much more heavily capitalised than most other parts of the economy. As a result the relative level of industrial labour productivity is unusually high.

Until 1978, industry was tightly controlled and investment fully funded by government. Expansion was fastest in the state–owned sector where the average enterprise was large and workers were a proletarian elite with complete job security and relatively generous welfare benefits. There was a second tier of collective enterprise where plants were smaller and less capitalised, and workers were less privileged. Most of the old small–scale handicraft operatives were moved into the collective sector, but some of the old handicraft activities were suppressed or disappeared.

In the reform period since 1978, government has operated with a much looser rein. The relative importance of the state sector has contracted considerably. Employment in state enterprises peaked at 35 million in 1992 and fell to 6 million in 2005. The process of attrition was cushioned by government; the operational surplus of state firms collapsed and government propped them up with funds borrowed from the banking system. The decay of state enterprise had significant social repercussions. The proportion of industrial workers enjoying generous social benefits and job security declined drastically.

There has been a huge expansion in industrial activity outside the state sector. In 1978 there were 265 000 collectives. By 1996 there were 1.6 million. The number of private enterprises rose from zero to 6.2 million in this period. The bulk of these were small–scale operations, most of them in rural areas and run by individuals, townships and village level governments. The success of these new firms was due to their lower labour costs than state enterprises, their modest capitalisation and their freedom to respond to market demand. Many benefited from special tax privileges granted by local authorities. Another major contribution to private–sector industry was the huge inflow of foreign direct investment.

Between 1978 and 1996 there was no change in the average size of state industrial enterprises , but downsizing in the rest of industry was spectacular with a decline from 112 to 8 persons. This reduced average firm size in industry as a whole from 175 to 14 (see Panel C of Table 3.21). In most planned economies, enterprises were bigger than in China. In 1987, the average Soviet industrial enterprise employed 814 workers. In Poland it was not too different and in Czechoslovakia it was more than double the Soviet average. By contrast the average US establishment had 49 persons, Germany and the United Kingdom 30 persons, France 19 and Japan 16. China has transformed its industrial organisation so that its average is below that in most advanced capitalist countries and about the same as in Japan. However, the average size in China was much bigger than in India where the average establishment in all manufacturing had only 2.3 persons in 1984–85. (Information on firm or establishment size in other countries was derived from Kouwenhoven, 1996, for the USSR; Ehrlich, 1985, for Eastern Europe; van Ark, 1993, for capitalist countries; Lee and Maddison, 1997, for India.)

We now have a good indicator of the growth of industrial value added in real terms in Wu (2002) and Appendix B for mining, utilities and 15 manufacturing branches. We do not have a breakdown of value added performance in real terms for the state and non–state sectors, but the gross output evidence permits some strong inferences. It seems clear that labour productivity has increased much more slowly in the state sector since 1978 than in other parts of industry, judging from the relative movement in the current price figures for gross output per person engaged (Panel E of Table 3.21). The average level of labour productivity in state firms fell below that in the rest of industry, in spite of their higher capitalisation.

In the Maoist period, there were two phases in industrial policy. Until 1958, there was a rather cautious approach in taking over Chinese owned private enterprise. Most foreign owned assets (a third of the prewar factory sector) were expropriated at an early stage. Half of these were Japanese and were taken at the end of the war. Most other foreign firms were seized at the outbreak of the Korean war in retaliation for foreign trade embargoes. The property of Chinese nationals who co–operated with the Japanese had already been taken over by the KMT government. Between 1949 and 1957 there was a period of coexistence with the national capitalists. Private firms executed state orders or were operated as joint enterprises. Some private owners were used as managerial personnel after state takeovers. About 1.1 million persons received modest financial compensation for confiscated assets — 5 per cent a year for ten years on the assessed value of their property (see Riskin, 1987, p. 97).

Private industrial enterprise was completely eliminated in 1958 during the Great Leap Forward. At that time there was also a massive development of small–scale industry in rural areas by diversion of labour to backyard iron–smelting, manufacture of cement, fertilisers and farm tools. This was carried out as a quasi–military operation, in which 30 million unskilled peasants were removed from their farms on the mistaken assumption that they were surplus labour. Industrial employment shot up from 23 million in 1957 to 62 million in 1959, but catastrophic harvest failure and the uselessness of much of the new industrial output led to a sharp reversal of policy. By 1963, industrial employment had fallen back to 23 million.

After 1978, competition for state firms came from the huge growth of output in low–cost, low–wage township, village and individual enterprises in rural areas, from rapid expansion in the tax–favoured special enterprise zones (SEZ) in coastal areas and from imports which rose from $11 billion in 1978 to $660 billion in 2005. This competition plus looser state control caused a collapse in the operational surplus of state enterprise.

 ISBN: 978-92-64-03762-5 © OECD 2007

Table 3.21. **Characteristics of Industrial Performance, by Type of Ownership, China 1952-96**

	1952	1978	1996
		A. Number of Enterprises (000s)	
State Owned	n.a.	83.7	113.8
Other	n.a.	264.7	7872.7
Total	n.a.	348.4	7986.5
		B. Persons Engaged (000 at end year)	
State Owned	5 100	31 390	42 770
Other	7 360	29 520	66 610
Total	2 460	60 910	109 380
		C. Average Employment Per Enterprise (persons engaged, at end year)	
State Owned	n.a.	375	376
Other	n.a.	112	8
Total	n.a.	175	14
		D. Shares of Gross Output (per cent)	
State Owned	41.5	77.6	28.5
Other	58.5	22.4	71.5
Total	100.0	100.0	100.0
		E. Gross Value of Output Per Person Engaged (per cent of average)	
State Owned	101.5	150.6	72.8
Other	98.9	46.2	117.4
Average Level	100.0	100.0	100.0
		F. Ratio of Value Added to Gross Output (per cent)	
Total	35.6	37.9	29.2

Source: Panel A 1978 from *Statistical Yearbook of China 1984*, p. 193; 1996 from *China Statistical Yearbook* 1997, p. 411. Panel B 1952 from 1984 *Yearbook*, pp. 109 and 114; 1978-96 from 1997 *Yearbook*, pp. 98 and 109. Panel C derived from A and B. Panel D from 1997 *Yearbook*, p. 411. Panel E derived from B and D. Panel F 1952 derived from col. 5 of Table B.1. The fall in the GVA/GO ratio after 1978 is partly due to the rapid growth of small enterprises outside the state sector, but also reflects changes in output structure. The 1997 *China Statistical Yearbook, pp.* 424 and 428, shows 1996 gross value added and gross output for firms with independent accounting systems. The value added ratio was 32 per cent for state and 26 per cent for non-state enterprises. http://dx.doi.org/10.1787/087734851051

Table 3.22. **Comparative Performance Levels in Chinese, Japanese, Soviet/Russian and US Manufacturing, 1952-94**

	Gross Value Added (1985 $ million)				Employment (000s)			
	China	Japan	United States	USSR/Russia	China	Japan	United States	USSR/Russia
1952	11 058	25 020	324 041	84 602	11 000	7 100	17 174	15 363
1978	105 185	357 958	730 655	395 739	53 320	13 260	21 784	32 913
1994	425 934	688 839	930 917	144 969	96 130	14 960	20 157	17 546
	Gross Value Added Per Person Engaged (1985 $)				Labour Productivity as per cent of US (US = 100.0 in each year)			
1952	1 005	3 524	18 868	5 507	5.3	18.7	100.0	29.2
1978	1 973	26 995	33 541	12 024	5.9	80.5	l00.0	35.8
1994	4 431	46 045	46 183	8 262	9.6	99.7	100.0	17.9
	Manufacturing Employment as per cent of Total Employment							
1952	5.3	18.4	25.4	18.3				
1978	13.2	24.5	22.2	25.7				
1994	15.6	23.2	16.2	25.3				

Source: The absolute levels of performance are converted to 1985 $ using PPP converters (unit value ratios) from a series of ICOP studies (Szirmai and Ren, 1995; Pilat, 1994; and Kouwenhoven, 1997). Their benchmark levels are all binaries comparing the respective countries with the United States. I used their Paasche converters (at US relative prices) with the United States as the link country. The benchmarks were merged with the relevant value added time series. Employment for 1952 generally from these sources, otherwise from OECD sources and Maddison (1998). http://dx.doi.org/10.1787/087816365374

Figure 3.4. **Gross Value Added and Labour Productivity in Chinese Industry and Construction, 1952–2003**
(Indices, 1952 = 1.00, Vertical Log Scale)

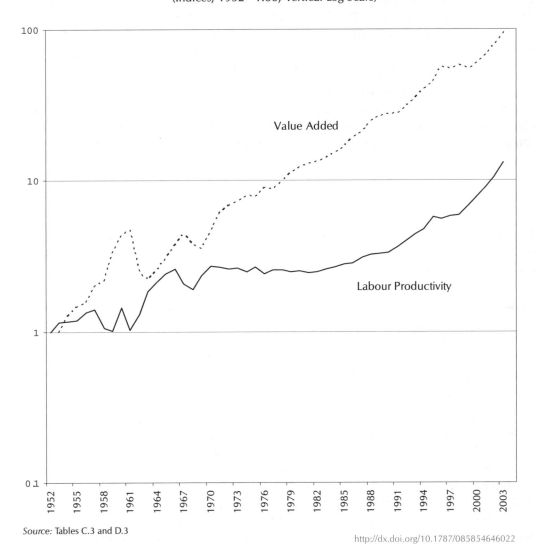

Source: Tables C.3 and D.3

http://dx.doi.org/10.1787/085854646022

The termination of Soviet aid to Chinese industry in 1960 was a serious blow, as it stopped many ambitious investment projects which were semi–finished. There was also a dip in industrial output in 1967–68 during the disturbances of the Cultural Revolution.

The "third–front" programme of the 1960s reduced the productivity of industrial investment, for it involved the strategically inspired location of plants in remote areas when a nuclear war was thought to be imminent. This programme, like the Great Leap Forward, was also a failure. Transport difficulties hindered access to markets and raw materials and slowed down construction. In the 1970s it was abandoned in favour of development in coastal areas.

The combination of major policy errors and poor governance led to massive waste of investment and labour resources. From 1952 to 1978, industrial labour productivity grew 3.7 per cent a year, but there were huge inputs of capital. Chen *et al.* (1988) estimate that net fixed capital stock in state industrial enterprises rose by 13.3 per cent a year from 1952 to 1978. If this were valid for industry as a whole, it would mean that total factor productivity growth for this period grew at only 0.5 per cent a year (giving labour a weight of 0.6 and capital 0.4). Between 1978 and 2003, industrial labour productivity rose by 6.5 per cent a year (see Table 3.20).

 ISBN: 978-92-64-03762-5 © OECD 2007

State manufacturing now represents about 10 per cent of GDP, down from 31 per cent in 1978. The government moved slowly in shutting down enterprises in default on bank loans and inter–enterprise debt. Wholesale privatisation, as in Russia, did not seem a promising option. Large debts were rolled over or written off. Many continued to produce goods for which there was little demand and they accumulated large inventories of unsaleable goods. The government appears to have spent $450 billion since 1998 bailing out and recapitalising the state-owned banks which financed these enterprises.

State manufacturing enterprises are part of the wreckage of collectivism with which the government will probably have to live for some years. Until a general social security system is created, it is politically difficult to abandon all the workers and management in these enterprises. As the private sector becomes more prosperous and pays higher wages, it will attract more workers from the state sector.

The Service Sector

Commerce is a sector which has experienced major swings in government policy. From 1952 to 1978 activity was severely squeezed and subjected to debilitating controls. Since 1978 retail trade and restaurant activity has been almost completely liberated and the ownership structure has reverted to what it was in 1952.

From 1952 to 1978 the number of people engaged in retail outlets, catering establishments and sundry convenience trades fell from 9.5 to 6.1 million even though the population had risen by two–thirds. The number of outlets fell from 5.5 to 1.3 million. There was also a big fall in rural and street market activity and a virtual disappearance of pedlar trade. The removal of private initiative in these simple activities meant a considerable fall in the quality of life for consumers, reinforced the effect of shortages and gave producers little guidance on consumer demand[4].

After 1978, when the service sector was released from official constraints, it grew very fast, particularly in rural areas. Not much capital or formal education was required to start a new business, so the barriers to entry were small. By 1996, 93 per cent of retail outlets were private, 96 per cent for restaurants and 53 per cent in wholesale trade. The number of retail outlets rose more than 13–fold, restaurants and catering establishments more than 20–fold. Employment in this sector rose from 11 million in 1978 to nearly 50 million in 2002; output increased nearly 11–fold from 1978 to 2003. Consumer satisfaction increased accordingly. It is difficult to understand why the old policy of complete elimination of petty capitalism in this sector was ever part of the socialisation strategy.

The Transformation of Relations with the Outside World

China's trading links in the 1950s were heavily concentrated on the USSR and other communist countries. This reflected political affinities and the Stalin–Mao agreements in February 1950 by which the Soviet Union agreed to provide an initial loan of $300 million to finance the purchase of capital equipment, together with a substantial supply of technicians and Soviet blueprints. It was reinforced by the trade embargoes imposed by European countries, Japan and the United States at the end of 1950 after China had sent "volunteers" to help expel UN forces from North Korea. The embargoes were lifted by Britain, Japan and most others in 1957, but the United States froze Chinese assets and maintained a total ban on all transactions with China until 1971.

Foreign trade was a state monopoly and was heavily concentrated on imports of capital goods and technology. Capital equipment from the communist bloc represented about a third of investment in machinery in the 1950s (see Chao, 1974) and was also very important for the military. The Soviet projects included machine tools, trucks, tractors, oil industry development, electric generating equipment, jet aircraft and submarine construction as well as experimental reactors and other nuclear related technology. In 1958 the USSR reneged on its offer to supply nuclear weapons, but its earlier help must have facilitated development of China's first atomic bomb in 1964 and its first hydrogen weapon in 1969. Chinese–Soviet relations soured in the late 1950s. Soviet loans were terminated and Soviet technicians were suddenly withdrawn in 1960. China had counted on Soviet co–operation to build 290 major projects by 1967, but only 130 of these had been completed when the split occurred. Many plants in steel and hydroelectricity were left partially finished when Soviet experts withdrew (taking their blueprints with them). The damage to Chinese investment and industrial development was the more significant as it occurred in the middle of the disorganisation and chaos created by the Great Leap Forward. Food shortages obliged China in the 1960s to make large grain imports from Australia and Canada which reduced the funds available to finance machinery imports.

In the course of the 1960s, China's situation was very isolated. Export volume fell a fifth from 1959 to 1970. Imports from communist countries dropped from 66 per cent of the total in 1959 to 17 per cent in 1970, it had no trade at all with the United States and foreign credits were restricted to short or medium term deals with West European countries and Japan to install plants for chemical products, fertilisers and plastics. At the same time China had to repay debts to the USSR and embarked on an aid programme providing credits of about $1 billion to Asian and African countries in the 1960s. From 1950 to 1964, remittances by overseas Chinese averaged only $30 million a year compared with $180 million in 1929. The position of China was much less fortunate than that of most other Asian countries in terms of access to world markets (see Tables 3.23 and 3.24) and capital flows. South Korea received external finance equal to 7.8 per cent of its GDP in 1952–78 and Taiwan 2.5 per cent. It was fortunate for China in this grim period that its large export surplus with Hong Kong provided substantial foreign exchange and trading agency connections for exports and a channel for evading foreign embargoes.

The new political leadership which emerged after the mid–1970s decided to abandon the previous policies of autarkic self–reliance and open the economy to the benefits several other Asian countries had derived from an expanding world economy. There was a move away from central control of foreign trade and payments. Foreign trade decisions were decentralised to authorised enterprises and provincial authorities and the previously rigid barriers between foreign and domestic prices were gradually removed, making trade more subject to market forces. Between 1957 and 1970 the exchange rate was unchanged, between 1970 and 1980 it was appreciated, between 1980 and 1995 there was a five–fold devaluation of the yuan against the dollar. Between 1995 and 2005 it remained fixed at 12 US cents to the yuan (8.33 yuan to the US dollar). This made Chinese goods very competitive and was a major reason for the huge increase in exports. In order to prevent the yuan from appreciating, the central bank bought large amounts of US government securities and eventually built up foreign exchange reserves of more than a trillion US dollars. This seems rather excessive; better use could have been found for some of these assets, but they serve to protect China's political independence and international leverage. Since 2005, the Chinese authorities have allowed the yuan to appreciate slightly.

A major element in the new policy stance was the creation of special enterprise zones (SEZ). These were free–trade areas where imported inputs and exports were duty free, where wages were very low by international standards and where there were substantial tax holidays for new enterprises. Four were created in 1980: Shenzhen (near Hong Kong), Zhuhai (near Macao), Shantou in Kwangtung and Xiamen (the old trading port of Amoy) in Fukien province, opposite Taiwan. Shenzhen was the biggest (328 square kilometres) and grew from a rural town of 23 000 inhabitants in 1979 to a huge agglomeration with 17 million inhabitants in its metropolitan and peripheral area today. Shenzhen

ISBN: 978-92-64-03762-5 © OECD 2007

became part of the greater Hong Kong economy and the bulk of Hong Kong industry was relocated in this low wage area. Hong Kong's shipping agencies, financial facilities and worldwide contacts ensured booming exports for the new factories located in the zone. In 1984 fourteen coastal cities were opened to greater foreign economic activity. The Yangtse delta towns and Shanghai were also involved in the process and the island of Hainan became a fifth SEZ in 1988.

Chinese export volume doubled from 1952 to 1978 and rose 28–fold from 1978 to 2003. In 1978, exports (in current yuan) were equal to 5.2 per cent of GDP (as officially measured) and by 2003 this had risen to 26.6 per cent. However, these proportions exaggerate the importance of exports which are sold at world prices, whereas the general price level in China is much lower. If one relates Chinese exports in US constant dollar terms to estimates of GDP in constant international dollars using a PPP converter rather than the exchange rate, the export share is much smaller — rising from 1.7 per cent of GDP in 1978 to 7.3 per cent in 2003 (see Table 3.25 and Appendix C). These ratios give a more realistic picture of the economic significance of exports. In 2003 China's exports were 8 per cent of the world total, a substantial rise on the 1978 situation when their share was 0.8 per cent.

Table 3.23. Volume of Merchandise Exports, Seven Countries, 1929–2003
(annual average compound growth rates)

	1929–52	1952–78	1978–2003
China	1.1	2.6	14.3
Japan	−0.2	13.2	4.1
South Korea	−13.1	26.1	11.2
Taiwan	1.7	16.6	7.8
Germany	−2.3	10.0	4.8
United Kingdom	1.6	4.6	3.1
United States	2.3	5.2	5.9

Source: Maddison (1995a) updated.

http://dx.doi.org/10.1787/086366743252

Table 3.24. Value of Merchandise Exports in Constant Prices, Seven Countries, 1929–2003
(million 1990 dollars)

	1929	1952	1978	2003
China	6 262	8 063	16 076	453 734
Japan	4 343	4 163	147 999	402 861
South Korea	1 292	51	21 146	299 578
Taiwan	261	385	20 693	134 884
Germany	35 068	20 411	241 885	785 035
United Kingdom	31 990	45 597	148 487	321 021
United States	30 368	51 222	190 915	801 784

Source: China from Table 3.26, other countries from Maddison (1995a), updated from Asian Development Bank, OECD, *Economic Outlook*, IMF *International Financial Statistics* and national sources for Taiwan.

http://dx.doi.org/10.1787/086410775572

From the early 1970s onwards, opportunities to participate in world trade on a more or less normal basis improved steadily. In 1971, China entered the United Nations. In 1972 relations with Japan and the United States were transformed by state visits, leading to diplomatic recognition by Japan and *de facto* recognition by the United States. The US embargo on trade and transactions was lifted. After establishment of formal diplomatic relations in 1979, property claims were settled, assets were unfrozen and China was granted most favoured nation tariff treatment by the United States. China joined the IMF and the World Bank in 1980, and the Asian Development Bank in 1986. In 1982, it was granted observer status in the GATT and began a long battle for membership of the World Trade Organization (WTO) which ended successfully in 2001.

Box 3.1. **China's Emergence from International Isolation, 1949–2001**

1949 Oct	People's Republic of China created. Diplomatic recognition by Burma, India and communist countries in 1949, by Afghanistan, Denmark, Finland, Israel, Norway, Pakistan and the United Kingdom in 1950.
1950 Feb	USSR agrees to provide financial and technical assistance — eventually $1.4 billion in loans and 10 000 technicians. China recognises independence of Outer Mongolia, agrees to joint Soviet–Chinese operation of Manchurian railways, Soviet military bases in Port Arthur and Dairen, and Soviet mining enterprises in Sinkiang.
1950 June 25	North Korea invades South Korea, penetrating deeply to Pusan.
1950 June 27	US changes its neutral line on Taiwan, sends in 7th Fleet.
1950 Oct	China sends "volunteers" (eventually 700 000) to N. Korea to push back UN forces advancing towards Chinese border on Yalu River.
1950–I	China retakes Tibet.
1953 July	Korean armistice.
1954	India cedes former British extraterritorial claims to Tibet.
1958	China menaces Taiwan in Quemoy and Matsu incidents. Khrushchev retracts offer of atomic aid.
1959	Revolt in Tibet, Delai Lama flees to India.
1960	USSR withdraws Soviet experts, abandons unfinished projects.
1962	Border clash with India over Aksai–chin road from Sinkiang to Tibet.
1964	First Chinese atom bomb test, 1969 first hydrogen bomb test.
1963–69	Border clashes with USSR in Manchuria. China questions legitimacy of Soviet/Chinese boundaries in Manchuria and Sinkiang.
1971 April	US lifts trade embargo on China.
1971 Oct	China enters United Nations, Taiwan ousted.
1972 Feb	President Nixon visits China.
1972 Sep	Visit of Prime Minister Tanaka to normalise diplomatic relations with Japan.
1973	US and China establish *de facto* diplomatic relations.
1978 Dec	US establishes formal diplomatic relations, derecognises Taiwan.
1979 Feb–Mar	Border war with Vietnam after expulsion of ethnic Chinese and Vietnamese destruction of Khmer Rouge regime in Cambodia.
1980	China becomes member of World Bank and IMF.
1986	China joined Asian Development Bank.
1997	Hong Kong restored to China.
1999	Macao restored to China.
2001	China admitted to the World Trade Organization.

Source: MacFarquhar and Fairbank (1987 and 1991).   http://dx.doi.org/10.1787/086054076302

In the 1950s, China's exports were concentrated on food, raw materials and textiles. Over time the share of light manufactures rose and by 1978 manufactures were half of the total. By 2005 the structure of exports was highly diversified, with 86 per cent consisting of a wide range of manufactures. Its import structure has also diversified (see Table 3.27). Capital goods and intermediate imports predominate, but there are imports of some consumer manufactures which contribute to competitive pressures in domestic markets. Food imports were relatively low. The geographic distribution of trade has been highly diversified since the 1970s (see Table 3.26).

In 1978 China had no foreign debt and virtually no foreign direct investment. The annual inflow of direct foreign investment rose from $3.5 billion in 1990 to $60 billion in 2005; the total inflow from 1979 to 2005 was more than $620 billion (2006 *Yearbook*, p. 752). Part of these inflows came from overseas Chinese investors in various parts of the world who had the connections and know–how to operate in an environment where opportunities were great, but legal protection was far from watertight. Some came from mainland Chinese investors who recycled their capital via Hong Kong in order to

ISBN: 978-92-64-03762-5 © OECD 2007

Table 3.25. **Export Performance, China 1870–2003**

	Commodity Exports in 1990 prices $ million	Exports as % of GDP in 1990 int. $ million	Commodity Exports in current prices $ million	Chinese exports as % of world exports in current $
1870	1 398	0.6	102	2.0
1913	4 197	1.2	299	1.6
1929	6 262	2.3	660	2.0
1952	8 063	2.6	820	1.0
1978	15 639	1.7	9 750	0.8
1990	62 090	2.9	62 090	1.9
2003	453 734	7.1	438 230	5.8

Source: First column, exports in 1990 $ are derived by merging the volume index in Table E.4 with the 1990 export level. The second column is the ratio of the first column to the estimates of GDP in 1990 international dollars in Table C.3. Exports in current dollars from Table E.2. World exports in current prices from Maddison, 1995a, p.238, updated from IMF, *International Financial Statistics*.
http://dx.doi.org/10.1787/086442856352

Table 3.26. **Geographic Distribution of Commodity Trade, China 1952–2005**
(per cent of total)

	Former USSR	Other ex-Communist	United States	Hong Kong	Japan	Australia & Canada	Western Europe
	Destination of Exports						
1952	47.4	21.7	0.0	n.a.	n.a.	n.a.	n.a.
1959	49.3	23.1	0.0	n.a.	0.9	n.a.	n.a.
1965	11.1	20.9	0.0	17.4	10.9	2.7	14.7
1970	1.1	21.9	0.0	22.3	10.7	3.0	16.9
1978	2.5	12.9	3.2	22.3	19.3	2.2	12.5
2005	2.9	2.3	21.5	16.3	11.0	3.0	18.2
	Origin of Imports						
1952	54.2	15.8	0.0	n.a.	n.a.	n.a.	n.a.
1959	46.4	19.9	0.0	n.a.	0.02	n.a.	n.a.
1965	10.3	17.6	0.0	0.3	13.9	16.8	18.9
1970	1.1	15.8	0.0	0.5	26.7	12.9	29.4
1978	2.3	12.5	8.4	0.6	29.8	9.0	22.7
2005	2.4	0.9	7.4	1.9	15.2	3.6	11.7

Source: 1952, 1959 and 1965 from JEC (1975) pp. 631, 648–9; 1970 from JEC (1978) pp. 734–5; 1978 from JEC (1982), pp. 41–42 (and 115 for Japan 1959); 2005 from NBS, *China Statistical Yearbook*, 2006 pp. 720-743. http://dx.doi.org/10.1787/086458422005

Table 3.27. **Leading Items in Chinese Commodity Trade, 2005**
($ million)

	Exports	Imports
Textile Products	107 661	23 445
Machinery, Electrical Equipment, Videos, etc.	322 008	271 119
Footwear, Hats, Jewelry, etc.	28 306	4 141
Leather, rubber and plastic goods	38 887	44 317
Chemical Products	31 853	50 583
Optical, Photographic and other Instruments	28 398	51 188
Transport Equipment	28 410	19 835
Metals and Metal Products	57 086	56 593
Wood and Paper Products	12 684	16 749
Food and Related Products	26 462	22 188
Minerals	33 177	95 667
Other	47 023	4 119
Total	761 953	659 953

Source: NBS, *China Statistical Yearbook*, 2006, pp. 738-9. http://dx.doi.org/10.1787/086463786586

ISBN: 978-92-64-03762-5 © OECD 2007

benefit from the tax privileges in the special economic zones. The zones have been an important vehicle for the development of a capitalist class in China, as well as a successful instrument for transfer of technology. There have of course been distortions in resource allocation due to the privileges granted to entrepreneurs in the special zones. The SEZs were tax havens for domestic as well as foreign investors. Significant Chinese investment was located in the zones which might have gone to other areas if the tax incidence had been uniform throughout the country. Tax and tariff incentives intended to foster transfer of technology and strengthen China's exports also led to illicit movement of duty–free consumer goods which were smuggled out of the SEZs (most notoriously in Hainan in 1984–85) and sold on the domestic market at much higher prices. These special privileges had something of the same effect as those the treaty ports enjoyed in the nineteenth century — they augmented inequalities in income between coastal and inland areas.

By comparison with the inflow of foreign direct investment, Chinese borrowing has been relatively modest, a total of $147 billion between 1979 and 2005, most of it long or medium term. The debt structure presents negligible exposure to sudden changes in foreign confidence; the Peoples' Republic has never been in arrears on foreign debt and has very large foreign exchange reserves. In this respect, its opening to the world economy has been remarkably trouble free by comparison with the situation in some other Asian and Latin American countries and in the former Soviet bloc.

Macromanagement and the Changing Role of Fiscal and Monetary Policy

From 1952 to 1978, the government ran a command economy. It provided the finance for investment and decided its allocation by sector. Inputs of materials and labour were controlled by government fiat, prices were controlled and important consumer items were both subsidised and rationed. The banking and financial sector was limited in size and did as it was directed. The government had a tight control of foreign trade and there was virtually no foreign investment.

The fiscal and planning systems were closely integrated. The predominant item in government spending was "economic construction" which included investment, administrative and support activities in the major productive sectors of the economy. Some of the investment and running costs of collective farms, state and co–operative enterprises were also met out of their own funds, but negligible amounts were financed by bank borrowing, issuance of bonds or shares as would be the case in a capitalist economy.

On the revenue side, the state derived a large part of its income from the enterprises it was financing. Except for the years of the Great Leap Forward and the beginning of the Cultural Revolution, fiscal policy in the Maoist period was relatively cautious and revenues were generally greater than expenditure. The early loans from the Soviet Union were fully repaid by 1965 and by 1978 there was no foreign or domestic debt. The rate of inflation was relatively modest; it averaged 1.7 per cent a year from 1952 to 1978.

After 1978, the nature of the economy changed fundamentally. The direct role of government in financing and controlling development was dramatically reduced. The previous budgetary contribution of state enterprises disappeared and was replaced by large net subsidies Most taxes are now collected by local authorities which have a strong financial interest in the profitability of the enterprises they run. They grant large tax relief and tax incentives for such activity, which is the second major reason for the proportionate fall in government revenue. The proportionate size of government revenue in 2005 had fallen to 17 per cent of GDP compared with 31 per cent in 1978. Government expenditure fell drastically in response to the squeeze in revenue. Nevertheless, the rise in government domestic debt was fairly modest; it was less than 16 per cent of GDP in 2005. From 1978 to 2003, inflation was much bigger than in the Maoist period (the annual inflation rate averaged 5.5 per cent).

ISBN: 978-92-64-03762-5 © OECD 2007

Table 3.28. **Size and Structure of Government Revenue and Expenditure, China 1952–2005**
(per cent of officially estimated GDP in current prices)

| | Net Government Revenue by Category | | | |
	Total	Taxes	Net Revenue from Enterprises	Other
1952	25.6	14.4	8.4	2.8
1965	27.6	11.9	15.4	0.3
1978	31.2	14.3	15.8	1.1
1995	10.3	10.1	−0.6	0.9
2005	17.3	15.7	-0.1	1.7

| | Government Expenditure by Category | | | | | |
	Total	Economic Construction	Culture & Education	Defence	Administration	Other
1952	25.9	10.8	3.1	8.5	2.3	1.2
1965	27.1	14.8	3.6	5.1	1.5	2.1
1978	31.1	19.7	4.0	4.6	1.5	1.0
1995	11.4	4.8	2.9	1.1	1.7	1.0
2005	18.5	5.1	4.9	1.4	3.6	3.6

Sources: Expenditure and revenue 1952 and 1965 from SSB, *China Statistical Yearbook* 1993, pp. 187-189, 1978–2005 from NBS 2006 *Yearbook*, pp. 281-283. They refer to central, provincial and local levels of government and exclude borrowing.
http://dx.doi.org/10.1787/086465677373

The reform programme involved decontrol of productive decisions in agriculture and gave scope for a massive expansion of entrepreneurship and productive activity in enterprises run by local government and private individuals. The expanded capitalist sector was able to recruit workers at low wages, with no job security, no social security and without trade unions to protect their interests. The decline in the role of state enterprise involved a substantial reduction in the extensive benefits for health, education, housing, pensions and employment security which state employees had enjoyed. The state itself makes negligible provision for pensions and social welfare (about 0.04 per cent of GDP in 2005). In the 1990s it started to impose charges for education. These are a minor item in budget receipts (1.1 per cent in 2005), but they are a significant burden for poor families.

In Russia, the transition from a command to a market economy was brutal and destroyed private savings. In China, it was more skillfully managed. There was no hyperinflation. The government remained internationally creditworthy and there was no capital flight. There were some years when sharp deflation was necessary to stabilise the growth path but these were handled with skill. As a result of this and the acceleration of economic growth and personal income, private savings increased enormously.

The explosive growth of household savings and the rapid monetisation of the economy were the most important elements preventing a financial crisis. Most private savings have been placed in the state banking system and the government also made significant seigniorage gains from the monetisation process. The new funds have more than offset the sharp decline in the operational surplus of state enterprise and the disappearance of budgetary savings. Before the reform period, household savings were negligible but they are now more than a quarter of household income. In 1978 the money supply (money and quasi money) was less than a third of GDP, but by 2005 it was bigger than GDP. Until 1978, the Peoples' Bank of China was part of the Ministry of Finance and controlled virtually all financial and insurance transactions. Since 1978, the government has created a much more complex banking structure. The Peoples' Bank is now a central bank, there are four big commercial banks, a larger number of investment banks, insurance companies, and urban and rural credit co–operatives. The banks attract customers by paying interest on deposits and expanding the branch network. In 1981 bond issues were initiated. At first a large part of bond sales were forced saving, but interest rates were raised and in 1988 a secondary market was created. The Shanghai stock exchange had been closed in 1949 and was reopened in 1990; the new Shenzhen exchange followed in 1991. Between them they listed more than 1 200 companies at the end of 2006 and the capitalised value of the 840 firms listed on the Shanghai stock exchange was $915 billion. In 2006, the Shanghai exchange, together with the Hong Kong exchange (whose capitalisation is bigger), launched a successful IPO and sold $21.9 billion shares in the Industrial and Commercial Bank of China.

A striking feature of the change in the Chinese budget situation is the drastic reduction in the official statement of military expenditure, which fell from 4.6 per cent of GDP in 1978 to 1.4 per cent in 2005 (see Table 3.28). This is mainly due to the fact that the military were encouraged to finance themselves by economic activity. Army personnel are engaged in a wide range of manufacturing, including pharmaceuticals, optical equipment, steel, explosives and weaponry. They deal in property, finance, hotel and travel services. They engage in joint ventures and are major exporters. This probably reduces military preparedness and it is likely to have created some elements of corruption, but it seems to have improved morale, particularly in the upper ranks and has probably strengthened military support for the reform process.

Notes

1. Buck's survey covered provinces representing 83.5 per cent of the cultivated area. The biggest uncovered area was in the four provinces of Manchuria which had about 15.4 per cent of cultivated area and where farms were bigger (see Liu and Yeh, 1965, p. 129 who give estimates of cultivated area for 30 provinces).

2. These are the figures for Buck's survey area. Including Manchuria, the multiple cropping ratio was 1.32

3. Skinner (May 1965, p. 372) comments thus on the market closures: "Traditional marketing weeks which had recurred in thousands of markets for centuries without break were abruptly discontinued.... The abolition of the periodic marketing system in most parts of China quickly induced near paralysis in commodity distribution."

4. If one compares the official figures for employment in commerce in 1952 and 1957 in Table 3.24 with the Liu and Yeh (1965) estimates for the same years in Table D.5, it is clear that the former take no account of peddlers, so that they understate the decline in service activities.

ISBN: 978-92-64-03762-5 © OECD 2007

Chapter 4

Problems and Prospects: the Outlook for China and the World Economy, 2003–2030

As a consequence of successful policy, Chinese per capita income rose by 6.6 per cent a year from1978 to 2003, faster than any other Asian country, very much better than the 1.8 per cent a year in the United States and Western Europe and four times as fast as the world average. Per capita GDP rose from 22 to 63 per cent of the world average and China's share of world GDP rose from 5 to 15 per cent. It became the world's second biggest economy after the United States. In 1998, when most east Asian countries were caught in a foreign exchange crisis and had substantial recessions, the impact was small in China[1]. With the rather cautious assumptions we have made, China will probably surpass the United States as the number one economy in terms of GDP before or shortly after 2015. It is likely to account for about a quarter of world GDP in 2030, with a per capita income about one third larger than the world average. Its influence on the performance of the world economy and its geopolitical leverage will certainly be greater in 2030 than in 2003.

China is still a relatively low–income country. In 2003 its per capita income was only 17 per cent of that of the United States, 23 per cent of Japan, 28 per cent of Taiwan and 31 per cent of Korea. Countries at China's distance from the technological frontier have a capacity for fast growth if they mobilise and allocate physical and human capital effectively, adapt foreign technology to their factor proportions and utilise the opportunities for specialisation which come from integration into the world economy. China demonstrated a capacity to do these things in the reform period.

It is likely that the catch–up process will continue in the next quarter century, but it would be unrealistic to assume that the future growth trajectory will be as fast as it was from 1978 to 2003. In that period there were large, once–for–all, gains in efficiency of resource allocation in agriculture, an explosive expansion of foreign trade and accelerated absorption of foreign technology through large–scale foreign direct investment. The pace of progress will slacken as China gets nearer to the technological frontier. I have assumed that per capita income will grow at an average rate of 4.5 per cent a year between 2003 and 2030, but that the rate of advance will taper off over the period. Specifically, I assume a rate of 5.6 per cent a year to 2010, 4.6 per cent between 2010 and 2020 and a little more than 3.6 per cent a year from 2020 to 2030. By then, in our scenario, it will have reached the same per capita level as Western Europe in 1990 and of Japan in 1986, when their catch–up process had ceased. As it approaches this level, technical advance will be more costly as imitation is replaced by innovation. However, by 2030 the technical frontier will have moved forward, so there will still be some scope for catch–up thereafter.

ISBN: 978-92-64-037625 © OECD 2007

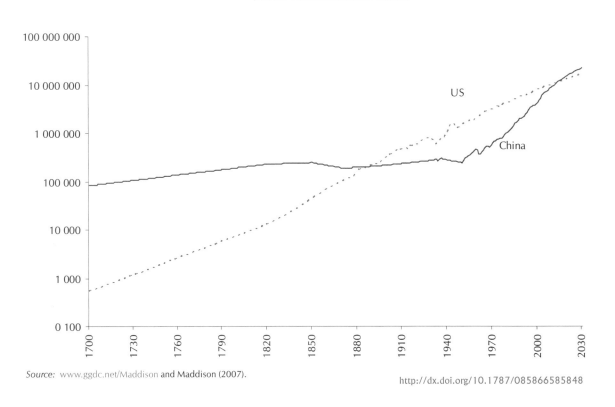

Figure 4.1. **Comparative Levels of GDP, China and the United States, 1700-2030**
(million 1990 International dollars)

Source: www.ggdc.net/Maddison and Maddison (2007).

http://dx.doi.org/10.1787/085866585848

In the reform period, China was able to increase employment nearly twice as fast as population because changes in demographic structure raised the proportion of working age from 54 to nearly 70 per cent of the population and there were substantial increases in the activity rate of women. By 2030, it seems likely that population growth will decelerate significantly and the proportion of working age will fall somewhat. There will probably be some reduction in average working hours as wages rise and leisure activities become affordable. There will be slower proportionate improvement in the educational level of the labour force; it increased six–fold from 1952 to 2003 and is unlikely to rise by more than half by 2030. Thus one might reasonably expect quality adjusted labour input to grow by half a per cent a year from 2003 to 2030, compared with 3.2 per cent in 1978–2003 (see Table 3.9).

In 1998, I made projections for Chinese growth from 1995 to 2015. At that time it seemed that China faced three big domestic problems: a) to shut down a very large number of loss–making state enterprises; b) to transform its financial system which operated with an important and increasing proportion of non–performing assets; and c) to strengthen the weak fiscal position of central government. These are classic problems in the transition from a command to a market economy. The failure to solve them in most of the economies of the former USSR was a major reason for their dismal performance in the 1990s. However, China was more successful in solving or significantly mitigating these problems than I expected and its integration into the world economy much more rapid.

My tables present a comparative picture of China's relative position in the world economy, its performance in the reform period 1978–2003 and its prospects for 2003–2030. Chinese performance and prospects are compared with the outlook for four other large countries — India, Japan, Russia and the United States. Together with China they accounted for 50 per cent of world GDP in 2003. I also show the prospects for the seven major regions which account for the other half of world income.

ISBN: 978-92-64-03762-5 © OECD 2007   94

It is clear from Tables 4.1a and b that China performed better than the other four big countries in the 1990–2003 period. The most striking contrast is with Russia which was also engaged in an effort to transform a command to a market economy. In 1990, China's GDP was less than twice as big as Russia's, but by 2003 it was more than six times as large. It is worth summarising the reasons for China's superior performance.

Table 4.1a. **Comparative GDP Performance of China, Russia, Japan, India and the United States, 1990–2030**

| | GDP levels in billion 1990 PPP dollars | | | | | China as per cent of | | | |
	Russia	Japan	China	US	India	Russia	Japan	US	India
1990	1 151	2 321	2 124	5 803	1 098	185	92	37	199
1991	1 093	2 399	2 264	5 792	1 112	207	94	39	204
1992	935	2 422	2 484	5 985	1 169	266	103	42	212
1993	854	2 428	2 724	6 146	1 238	319	112	44	220
1994	745	2 455	2 997	6 396	1 328	402	122	47	226
1995	715	2 504	3 450	6 558	1 426	483	138	53	242
1996	689	2 590	3 521	6 804	1 537	511	136	52	229
1997	699	2 636	3 707	7 110	1 611	530	141	52	230
1998	662	2 609	3 717	7 407	1 716	561	142	50	217
1999	704	2 605	3 961	7 736	1 820	563	152	51	218
2000	774	2 667	4 319	8 019	1 900	558	162	54	227
2001	814	2 673	4 781	8 079	2 009	587	179	59	238
2002	852	2 664	5 374	8 209	2 080	631	202	65	258
2003	914	2 699	6 188	8 431	2 267	677	229	73	273
2015	1 300	3 116	12 271	11 467	4 665	944	394	107	263
2030	2 017	3 488	22 983	16 662	10 074	1 139	659	138	228

Source: 1990-2003 from www.ggdc.net/Maddison; 2015 and 2030 derived from Tables 4.2 and 4.3.

http://dx.doi.org/10.1787/086618665424

Table 4.1b. **Comparative Per Capita GDP Performance of China, Russia, Japan, India and the United States, 1990–2030**

| | Per capita GDP levels in 1990 PPP dollars | | | | | China as per cent of | | | |
	Russia	Japan	China	US	India	Russia	Japan	US	India
1990	7 779	18 789	1 871	23 201	1 309	24	10	8	143
1991	7 373	19 355	1 967	22 849	1 299	27	10	9	151
1992	6 300	19 482	2 132	23 298	1 341	34	11	9	159
1993	5 752	19 478	2 312	23 616	1 390	40	12	10	166
1994	5 020	19 637	2 515	24 279	1 463	50	13	10	172
1995	4 813	19 979	2 863	24 603	1 538	59	14	12	186
1996	4 645	20 616	2 892	25 230	1 630	62	14	11	177
1997	4 717	20 929	3 013	26 052	1 680	64	14	12	179
1998	4 475	20 662	2 993	26 824	1 760	67	14	11	170
1999	4 776	20 594	3 162	27 699	1 835	66	15	11	172
2000	5 277	21 051	3 421	28 403	1 885	65	16	12	181
2001	5 573	21 062	3 759	28 347	1 963	67	18	13	191
2002	5 865	20 969	4 197	28 535	2 012	72	20	15	209
2003	6 323	21 218	4 803	29 037	2 160	76	23	17	222
2015	9 554	24 775	8 807	35 547	3 663	88	36	25	240
2030	16 007	30 072	15 763	45 774	7 089	98	52	34	222

Source: 1990-2003 from www.ggdc.net/Maddison; 2015 and 2030 derived from Tables 4.2 and 4.3.

http://dx.doi.org/10.1787/086618665424

ISBN: 978-92-64-037625 © OECD 2007

1) Chinese reformers gave first priority to agriculture. They ended Mao's collectivist follies and offered individual peasant households the opportunity to raise their income by their own efforts. Russian reformers more or less ignored agriculture as the potential for individual peasant household enterprise had been killed off by Stalin in the 1920s. The Chinese government encouraged small-scale manufacturing production in township and village enterprises. Local officials and party elite got legal opportunities for greatly increasing their income if they ran the enterprises successfully.

2) China did not disintegrate as the USSR did. The proportion of ethnic minorities is much smaller in China, and in spite of its size, China is a nation state rather than an empire. By patient diplomacy and accepting capitalist enclaves it grew by reintegrating Hong Kong and Macao as special administrative regions.

3) In the reform era, China benefited substantially from the great number of overseas Chinese. A large part of foreign investment and foreign entrepreneurship has come from Hong Kong, Singapore, Taiwan and Chinese in other parts of the world.

4) China started from a very low level of productivity and income. In 1978, when the reform era began, per capita income was less than 15 per cent of that in the USSR and its degree of industrialisation was much smaller. If the right policies are pursued, backwardness is a favourable position for a nation which wants to achieve rapid catch-up. The very fact that the Chinese income level was so much lower than that of Hong Kong, Japan, Malaysia, South Korea, Singapore and Taiwan made it easier to capture the advantages of backwardness and make big structural changes. It means that its period of super-growth can stretch further into the future than theirs.

5) Chinese family planning policy reduced the birth rate and changed the population structure in a way that promoted economic growth. From 1978 to 2003 the proportion of working age rose from 54 to 70 per cent. In China, life expectation has risen. In Russia it has fallen.

6) The leadership was very sensitive to the dangers of hyper-inflation which China had experienced when the KMT were in charge. Instead of destroying private savings as in Russia, they were encouraged and have increased enormously. They are the main reason that it was possible to raise investment to such high levels. Russian shock therapy involved a period of hyper-inflation, large-scale capital flight, currency collapse and default on foreign debt. China remained internationally creditworthy and had negligible capital flight. Its tax incentives attracted large scale foreign investment, which facilitated its technological advance.

7) The state sector was not privatised, but waned by attrition. There are now many wealthy entrepreneurs in China and some have enjoyed official favours, but China did not create super-rich oligarchs by selling off state enterprises at knock-down prices as Russia did. In Forbes Magazine's listing of the world's 100 richest billionaires in 2007, 13 were in Russia, 3 were in Hong Kong and none were in China.

8) China has made massive strides to integrate into the world economy. It gave high priority to promotion of manufactured exports and set up tax-free special enterprise zones near the coast. Exports were also facilitated by maintaining an undervalued currency. The rebound in the Russian economy since 1998 has been largely driven by the rise in the price of its exports of oil and natural gas. If Hong Kong is included, China is now the biggest exporter, acounting for nearly 11 per cent of the world total. In 2006, exports were $1 286 billion including Hong Kong, Germany was second, with $1 126, the United States third with $1 038, Japan fourth with $650 billion and Russia was seventh with $305 billion (see IMF, 2007).

China still has some of the problems I cited in my 1998 projections, i.e. a) the fiscal resources of central government need to be substantially enhanced to finance social expenditure on education and health and to mitigate inequality of income and opportunity between different regions; b) government still has to shut down loss-making state enterprises, but their proportionate importance is much reduced; and c) considerable progress has been made in improving the solvability and efficiency of the banking system, which operated with a large proportion of non–performing assets. Most of these have been written off and China has attracted foreign participation in state banks by selling shares on the Hong Kong and Shanghai stock markets. In the two years following June 2005, more than $60 billion was raised this way and some foreign banks have been allowed to operate in China. China has accumulated $1.2 trillion in foreign exchange reserves and has begun to make foreign investment on a substantial scale to secure its future supply of raw materials and energy. Its integration in the world economy has been furthered by reduction of its own trade barriers and the greater security of its access to foreign markets thanks to its membership of the World Trade Organisation. There are however, some other important problems.

Energy and the Environment

The Chinese economy has expanded very fast and energy consumption has risen a good deal. Electricity production increased ten–fold between 1978 and 2005 and its availability at rather low prices transformed living conditions in many urban households, with the spread of electric light, television, washing machines, microwaves, fans and air conditioners. Car ownership has also risen and is likely to be the most dynamic element in private consumption. In 2006 there were about 19 millon passenger cars in circulation, (one for every 70 persons). This compared with 140 millon and one for every two persons in the United States (see www.autoexecmag.com). Judging by the average west European relationship of car ownership to per capita income, it seems likely there will be 300 millon passenger cars in China (one for every five persons) in 2030.

Per capita energy consumption has doubled since 1973. There was a surprisingly large improvement in the efficiency with which energy is used. In 1973, 0.64 tons of oil equivalent were used per thousand dollars of GDP, by 2003, this had fallen to 0.22 tons. The International Energy Agency (IEA, 2006) projects a further fall to 0.11 tons in 2030 in its "A" scenario, which takes account of energy efficiency policies governments can reasonably be expected to adopt (see Table 4.2). Energy efficiency was better in China than in the United States in 2003 and this is expected to be true in 2030.

The "R" scenario of IEA provides an estimate of how energy demand may increase if governments do nothing beyond their present commitments to energy economy. Here again the IEA expects China to be more efficient than the United States (see last column of Table 4.2).

However, the environmental impact of energy use in China is particularly adverse because its dependence on coal is unusually large and carbon emissions are proportionately much bigger from coal than those from oil or gas. In 2003, 60 per cent of energy consumption came from coal, compared to 23 per cent in the United States, 17 per cent in Russia and 5 per cent in France. Eighty per cent of its electricity is generated by coal powered plants. This means that the ratio of carbon emissions to energy consumption is higher in China than in most countries. In the IEA "A" scenario, China is expected to emit 0.8 tons of carbon per ton of energy used in 2030, compared with 0.63 in the United States and a world average of 0.60 (see Table 4.2).

Chinese coal is particularly dirty; sulfur dioxide and sooty particles released by coal combustion have polluted the air in its major cities and created acid rain, which falls on 30 per cent of its land mass. There are more than 20 000 coal mines and nearly 6 millon miners, whose productivity is low and whose working conditions are dangerous. Several thousand are killed every year in mining accidents. In north China there are some coal seams near the surface which burn continuously in unstoppable fires. These environmental problems are likely to be bigger in China than in the rest of the world, as it is more difficult and more costly to reduce the proportionate role of coal. The IEA projection assumes that China will use about 48 per cent of the world's coal output in 2030 compared with 36 per cent in 2004. The government made a major effort to offset carbon emissions by reforestation of 4 millon hectares a year in 2000–2005 and is seeking to develop new and more efficient energy techniques. It has negotiated deals to invest in future oil supplies from Angola, Iran, Sudan and Venezuela. In 2005,

ISBN: 978-92-64-037625 © OECD 2007

Table 4.2. **Intensity of Energy Use and Carbon Emissions, China, the United States and World, 1973-2030**
(energy in million metric tons of oil equivalent; carbon emissions in million tons)

	1973	1990	2003	2030A	2030R
		China			
Total Energy Use	472	880	1 409	2 630	2 971
tons per capita	0.54	0.78	1.09	1.80	2.04
tons/$1000 GDP	0.64	0.41	0.22	0.11	0.13
Carbon Emissions	244	615	1 043	2 100	2 487
per capita emissions	0.28	0.52	0.81	1.44	1.71
emission/energy use	0.52	0.70	0.74	0.80	0.83
		United States			
Total Energy Use	1 736	1 928	2 281	2 889	3 131
tons per capita	8.19	7.71	7.86	7.94	8.61
tons/$1000 GDP	0.49	0.33	0.27	0.17	0.19
Carbon Emissions	1 283	1 321	1 562	1 828	2 081
per capita emissions	6.05	5.28	5.38	5.02	5.72
emission/energy use	0.74	0.69	0.68	0.63	0.66
		World			
Total Energy Use	6 248	8 811	10 760	14 584	16 203
tons per capita	1.60	1.68	1.71	1.78	1.98
tons/$1000 GDP	0.39	0.32	0.26	0.15	0.17
Carbon Emissions	4 271	5 655	6 736	8 794	10 447
per capita emissions	1.09	1.08	1.07	1.08	1.28
emission/energy use	0.68	0.64	0.63	0.60	0.64

Source: Primary energy consumption, 1973-2003, from IEA (2005a), Carbon emissions, 1990-2003, from IEA (2005b), 1973 supplied by IEA. I converted CO2 to carbon by dividing by 3.667 (the molecular weight ratio of carbon dioxide to carbon). Projections for 2030 were derived from the "alternative scenario" of IEA for that year in *World Energy Outlook 2006*, pp. 528-9, 534-5 and 552-3. I adjusted the IEA projections for 2030 by the difference between their GDP projections and mine (a downward coefficient of 0.875 for China, 1.069 upward for the United States, and .9478 downward for the world). The "alternative A scenario" takes account of energy-efficiency policies countries might reasonably be expected to adopt over the projected period; the IEA "reference R scenario" (pp. 492-517) provides a "baseline vision" of how energy demand would evolve if governments do nothing beyond their present commitments. GDP in 1990 Geary-Khamis PPP dollars and population from www.ggdc.net/Maddison;

http://dx.doi.org/10.1787/086648176475

the Chinese company CNOOC made an $18.5 billion offer to buy the American oil company Unocal, but the transaction was blocked by opposition in the US Congress. It has made an agreement with the European Union for joint research to develop a near–zero emissions technology (carbon capture and storage) in a pilot coal plant in China (see Stern Review, 2006); however, the results will not be available for several years and it is not clear how cost–effective they will be. In the long run, there would be substantial benefits if China acquires pipeline access to Russian natural gas.

Regional Inequality

Regional inequality in China is extreme. Table F.2 shows a ten–to–one range of per capita GDP in China's 31 administrative regions in 2005. Average income for China as a whole was 14 000 yuan a year. Shanghai led with an annual income per person of 52 000, Beijing second with 45 000 and Tianjin third with 35 000. Guizhou was lowest with 5.3 thousand, Gansu next with 7.5 and Yunnan third with 7.8. The top three had a combined population of nearly 44 millon and the bottom three nearly 108 millon. The income spread narrowed from 14:1 in 1978 to 10:1 in 1995. Since then it has hardly changed; Shanghai has always been top and Guizhou bottom (SSB, 1997). These spreads are not adjusted for price difference between areas, but this is usually the case for other countries where such estimates are available. The Chinese regional divergence seems extreme by international standards. I found a spread of 8:1 in Brazil, 6:1 in Mexico and 2:1 in the United States in the 1980s (see Maddison, 1992, p. 79). However, the inter–regional spread in India (between Goa and Bihar) increased from 5.5 in 1993–94 to 10.1 in 2002–03 (see Indiastat.com). The divergence in China could be narrowed by major investment in transport and other infrastructure, improved education opportunity in the low income areas, removal of barriers to migration between different areas and elimination of the tax enjoyed by special enterprise zones in eastern China. However, the mitigation of inter–regional income divergence is likely to be a slow process.

Rural–Urban Inequality

The spread between average rural and urban income is bigger than in other Asian countries. In 2002 it was 3.2/1 in China and varied from 1.3/1 to 2.2/1 elsewhere in Asia. The gap was biggest (3.5/1) in China's western provinces and lowest (1.9/1) in the eastern provinces. An important reason for the gap is the household registration system (*hukou*) established in the Maoist period to control population movement. It is reinforced by legislation to penalise immigrant workers who seek unregistered employment in urban areas. Despite some easing in the system, they are still denied public services such as health and education, they have difficulty in getting housing and employers who hire them may suffer financial penalties. Hence they are in a weak bargaining position and get low wages for long hours. Their wages are often in arrears and sometimes fail to be paid. Sicular *et al.* (2007) estimate that unregistered households are about 17 per cent of the urban population and that their average income is 60 per cent lower than that of registered urban households. However, it is 40 per cent bigger than that of rural households. The urban–rural spread of 3.2/1, cited above, refers only to registered urban households, it is reduced to 3/1 if all urban households are included. If the urban–rural differential is further adjusted for differences in cost of living, it is about 2.1/1. It is clear that the discriminatory registration system is a major source of social discontent, which is in need of remedy.

The Legal System and Private Property Rights

China has made giant strides in moving towards a market economy and its legal system allows private enterprise to flourish. Property rights have recently been strengthened, but are a good deal weaker and more ambiguous than they would be in a capitalist economy. Land is still state or "collective" property. Peasants can get 30 year leases for their farms and urban householders can get 70 year leases on their houses; thereafter, their property reverts to the state. It is difficult to sell such properties or use them as collateral for loans. Paradoxically for a socialist country, property rights are weaker for ordinary citizens than they are for domestic or foreign capitalists. Urban developers find it easier than would be the case in a capitalist country to expropriate land of peasants or poor urban residents and demolish their homes without adequate compensation. Influential party officials are able to enrich themselves by conniving in such transactions. These problems have led to increased public protests and punishment of party officials for corruption. The equity and efficiency of the economy would benefit if property rights were strengthened and the judiciary were less subject to official pressure.

ISBN: 978-92-64-037625 © OECD 2007

The Outlook for the World Economy: 2003–2030

Developments in the world economy in the last half century have been quite complex. Over the years 1952 to 1978, world per capita income grew faster than ever before, at 2.6 per cent a year — 50 times as fast as in 1500–1820, and nearly 3 times as fast as in 1820–1952. In this golden age, all parts of the world economy showed substantial improvement on past performance. The United States — the lead country in terms of productivity and per capita income — grew more slowly than the world average, but continued to experience relatively high rates of total factor productivity growth, which can be taken as evidence of rapid advance at the technological frontier (see Table 3.9). There was a remarkable degree of catch–up in Japan and the advanced capitalist countries which substantially reduced the per capita income gap between themselves and the lead country. There was significant catch–up (from lower levels of income) in Other Asia, Eastern Europe and the USSR. Latin American per capita growth was the same as the world average. In China and Africa, real per income grew faster than ever before, but grew less than the world average[2].

Table 4.3. **World Economic Growth Performance and Projections 1952–2030**
(annual average compound growth rates)

	1952-1978		1978-2003		2003–2030	
	Per capita GDP	Population	Per capita GDP	Population	Per capita GDP	Population
West Europe	3.66	0.65	1.84	0.32	1.7	0.05
United States	2.24	1.34	1.85	1.06	1.7	0.84
Western Offshoots	2.54	1.89	1.76	1.21	1.7	0.70
Japan	6.69	1.10	2.11	0.40	1.3	-0.33
The Rich	**3.34**	**0.97**	**1.93**	**0.62**	**1.73**	**0.32**
China	2.33	2.02	6.57	1.19	4.5	0.46
India	1.66	2.16	3.27	1.95	4.5	1.13
Other Asia	3.58	2.44	2.25	2.05	2.5	1.29
Russia	3.39	1.02	-1.48	0.22	3.5	-0.49
Other former USSR	2.86	1.69	-2.14	0.56	2.0	0.43
Eastern Europe	3.75	0.96	0.48	0.20	2.0	-0.21
Latin America	2.62	2.65	0.53	1.82	1.5	0.97
Africa	1.83	2.45	0.16	2.63	1.0	1.98
The Rest	**2.72**	**2.14**	**2.00**	**1.72**	**3.01**	**1.08**
World	**2.62**	**1.91**	**1.55**	**1.55**	**2.23**	**0.98**

Source: Per capita GDP, 1952-2030, from www.ggdc.net/Maddison and Maddison (2007); population, 1952-2030, from International Programs Department, US Census Bureau, www.census.gov/ipc.
Western Offshoots are Australia, Canada and New Zealand.

http://dx.doi.org/10.1787/086681472672

In 1978–2003, world economic growth was much slower. The deceleration in the lead country was mainly due to a sharp drop in total factor productivity performance, suggesting strongly that the pace of advance at the technological frontier had weakened. There was a sharp slowdown in Japan and the other advanced capitalist countries, because of the weaker growth at the technological frontier and the fact that they were operating much nearer to it. Hence they had eroded a good part of their potential for rapid catch–up.

The Asian economies were the most dynamic in 1978–2003. Growth of per capita income accelerated sharply in China. There was substantial improvement in India and a milder acceleration elsewhere.

A slowdown in the advanced capitalist countries was to be expected as their scope for rapid catch–up was more or less exhausted. The acceleration in a significant number of Asian countries was also understandable as their scope for catch–up was quite large. If the world economy had consisted only of these two groups, one could have interpreted the pattern of development as a fairly clear–cut demonstration of the possibilities for "conditional convergence" suggested by neo–classical growth theory. However, catch–up in the poorer economies was not automatic or generalised. They could exploit their catch–up potential only if they adopted policies propitious for growth, mounted high rates of investment in physical and human capital, increased labour force participation, opened their economies to foreign trade and specialisation, pursued macroeconomic policies which smoothed the growth process and microeconomic policies which promoted increased efficiency of resource allocation. Such policies were characteristic of China and the dynamic Asian economies.

Growth theory provides little help in explaining the 1978–2003 experience in other parts of the world. The biggest shock was the disintegration of the USSR into 15 independent states. The net impact was a large drop in per capita income in Russia, a bigger fall in the other republics of the former USSR and a sharp slowdown in Eastern Europe. In the Middle East, Latin America and Africa, growth in the golden age had not been due to any great virtues of domestic policy, but was significantly dependent on the diffusion effects of high growth momentum in the advanced capitalist countries. The sharp slowdown in the capitalist core sparked off debt crises, inflation, fiscal and monetary problems in Latin America and Africa. In the Middle East falling oil prices and wars affecting Iran, Iraq and Lebanon were major disturbing forces.

The projections for world development in 2003–2030 in Tables 4.4 and 4.5 are mainly from Maddison (2007). They have two components: growth of population and per capita GDP. The GDP projections are derivative. The demographic projections are those of the US Census Bureau and cover 224 countries (see www.census.gov/ipc and www.ggdc.net/Maddison). The projections of per capita GDP are much more aggregative. They cover seven major regions, the four countries with the biggest shares of world GDP and Russia. They are not the result of an econometric exercise, but are based on an analysis of changes in the momentum of growth in different parts of the world economy and my assessment of the likelihood of their continuation or change. They were conceived as the likely continuation or deviation from the momentum of growth in 1990–2003.

For the advanced capitalist group, (Western Europe, the United States, the other Western Offshoots and Japan), I assume that their aggregate per capita GDP will grow at about the same rate as in 1990–2003. This does not mean that all component countries will advance at the same pace. France, Germany, Italy and Japan advanced more slowly than the United States in 1990–2003, but Ireland made a remarkable bound forward, while Australia, Spain and the United Kingdom had a respectable degree of catch–up. Labour input per head of population is generally lower in Western Europe than in the United States, so the gap in performance is substantially smaller in terms of productivity than in per capita GDP.

It is reasonable to expect some reversal of the previous declines in per capita income in the countries of the former Soviet Union and an acceleration of growth in eastern Europe, Latin America, Africa and most of Asia. For China, I have assumed a slowdown in per capita growth for reasons already explained, but it will still be a very dynamic economy and its dynamism will be a major force driving growth of the world economy, which will offset the diminished relative role of the advanced capitalist group (see Table 4.6).

The overall world projection shows slower demographic growth than in 1978–2003, but a significant acceleration in per capita income. World per capita GDP is projected to grow at 2.2 per cent a year, much faster than performance (1.55 per cent) in 1978–2003, but slower than the 2.6 per cent in the golden age (1952–78).

ISBN: 978-92-64-037625 © OECD 2007

The expected changes in performance are shown in Tables 4.4 and 4.5. Changes in economic leverage inevitably have geopolitical repercussions, making present membership of groups like the UN Security Council or the G–8 summiteers obsolete. They will also reduce the capacity of the United States to play a hegemonial role. Changes in these arrangements would be needed to maintain peaceful co–existence between the major powers, to reduce the size and spread of nuclear arsenals and to mitigate the spread of various brands of religious fundamentalism. Major failures in these areas would probably make my relatively cautious economic projections seem euphoric.

Table 4.4. **Per Capita GDP: the World and Major Regions, 1952–2030**

	Level in 1990 international PPP $					Average annual rate of change	
	1952	1978	1990	2003	2030	1990-2003	2003-2030
Western Europe	4 963	12 621	15 965	19 912	31 389	1.71	1.7
United States	10 316	18 373	23 201	29 037	45 774	1.74	1.7
Other Western Offshoots	7 688	14 745	17 902	22 853	36 025	1.90	1.7
Japan	2 336	12 585	18 789	21 218	30 072	0.94	1.3
"The Rich"	6 149	14 455	18 781	23 345	37 086	1.69	1.73
Eastern Europe	2 207	5 749	5 440	6 476	11 054	1.35	2.0
Russia	3 120	7 420	7 779	6 323	16 007	-1.58	3.5
Other former USSR	2 696	5 607	5 954	4 461	7 614	-2.20	2.0
Latin America	2 588	5 070	5 072	5 786	8 648	1.02	1.5
China	538	978	1 871	4 803	15 763	7.52	4.5
India	629	966	1 309	2 160	7 089	3.93	4.5
Other Asia	978	2 441	3 078	4 257	8 292	2.53	2.5
Africa	928	1 488	1 449	1 549	2 027	0.52	1.0
"The Rest"	1 157	2 324	2 718	3 816	8 504	2.64	3.01
World	2 260	4 432	5 162	6 516	11 814	1.81	2.23

Source: Maddison (2007).   http://dx.doi.org/10.1787/086728413344

Table 4.5. **Growth of GDP: the World and Major Regions, 1952–2030**

	Levels in billion 1990 PPP dollars					Average annual rate of change	
	1952	1978	1990	2003	2030	1990-2003	2003-2030
Western Europe	1 532	4 609	6 033	7 857	12 556	2.05	1.75
United States	1 625	4 090	5 803	8 431	16 662	2.91	2.56
Other Western Offshoots	196	611	862	1 277	2 414	3.07	2.39
Japan	202	1 446	2 321	2 699	3 488	1.17	0.95
"The Rich"	3 556	10 753	15 020	20 265	35 120	2.33	2.06
Eastern Europe	198	662	663	786	1 269	1.33	1.79
Russia	329	1 018	1 151	914	2 017	-1.76	2.98
Other former USSR	217	697	837	638	1 222	-2.17	2.43
Latin America	453	1 749	2 240	3 132	6 074	2.61	2.48
China	306	935	2 124	6 188	22 983	8.56	4.98
India	234	625	1 098	2 267	10 074	5.73	5.68
Other Asia	400	1 865	3 099	5 401	14 884	4.36	3.83
Africa	221	664	905	1 322	2 937	2.96	3.00
"The Rest"	2 357	8 216	12 117	20 649	61 460	4.19	4.12
World	5 913	18 969	27 136	40 913	96 580	3.21	3.23

Source: Maddison (2007).   http://dx.doi.org/10.1787/086771851824

Table 4.6. **Shares of World GDP, 1700–2003 (Per cent of World Total)**
(per cent)

	1700	1820	1952	1978	2003	2030
China	22.3	32.9	5.2	4.9	15.1	23.1
India	24.4	16.0	4.0	3.3	5.5	10.4
Japan	4.1	3.0	3.4	7.6	6.6	3.6
Western Europe	21.9	23.0	25.9	24.2	19.2	13.0
United States	0.1	1.8	27.5	21.6	20.6	17.3
USSR	4.4	5.4	9.2	9.0	3.8	3.4

http://dx.doi.org/10.1787/086785463850

Source: Maddison (2007).

ISBN: 978-92-64-037625 © OECD 2007

Notes

1. In 1998, per capita income dropped 1.3 per cent in China and Japan, 14.3 per cent in Thailand, 14.1 in Indonesia, 9.3 in Malaysia, 7.7 in Korea, 5.7 in Hong Kong, 3.5 in Singapore and 2.6 per cent in the Philippines. It should be noted that the divergence between my GDP estimate and the official figure of the National Bureau of Statistics (NBS) is very large for 1998. NBS show a 6.8 rise in per capita GDP in 1998.

2. In analysing growth performance and potential, it is useful to go beyond the estimates of per capita product. Growth accounts such as those in Table 3.9 for China, Japan, Korea and the United States are a basic guide to such analysis, as they illuminate the causal processes of economic growth and provide some idea of the role of factor accumulation and factor productivity.

Appendix A

Performance in Farming, Fishery, Forestry and Agricultural Sidelines, China 1933–95

The original statistical monitoring system of the Chinese State Statistical Bureau (SSB) was in most respects a copy of the Soviet material product approach and its methods of data collection reflected the ubiquity of state control.

The SSB was created in 1952 and its aggregate estimates for agriculture are available on an annual basis from that year. The first major statistical publication (SSB, 1960) provided detail for 1949–58 on output of twenty major crops, some categories of livestock and some farm inputs, but aggregate agricultural performance was indicated only by gross output values at current prices. Thereafter, there was a 20–year period in which published material on agricultural performance was scarce and often distorted for political reasons, particularly during the Great Leap Forward and Cultural Revolution. The SSB was actually abolished in 1968 and its staff dispersed. The provincial offices also seem to have been disbanded. The statistical system was reestablished in 1972, but most of the old staff had disappeared, many old records had been destroyed and no new graduates with the requisite training had been produced in the years when universities had been closed. In 1981 the World Bank reported that the central staff of SSB had only 200 people compared with 400 in 1966.

In the 1980s, after China had joined the UN, World Bank and IMF, it began to shift gradually to the standardised system of national accounts used by Western countries. Vestiges of the old concepts remain and the statistical reporting system has not yet changed much. The new hybrid system can be seen most clearly in the official 1987 input/output table. Table A.1 shows the major entries for agriculture as a whole and for farming. In particular, it shows very clearly the relationship between the Western concept of gross value added and net material product, which was the main indicator of performance in the most sophisticated version of the former Chinese system. In fact the difference between the two magnitudes is rather small for agriculture.

A time series showing the three major official Chinese measures of aggregate agricultural performance: gross output, net material product (NMP) and gross value added (GVA) in "comparable" (quasi–constant) prices can be found in Table A.2. The gross product measure exaggerates performance because it makes no deduction for inputs used in production. According to the World Bank (1992) p. 30, net material product was derived by deducting 13 separate input items from gross output. These were seeds, animal feed, breeding and veterinary costs, fertilisers, fuel, pesticides and other farm chemicals, electric power for production, cost of small implements, depreciation, inputs to sideline products, equipment repairs and production support services., and other physical inputs, but no deduction was made for inputs of "non–productive" services. Gross value added shows agriculture's contribution to gross domestic product and is comparable in concept to Western measures of performance. It is equal to net material product, minus "non–productive" services plus depreciation.

ISBN: 978-92-64-03762-5 © OECD 2007

In the 1980s, the availability of statistical information improved a good deal with the publication of the *China Statistical Yearbook* covering all fields of economic activity. The *China Agriculture Yearbook* contained a statistical section which gave little more than the first mentioned source, but a special comprehensive retrospective volume (Ministry of Agriculture, 1989) covered the whole period 1949–86. It showed output estimates for about 50 crop and livestock items, a measure of aggregate gross agricultural output at "comparable" prices (pp. 106–9) with a breakdown into five major branches (crops, livestock, fishery, forestry and farm "sidelines" – the latter item referred to rural handicrafts, hunting and gathering activities). In the 1990s, this index of gross output was revised to show somewhat slower growth. Retrospective estimates of net material product of agriculture were provided for 1952–93. In 1997, retrospective official estimates of agricultural gross value added at comparable prices became available back to 1952. All these three indicators are available at current and "comparable" prices. However, no breakdown is published between farming, fishery, forestry and sidelines.

As I wanted to check the growth rates and levels of output shown in the official figures and to make an international comparison of Chinese and US farm performance, I constructed my own estimates of agricultural performance at constant prices. Table A.3 summarises my results for agriculture as a whole. Table A.4 shows my estimates of farm gross output and value added for six benchmark years from 1933 to 1994. I used Food and Agriculture Organization (FAO) 1987 prices as weights, FAO quantities for 1975, 1987 and 1994, SSB quantities for 1952, 1957 and 1978 and quantities of Liu and Yeh (1965) for 1933. I had quantitative information for 136 crop and livestock items and prices for 103 of these. For 24 items I felt it was reasonable to estimate shadow prices by assimilating non–priced items with prices for similar products. My aggregate for Chinese farm output therefore covers 125 items. I used the Chinese input–output table to estimate 1987 inputs and extrapolated these to other years using official indicators of the movement of major input items as explained in the notes to Table A.4. Tables A.5, A.6 and A.7 provide rough estimates for fishery, forestry and "sideline" output.

I used 1987 weights throughout because of the availability of a detailed input–output table for that year. Normally, the effect of taking late weights for a 61 year period would tend to understate the growth rate, but this is much less important in agriculture than in industry, because there are no new products and much less change in the product mix than in other sectors of the economy.

My estimates show slightly faster growth than the official figures for 1952–78. I found a growth rate of gross value added of 2.2 per cent a year, compared with the official 2.1 per cent. For 1978–95 my estimates show the same growth as the official 5.1 per cent. For 1952–95 as a whole my growth rate is 3.4 per cent a year, compared with the official 3.3 per cent. For farming I found a growth rate of 3.0 per cent for 1952–94, for fishery 5.7 per cent, forestry 7.1 per cent and "sidelines" 5.6 per cent.

My estimates show a significantly higher level of value added than the official figures. For the benchmark year 1987 my agricultural gross value added was 38l billion yuan compared with the official 320 billion. The difference arises entirely from the farm sector where I have 326 billion yuan compared to the official 265 billion. For the other three sectors I used the official estimates.

For 1952 and 1957 my estimate of agricultural output is 14 per cent higher than the official figures, 18 per cent or over from 1978 onwards. It is not easy to explain this difference in results, because the statistical information in the Chinese official sources is rather limited. Published quantitative information is or has been available for about 50 items compared with 125 in FAO sources. For the 50 SSB items there are no significant differences from FAO data, but it seems quite possible that the official estimates do not give very full coverage to items like fruits, vegetables or nuts, which are not subject to compulsory delivery. Official price information is rather scarce and seems to refer mainly to consumer rather than producer prices. Tables A.22a and A.22b compare a range of official estimates with those of the FAO. One does not find striking differences, but it is not clear what prices were actually used in the official measures. Table A.22c shows there was still a significant degree of segmentation in Chinese farm markets in 1987. The biggest segment for cereals was peasant self–consumption, where prices must necessarily be imputed. The first "market" segment consists of items for which the government set a compulsory delivery. Quotas for 1987 were 18 per cent of the rice crop, 33 per cent for wheat, 40 per cent for maize and 50 per cent for soybeans. The second segment consisted of "above quota" deliveries for government purchase (where prices are higher). The highest prices prevail on the free market. Both the official and the FAO valuations of output seem to be somewhere between the quota and the above–quota prices and the official valuations are probably lower.

It seems likely that my estimates of farm output are higher than the official figures for a mixture of reasons. Part of the explanation may be differences in valuation, part may be due to differences in coverage.

Albert Keidel (World Bank, 1994, pp. 12, 15, 16) suggests that the official estimates understate 1987 farm output because of undervaluation and undercoverage. He maintains that in Chinese statistical practice farm self–consumption of grains is generally valued below market prices. He suggests an upward revaluation of grain output by 20 per cent to correct for this (which would add about 8 per cent to the value of farm output). He believes that the quantity of grain and vegetable output is not recorded fully and that the official estimates for these items should be augmented by 10 per cent and 30 per cent respectively to correct for this. This would probably add another 6 per cent to the value of farm output in 1987.

Measures of 1933 Farm Performance

Official estimates of farm performance do not provide any link with prewar years, but this is essential if one is to get a reasonable perspective on postwar performance.

My estimate of farm performance in 1933 was derived by linking aggregate output of a sample of 28 items in 1933 and 1975 (see Table A.21). I used all the 1933 information provided by Liu and Yeh (1965) which could be matched with the same items for 1975. The sample represented 73 per cent of 1975 gross output and I assumed that coverage was the same in 1933. The main differences between their 1933 measure and mine are use of a different weighting base, my link with 1975 rather than 1957 and the fact that I matched a slightly smaller number of products. For value added I estimate 1933 to be 94 per cent of 1957 compared with an average of 96.2 for their two measures.

Table A.21 also shows 1931–7 output derived from Perkins (1969) for 22 items I was able to match. They show prewar farm output output about 10 per cent lower than I derived from the Liu and Yeh data for 1933. The main difference is that Liu and Yeh used prewar crop yield estimates which in some cases were higher than those which prevailed in 1957. Perkins did not accept that crop yields could have fallen. He assumed that 1957 yields prevailed in the 1930s in every province. He made some adjustments to the figures for area cultivated and used lower figures than Liu and Yeh for the 1930s stock of most animals. Table A.21 permits a detailed comparison of the Perkins and Liu and Yeh estimates for the 1930s for the items one can match and the difference in the aggregate results can be seen in Table A.4. I prefer the figures based on Liu and Yeh as they are more fully documented. The Perkins assumption that 1957 yields prevailed in 1933 seems a bit arbitrary. It seems quite feasible that 1957 yields were lower than in 1933 after 12 years of war and the disruption caused by agrarian reform and collectivisation.

ISBN: 978-92-64-03762-5 © OECD 2007

Chinese Farm Performance in International Perspective

Another way of getting a perspective on Chinese performance is through comparisons with other countries. Table A.11 compares Chinese and US farming in 1987 using detailed FAO information on prices and quantities of individual commodity output, feed and seed and taking non–farm inputs from the respective input–output tables (Tables A.12 and A.13).

It is clear that China had the bigger farm economy with a value added 2.3 times that in the United States (at 1987 US prices). Value added per head of population was 51 per cent of the 1987 US level but Chinese labour productivity in 1987 was only 1.8 per cent of that in the United States. Table A.14 merges the benchmark levels with time series for the two countries. It can be seen that Chinese labour productivity has fallen substantially relative to that in US farming. In 1933, it was 7.1 per cent of the US level; in 1952, 5.1 per cent; in 1978, 2.2 per cent and in 1994 only 1.6 per cent.

Table A.15 shows the results of an earlier 13 country comparison on similar lines for 1975, using detailed FAO information on quantities and prices of gross output and inputs of feed and seed, together with non–agricultural input information from various sources. The 1975 information on China has since been revised downwards by the FAO and better information is now available on Chinese non–agricultural inputs, but nevertheless the results of this earlier study throw a good deal of light on comparative performance. In this earlier study, China ranked second lowest in terms of labour productivity in this group of countries.

Table A.16 also throws interesting comparative light on Chinese performance. It now has the second highest input of chemical fertiliser per hectare of cropland. Its input ratio is exceeded only by that of Japan.

Table A.1. **Input–Output Characteristics of Chinese Farming, Official Estimates, China, 1987**
(million yuan)

	Farming, Forestry, Fishery and Sidelines	Farming
Gross Value of Output	467 570	390 371
Total Inputs	147 367	125 712
of which from:		
Farming	56 017	52 572
Forestry, Fishery and Sidelines	12 831	3 444
Industry	61 450	54 331
Other Material Product	8 887	8 675
"Non–productive" Services	8 182	6 690
Gross Value Added	320 203	264 660
Basic Depreciation	9 050	7 180
Repair & Maintenance	1 059	888
Net Value Added	310 094	256 591
Gross Material Product	328 385	271 349
Net Material Product	318 276	263 281
Allocation of Gross Value Added		
Labour Income	262 213	217 873
Welfare Income	7 099	5 760
Profits & Taxes	28 368	23 167
Depreciation, Repair & Maintenance	10 109	8 068
Other	12 413	9 791
Total Gross Value Added	320 203	264 659
Gross Value of Output	467 570	390 371
Total Intermediate Uses	217 926	180 735
of which:		
Farming, Forestry, Fishery and Sidelines	68 848	56 017
Industry	136 490	118 093
Other Material Product	10 241	5 000
"Non–productive" Services	2 347	1 625
Final Uses	249 644	209 637
of which:		
Private Consumption	217 579	192 377
Social Consumption	710	655
Investment	9 590	1 409
Inventories	11 980	7 027
Net Exports	7 755	6 682
Reconciliation Item	2 031	1 487

Source: SSB, *Input-Output Table of China*, 1987 (in Chinese), 1991.

http://dx.doi.org/10.1787/087831265105

ISBN: 978-92-64-03762-5 © OECD 2007

Table A.2. **Official Measures of Aggregate Performance in Agriculture, China 1952–95**
(Farming, Fishery, Forestry and Sidelines)
(million 1987 yuan)

	Gross Value of Output	Net Material Product	Gross Value Added	Ratio GVA/GO
1952	133 173	116 485	112 038	84.1
1953	137 301	118 349	114 167	83.2
1954	141 962	120 329	116 072	81.8
1955	152 749	129 881	125 259	82.0
1956	160 473	135 705	131 085	81.7
1957	166 200	139 898	135 118	81.3
1958	170 195	140 131	135 679	79.7
1959	147 023	117 184	114 167	77.7
1960	128 379	97 381	95 457	74.4
1961	125 316	98 663	96 913	77.3
1962	133 040	103 322	101 283	76.1
1963	148 488	115 203	112 711	75.9
1964	168 730	130 346	127 276	75.4
1965	182 580	143 160	139 600	76.5
1966	198 428	153 643	149 683	75.4
1967	201 491	156 323	152 484	75.7
1968	196 563	153 294	150 132	76.4
1969	198 694	153 993	151 364	76.2
1970	210 147	162 846	163 016	77.6
1971	216 939	165 408	166 041	76.5
1972	214 675	163 661	164 585	76.7
1973	232 387	178 338	179 374	77.2
1974	240 643	185 444	186 768	77.6
1975	248 101	189 055	190 577	76.8
1976	247 036	185 327	187 216	75.8
1977	246 103	180 668	183 071	74.4
1978	266 079	187 773	190 577	71.6
1979	286 055	199 791	202 341	70.7
1980	290 184	196 223	199 316	68.7
1981	306 964	210 118	213 209	69.5
1982	341 588	234 905	237 858	69.6
1983	368 223	254 809	257 576	69.9
1984	413 369	287 669	290 852	70.4
1985	427 485	295 553	296 118	69.3
1986	441 868	304 569	305 977	69.2
1987	467 570	318 276	320 430	68.5
1988	485 815	325 411	328 497	67.6
1989	500 863	335 927	338 692	67.6
1990	538 951	361 088	363 453	67.4
1991	558 927	369 350	372 192	66.6
1992	594 617	387 752	389 670	65.5
1993	641 094	403 337	408 044	63.6
1994	696 228	n.a.	424 290	60.9
1995	772 003	n.a.	445 577	57.7

Source: An index of the gross value of agricultural output (farming, fishery, forestry and sidelines combined) at "comparable" prices can be found in *China: Statistical Yearbook,* 1993 edition, p. 52 and 1996, edition, p. 356. A disaggregation of gross output for the four main sectors can be found in the Yearbooks and in the historical statistics in Ministry of Agriculture (1989), but no such breakdown is available for the official measures of net material product or gross value added. The index of net material product (NMP) in "comparable" prices can be found in the 1993 *Yearbook,* p. 31 for 1952–92 and in the 1994 *Yearbook,* p. 28 for selected years through 1993. This measure has now been discontinued. Gross value added at "comparable" prices has superseded the net material product measure and the index is now available from 1952 in SSB\Hitotsubashi (1997), p. 70. 1987 values of gross output and net material product are from the official input–output table (see Table A.1) and GVA from SSB/Hitotsubashi (1997) p. 61. These 1987 values were merged with the volume indices to produce the estimates of levels of output 1952–95 at 1987 prices shown above. This is a hybrid measure in which 1987 is simply the numeraire. The underlying official volume indices were produced by linking segments with different weighting years.

http://dx.doi.org/10.1787/088237542127

ISBN: 978-92-64-03762-5 © OECD 2007

Table A.3. **Maddison Measures of Chinese Agricultural Performance, Benchmark Years, 1933–94**

	Gross Output		Gross Value Added		Mid–year Employment		Gross Value Added Per Person Engaged	
	Farming	Total AFFS	Farming	Total AFFS	Farming	Total AFFS	Farming	Total AFFS
	(million 1987 yuan)				(000s)		(1987 yuan)	
1933	151 106	n.a.	131 485	138 497	166 545	175 366	789	789
1952	140 132	149 614	120 440	127 891	161 097	171 070	748	748
1957	168 031	185 191	139 938	153 649	172 301	189 175	812	812
1978	272 424	305 373	200 612	225 079	256 747	288 060	781	781
1987	451 182	528 381	325 470	381 013	268 728	314 585	1 211	1 211
1994	604 939	728 018	417 536	503 098	279 487	336 760	1 494	1 494
	annual average compound rates of growth (per cent per annum)							
1933–78	1.3	n.a.	0.9	1.1	1.0	1.1	0.0	0.0
1952–78	2.6	2.8	2.0	2.2	1.8	2.0	0.2	0.2
1978–94	5.1	5.6	4.7	5.2	0.5	1.0	4.1	4.1

Source: The derivation of the estimates for farming is described in Table A.4. The much rougher estimates for fishery, forestry and sidelines are shown in Tables A.5, A.6 and A.7. Total endyear employment in farming, forestry, fishery and sidelines from SSB *China Statistical Yearbook* 1993, p. 79 and 1996 *Yearbook*, p. 92 adjusted to a midyear basis. 1933–52 employment movement from Liu and Yeh (1965), p. 69; their figure for 1952 farm employment was 18 million bigger than the official estimate which I use, but they included persons 7 years old and above (pp. 184–6), whereas SSB includes only males 16 to 60 years of age and females aged 16 to 55 (see World Bank, 1991, p. 16). No official figures are available for employment in farming. I simply assumed that the proportion in farming was the same as for value added (i.e. productivity levels were the same).

http://dx.doi.org/10.1787/088405744027

Table A.4. **Estimated Levels of Gross Output, Inputs and Value Added in Chinese Farming, Benchmark Years, 1933–94**
(million 1987 yuan)

	Gross Output	Feed Input	Seed input	Other Farm Inputs	Non–Farm inputs	Gross Value Added
1931–37*	135 786	6 081	3 905	4 005	3 781	118 014
1933	151 106	7 045	4 261	4 534	3 781	131 485
1952	140 132	7 705	4 131	4 746	3 110	120 440
1957	168 031	11 094	5 016	6 460	5 523	139 938
1975	247 602	18 210	7 407	9 760	22 455	189 768
1978	272 424	19 096	8 162	10 930	33 624	200 612
1987	451 182	32 558	7 425	16 033	69 696	325 470
1994	604 939	48 496	7 118	22 301	109 488	417 536

* The first row gives an estimate of prewar performance using the alternative assumptions of Dwight Perkins (see Table A.21 for details of the difference between his estimates and those of Liu & Yeh which I prefer).

Source: The first column estimates for 1975, 1987 and 1994 are aggregates derived from 125 FAO items, see Tables A.17 A.18 and A.19 for details. Gross output for 1933, 1952, 1957 and 1978 was derived from a sample of about three–quarters of the value of total output as shown in Tables A.20 and A.21. These sample totals were augmented to correct for non–coverage of items included in the 1975 benchmark. The second and third columns for 1975, 1987 and 1994 are from Tables A.17, A.18 and A.19. For other years feed inputs were estimated to move with the stock of animals; seed with the movement in grain and potato output. The fourth and fifth columns for 1987 were derived from the official input–output tables for that year (Table A.1). For other years the figures were extrapolated from the 1987 benchmark. Other agricultural inputs were taken to move with the total for feed and seed. Non–agricultural inputs were measured by a combined index of inputs of fertiliser, the movement in the weighted stock of different types of tractor, electricity consumption and the irrigated area (see Table A.8). The weight of an average large–medium tractor was 3.69 times that of small pedestrian tractor in 1978 as indicated in *China Statistical Yearbook* 1995, p. 334. The weights for these various non–agricultural inputs in the 1987 benchmark year were taken from the official input–output table for 1987.

http://dx.doi.org/10.1787/088422861605

ISBN: 978-92-64-03762-5 © OECD 2007

Table A.5. **Estimated Levels of Gross Output and Value Added in Chinese Fishery, Benchmark Years 1933–94**

	Physical Production of Aquatic Products (000 tons)	Gross Value of Output (million 1987 yuan)	Gross Value Added (million 1987 yuan)
1933	n.a.	3 449	2 909
1952	1 670	3 930	3 264
1957	3 120	7 343	5 911
1975	4 410	10 379	7 691
1978	4 655	10 956	7 801
1985	7 052	16 596	11 628
1986	8 236	19 384	13 551
1987	9 554	22 486	15 683
1990	12 370	29 114	19 914
1994	21 431	50 439	33 480

Source: 1987 gross output and value added from official input–output tables. Physical output from *China Statistical Yearbook*, 1993, p. 347 and 1996 ed., p. 380. Ratio of gross value added to gross output assumed to move in the same proportions as in farming. 1933–52 movement in gross value and gross value added from Liu and Yeh (1965), p. 140. A good deal of fishery output (48 per cent in 1987) was derived from fishpond breeding.

http://dx.doi.org/10.1787/088428561203

Table A.6. **Estimated Levels of Gross Output and Value Added in Chinese Forestry, Benchmark Years 1933–94**

	Official Index of Output Volume	Gross Value of Output (million 1987 yuan)	Gross Value Added (million 1987 yuan)
1933	n.a	1 519	1 430
1952	11.2	1 470	1 382
1957	35.9	4 707	4 289
1975	83.6	10 961	9 192
1978	100.0	13 112	10 564
1985	176.1	23 090	18 308
1986	169.8	22 264	17 616
1987	169.3	22 198	17 523
1990	179.3	23 510	18 200
1994	237.8	32 165	24 286

Source: 1987 gross output and value added from official input–output tables. Output volume index from Ministry of Agriculture (l989), pp. 106–8, for 1952–78, 1978–94 from *China Statistical Yearbook* 1993, p. 301 and 1996 ed., p. 356. Ratio of gross value added to gross output assumed to move in the same proportions as in farming. 1933–52 movement in gross value and gross value added from Liu and Yeh (1965), p. 140.

http://dx.doi.org/10.1787/088428561203

Table A.7. **Estimated Levels of Gross Output and Value Added in Agricultural Sidelines, Benchmark Years, China 1933–94**

(million 1987 yuan)

	Gross Value of Output		Gross Value Added	
	old definition	new definition	old definition	new definition
1933	n.a.	n.a.	(2 673)	1 129
1952	4 082	n.a.	2 805	1 185
1957	5 110	n.a.	3 511	1 483
1971	14 074	5 948	9 669	4 086
1975	24 504	7 205	16 834	4 952
1978	44 505	8 881	30 574	6 102
1985	202 098	23 910	138 836	16 426
1986	267 467	29 106	183 743	19 995
1987	n.a.	32 515	n.a.	22 337
1990	n.a.	40 285	n.a.	27 666
1994	n.a.	(40 475)	n.a.	(27 796)

Source: Benchmark 1987 gross value of output and gross value added from official input–output table. I assumed that the 1987 ratio between gross output and value added applied for the whole period covered in the table. Measurement of sideline performance is particularly difficult. Until 1971, this item covered output of village industries, as well as household handicrafts, hunting and gathering activities. After 1971 output of village industry was treated as industrial production. The figures for gross output 1952–86 are available in Ministry of Agriculture (1989), pp. 107 and 109. One can readily see the major boom in village industry after 1971 (i.e. the difference between columns 3 and 4 for value added). By 1978, the village industries constituted about 12 per cent of industrial output and probably more than a third in 1986, when figures on the old basis ceased to be available. For our purpose, I had to accept the discontinuity in the definition (i.e. old definition before 1971, new definition from 1971 onwards) as there was no satisfactory way of getting consistent coverage and allocating the village industry content of the early years to industrial production. The 1993 *Statistical Yearbook* and subsequent editions do not show movement in the volume of sideline output since 1991. I assumed the 1991–94 rate of growth to be the same as for 1987–91. I assumed the official estimate of sideline output volume after 1978 was underdeflated, and corrected for this as I did for industrial production in Appendix B. Liu and Yeh (1965), p. 66 do not include rural sidelines as an agricultural activity, but I assumed the 1933–52 movement was the same as they indicate for all handicrafts.

http://dx.doi.org/10.1787/088433521072

Table A.8. **Selected Traditional and Modern Inputs into Chinese Farming, Benchmark Years, 1933–95**

	Traditional			Modern			
	Night Soil	Animal Manure	Irrigated Area	Chemical fertiliser	Electricity Consumed in Rural Areas	Large and Medium Tractors in Use	Small Pedestrian Tractors
	(million tons of nutrient)		(million ha.)	(million tons of nutrient)	(billion Kwh)	(end year)	(000s at end–year)
1933	1.32	1.06	26.5	.000	.00	0	0
1952	1.50	1.17	20.0	.078	.05	1 307	0
1957	1.68	1.68	27.3	.373	.14	14 674	0
1975	2.41	2.75	41.9	5.369	18.34	(500 000)	(109)
1978	2.51	2.89	45.0	8.840	25.31	557 358	1 373
1987	2.85	3.22	44.4	19.993	65.88	880 952	5 300
1994	3.13	4.11	48.8	33.179	147.39	693 154	8 237
1995	3.16	4.48	49.3	35.937	165.57	671 846	8 646

Source: Irrigated area, 1933 from Perkins (1969), p. 64, 1952–94 from SSB, 1984 *Yearbook*, p. 175, and 1996 *Yearbook*, p. 361. Chemical fertiliser, electricity and tractors from SSB (1984), p. 175, and (1996), pp. 358–61, 1975 from JEC (1986), p. 455, and World Bank (1981), p. 162. Night soil (human excrement) and animal manure coefficients from Perkins (1969) multiplied by population and number of farm animals respectively. My total for night soil and animal manure is similar to that given in Chao (1970), pp. 310–11 for 1952 and 1957, but he also allows for inputs of other traditional fertilisers (compost, oilseed cakes, green manure, river and pond mud). His total for these other nutrients was 620 thousand tons in 1952 and 840 thousand in 1957. Wen (1993), pp. 14–17 has much larger estimates of inputs of traditional fertiliser: a total of night soil and animal manure nutrients of 8.04 million tons in 1952, 11.18 million in 1957 and 18.70 million in 1987. His figures for other traditional fertilisers are also very high: 1.91 million tons of nutrient in 1952, 2.46 in 1957, and 3.88 million in 1987. As inputs of chemical fertiliser grow, it is likely that the recuperation coefficient from night soil will fall, as its collection is both unpleasant and very labour intensive. In Japan this type of traditional fertiliser input ended in the 1960s. However, I assumed no change in the coefficient for China.

http://dx.doi.org/10.1787/088447761475

ISBN: 978-92-64-03762-5 © OECD 2007

Table A.9. **Stock of Animals (year end) and Meat Output, Benchmark Years, China 1933–95**

	Cattle & Buffaloes	Horses, Donkeys Mules & Camels	Hogs	Goats & Sheep	Total Animals	Output of Pork Beef & Mutton
			million			million tons
1931–37	37.90	25.59	68.36	48.10	179.95	n.a.
1933	40.10	26.00	70.20	72.20	208.50	2.08
1952	56.60	19.86	89.77	61.78	228.01	3.39
1957	63.61	20.21	145.90	98.58	328.30	3.99
1975	74.68	23.31	281.17	160.87	538.90	7.97
1978	70.72	23.17	301.29	169.94	565.12	8.56
1987	94.65	27.26	327.73	180.34	629.99	19.86
1994	123.32	26.87	414.62	240.53	805.34	36.93
1995	132.06	26.56	441.69	276.86	877.17	42.65

Source: SSB, *Statistical Yearbook, 1984*, pp. 159–60; 1996 *Yearbook*, pp. 356–8 and 378. 1933 stock of animals from Liu and Yeh (1965), p. 308. 1931–37 stock of animals from Perkins (1969), p. 287. Meat production in 1933 derived as described in the source note to Table A.21.

http://dx.doi.org/10.1787/088462457810

Table A.10. **Land Used for Farming, Benchmark Years, China 1933–95**
(thousand hectares)

	Pastoral Area	Cultivated Area	Sown Area	Multiple Cropping Coefficient	Cultivated Land Irrigated %
1933	n.a.	102 300	135 036	1.32	25.9
1952	194 000[a]	107 900	141 256	1.31	18.5
1957	n.a.	111 800	157 244	1.41	24.4
1975	319 000	99 700	149 545	1.50	42.0
1978	319 000	99 390	150 104	1.51	45.3
1987	385 000	95 889	144 957	1.51	46.3
1994	400 000	94 907	148 241	1.56	51.4
1995	400 000	94 971	149 879	1.58	51.9

a. 1947.

Source: Pastoral area from FAO, *Production Yearbook*, various issues. Cultivated area 1952–75 from Lardy (1983), p. 5. Sown area 1952–75 from SSB, *Statistical Yearbook*, 1984, p. 137 (mu converted to hectares on basis of 15 mu per hectare). Cultivated and sown area 1978–95 from SSB, *Statistical Yearbook*, 1996, pp. 355 and 368. Percentage irrigated from (Table A.8) divided by col. 2. 1933 cultivated area from Liu and Yeh (1965), p. 129, 1933 sown area and multiple cropping coefficient derived from Buck (1937), p. 268 adjusted to include Manchuria.

http://dx.doi.org/10.1787/087838746626

Table A.11. **Summary Results of China/US Comparison of Farm Output and Purchasing Power, 1987**

	China	United States
(1) Gross Value: Aggregate of 60 Matched Items (FAO data)		
million yuan	403 667	(380 400)
million dollars	(174 538)	126 306
(2) Purchasing Power Parity for Matched Items		
(yuan/dollar)	2.313	3.012
(3) Gross Value of all priced items in FAO sample		
(125 items specified for China, 95 for the US)		
million yuan	451 182	(402 960)
million dollars	(195 064)	133 785
(4) Gross Value Added (China yuan figures derived from		
Table A.4); US from I/0 table)		
million yuan	325 470	(186 127)
million dollars	(140 713)	61 795
(5) Population (thousands)	1 084 035	243 942
(6) Persons Engaged in Farming (thousands)	268 728	2 106
(7) Gross Value Added Per Capita		
yuan	300	(763)
dollars	(130)	253
(8) Gross Value Added Per Person Engaged		
yuan	1 211	(88 370)
dollars	(524)	29 342

Source: The first two entries are derived from Table A.24 which compares unit values for all the items in the FAO data set which can be matched. The aggregate PPP for all the matched items is 2.313 yuan per dollar when Chinese quantities are weighted by US prices (unit values), or 3.012 when US quantities are weighted by Chinese prices. The first of these is the Paasche PPP, the second is the Laspeyres PPP (to use the ICOP/ICP terminology). The exchange rate in 1987 was 3.722 yuan to the dollar. The PPPs derived from the sample (which covered 89 per cent of FAO gross value for China and 94 per cent for the United States are assumed to be valid for total gross value (item 3) and also for gross value added (item 4). Figures in brackets are derived by using the PPPs, original national currency estimates are not in brackets. In item (4), the Chinese value added figure of 325 470 million yuan is my estimate (see Table A.4); the US figure of $61 795 million is from the US input/output table (see Table A.13). Chinese farm employment from Table A.3, US from Table A.25, Chinese population from Table D.l, US population from Maddison (1995a).

http://dx.doi.org/10.1787/087847237233

ISBN: 978-92-64-03762-5 © OECD 2007

Table A.12. **1987 Breakdown of Output and Inputs within Chinese Farming, Forestry, Fishery and Sidelines**
(million 1987 yuan)

	Gross Output	Value Added	Inputs	Ratio of Inputs to Gross Output
	million yuan			
Grain	170 512	113 885	56 627	33.2
Other Crops	113 281	92 008	21 273	18.8
Animal Products	106 578	58 766	47 812	44.9
Farming	390 371	264 659	125 712	32.2
Forestry	22 198	17 523	4 675	21.1
Fishery	22 486	15 683	6 803	30.3
Sidelines	32 515	22 337	10 178	31.3
Total	467 570	320 203	147 367	31.5

Source: SSB (199l), pp. 146–7

http://dx.doi.org/10.1787/087862151431

Table A.13. **1987 Breakdown of Output and Inputs within US Farming, Forestry, Fishery and FFF Services**
(million 1987 dollars)

	Gross Output	Agricultural Inputs	Agricultural Service Inputs	Other Inputs	Value Added	Ratio of Inputs to Gross Output
Crops	86 742	5 439	6 542	28 040	46 721	46.14
Livestock & Livestock Products	87 484	40 596	4 003	27 811	15 074	82.77
Farming	174 226	46 035	10 545	55 851	61 795	64.53
Forestry & Fishery	7 456	195	1 288	2 265	3 708	50.27
F.F.F. Services	22 201	3 372		8 881	9 948	55.19
Total	203 883	49 602	11 833	66 997	75 451	62.99

Source: "Benchmark Input–Output Accounts for the US Economy", *Survey of Current Business*, April 1994, p. 106.

http://dx.doi.org/10.1787/088100765031

Table A.14. **Comparative Levels of Farm Value Added and Labour Productivity, China/United States, Benchmark Years, 1933–94**
(at 1987 US prices)

	Gross Farm Value Added		Farm Employment		Value Added per Person Engaged		
	China	US	China	US	China	US	China/US
	$ million		000s		$	$	%
1933	56 846	41 466	166 545	8 722	341	4 754	7.2
1952	52 071	37 522	161 097	5 946	323	6 310	5.1
1957	60 501	38 432	172 301	5 052	351	7 607	4.6
1975	82 044	46 422	262 740	2 931	312	15 838	2.0
1978	86 732	41 972	256 747	2 723	338	15 414	2.2
1987	140 713	61 795	268 728	2 106	524	29 342	1.8
1994	180 517	83 337	279 487	2 114	646	39 421	1.6

Source: Column 1 entry for 1987 from Table A.11 (item 4), extrapolated to other years using the last column of Table A.4. Col. 2 entry for 1987 from the last column of Table A.26. Col. 3 from Table A.3, col. 4 from Table A.25. Col. 5 is col. 1 divided by col. 3. Col. 6 is col. 2 divided by col. 4.

http://dx.doi.org/10.1787/088112002812

Table A.15. **Comparative Performance in Farming in 13 Countries in 1975**

	Gross Value Added in Farming	Gross Value Added Per Head of Population	Gross Value Added Per Person Engaged in Farming	Net Farm Exports
	1975 $ million	US = 100	US = 100	$ million
Argentina	8 933	157.7	43.9	4 035
Brazil	18 303	80.2	10.0	6 178
China	95 496	47.9	2.3	175
India	41 963	31.4	1.9	–88
Indonesia	9 631	33.3	2.4	234
Korea	2 524	32.9	3.6	–657
Mexico	6 024	46.0	6.7	44
France	12 082	105.4	39.8	791
Germany	6 976	51.9	30.1	–7 730
Japan	7 569	31.2	8.8	–4 107
Netherlands	3 347	112.6	90.0	2 208
United Kingdom	5 197	42.5	54.7	–7 133
United States	46 981	100.0	100.0	12 310

Source: Maddison (1995*b*) pp. 214–216. This comparison was carried out using 1975 Paasche PPPs (i.e. 1975 US prices throughout).

http://dx.doi.org/10.1787/088113885651

Table A.16. **Comparative Intensity of Fertiliser Consumption, 8 Countries, 1993/94**

	Total Consumption (000 tons of nutrient)	Cultivated Area (000 ha.)	Pasture Area (000 ha.)	Fertiliser Consumption: (Kg. Per ha. Cultivated)
Australia	1 488	46 486	413 800	32
Brazil	4 150	48 955	185 000	85
China	33 179	94 907	400 000	350
France	4 611	19 439	10 764	237
India	12 345	169 650	11 400	73
Japan	1 817	4 463	661	407
United States	20 350	187 776	239 172	108
USSR[a]	19 463	231 540	325 200	84

a.   1991.

Source: China (1994) from Tables A.8 and A.10 above. Other countries, 1993/94 fertiliser consumption from FAO, *Fertiliser Yearbook 1994*, and 1993 cultivated area from FAO, *Production Yearbook 1994*. These figures do not include animal and human manure which is used more intensively in China than in the other countries. Table A.8 above shows that Chinese use of manure was around 7 million tons (nutrient value) in 1994.

http://dx.doi.org/10.1787/088185328563

ISBN: 978-92-64-03762-5 © OECD 2007

Table A.17. **China 1994: Detailed Accounts for Quantities, Prices and Value of Farm Output**

	China 1994 Production	1987 Producer Price	Gross Value of Output (1987 prices)	Output destined for use as Feed		Output destined for use as Seed		Value of Feed/Seed (1987 prices)	Final Output
	1 000 MT	Yuan per ton	thousand yuan	1 000 MT	thousand yuan	1 000 MT	thousand yuan	thousand yuan	thousand yuan
Cereals	390 738		175 017 995	77 952	29 320 845	10 562	4 885 009	34 205 855	140 812 140
Wheat	99 299	474	47 067 726	2 000	948 000	4 618	2 188 742	3 136 742	43 930 984
Rice, paddy	175 933	480	84 447 840	2 000	960 000	4 304	2 065 997	3 025 997	81 421 843
Barley	3 200	505	1 616 000	190	95 859	147	74 235	170 094	1 445 906
Maize	99 277	366	36 335 382	70 000	25 620 000	1 139	416 801	26 036 801	10 298 581
Rye	600	362	217 200	12	4 344	53	19 005	23 349	193 851
Oats	600	320	192 000	150	48 042	34	10 880	58 922	133 078
Millet	3 696	382	1 411 872	500	191 000	56	21 392	212 392	1 199 480
Sorghum	6 333	475	3 008 175	2 800	1 330 000	43	20 199	1 350 199	1 657 976
Buckwheat	900	412	370 800	300	123 600	84	34 608	158 208	212 592
Triticale	900	390	351 000			85	33 150	33 150	317 850
Cereals, NES									
Roots and Tubers	156 363		27 425 075	70 625	12 291 801	2 802	504 361	12 796 162	14 628 913
Potatoes	48 766	180	8 777 950	25 200	4 536 000	2 802	504 276	5 040 276	3 737 675
Sweet potatoes	102 722	170	17 462 655	45 000	7 650 000	1	85	7 650 085	9 812 570
Cassava	3 501	260	910 369	350	91 000			91 000	819 369
Taro (coco yam)	1 343	200	268 603	65	13 001			13 001	255 602
Roots and tubers NES	31	**180**	5 498	10	1 800			1 800	3 698
Pulses	4 966		2 481 197	668	362 574	300	147 140	509 714	1 971 483
Dry beans	1 511	600	906 872	45	27 080	112	67 500	94 580	812 292
Broad beans	2 000	**420**	840 000			179	74 970	74 970	765 030
Dry peas	1 275	543	692 325	600	325 800	9	4 670	330 470	361 855
Lentils	100	**420**	42 000	23	9 694			9 694	32 306
Pulses, NES	80								
Nuts/oilseeds	60 950		79 695 362	6 136	4 560 172	1 811	1 581 079	6 141 251	73 554 111
Cashew nuts	12	**2 092**	25 104						25 104
Chestnuts	110	2 216	243 760						243 760
Almonds	18	**2 092**	37 656						37 656
Walnuts	210	2 092	439 314						439 314
Pistachios	25	**2 092**	52 300						52 300
Hazelnuts	9	**2 092**	18 828						18 828
Areca nuts									
Nuts, NES	26	**2 092**	54 392						54 392
Soybeans	16 011	808	12 936 888	2 000	1 616 000	854	689 899	2 305 899	10 630 989

http://dx.doi.org/10.1787/088206155215

Table A.17. continued (1)

	China 1994 Production 1 000 MT	1987 Producer Price Yuan per ton	Gross Value of Output (1987 prices) thousand yuan	Output destined for use as Feed 1 000 MT	thousand yuan	Output destined for use as Seed 1 000 MT	thousand yuan	Value of Feed/Seed (1987 prices) thousand yuan	Final Output thousand yuan
Groundnuts in shell	9 763	1 137	11 100 284			346	393 754	393 754	10 706 530
Coconuts	75	300	22 500						22 500
Oil palm fruit	450	360	162 000						
Palm kernels	37	360	13 320						13 320
Palm oil	150	670	100 500						100 500
Castor beans	260	3 051	793 260			2	7 322	7 322	785 938
Sunflower seed	1 367	866	1 184 170			20	17 601	17 601	1 166 569
Rapeseed	7 492	980	7 342 276	800	784 000	242	236 910	1 020 910	6 321 366
Tung nuts	435	735	319 386						319 386
Sesame seed	548	1 695	929 326			9	15 323	15 323	914 003
Melonseed	40	390	15 600	37	14 274	1	546	14 820	780
Tallowtree seeds	795	390	310 050						
Vegetable tallow	119	390	46 508						46 508
Stillingia oil	119	390	46 508						46 508
Seed cotton	13 023	2 842	37 011 366						
Cottonseed	8 682	650	5 643 301	3 277	2 129 738	325	211 458	2 341 196	3 302 105
Linseed	511	750	383 550			10	7 800	7 800	375 750
Hempseed	25	700	17 500	23	16 160	1	466	16 625	875
Oilseed NES	637	700	445 716						445 716
Vegetables	170 626		56 374 813	2 207	270 501			270 501	56 104 312
Cabbages	12 887	200	2 577 330	625	125 000			125 000	2 452 330
Asparagus	2 307	240	553 782						553 782
Lettuce	4 200	240	1 008 000						1 008 000
Spinach	4 200	240	1 008 000						1 008 000
Tomatoes	12 028	300	3 608 388						3 608 388
Cauliflower	3 459	200	691 878	102	20 400			20 400	671 478
Pumpkins, squash, gourds	2 253	300	675 767	66	19 800			19 800	655 967
Cucumbers, gherkins	10 542	240	2 530 123	315	75 600			75 600	2 454 523
Eggplants	7 323	300	2 196 832						2 196 832
Chillies, peppers	5 021	300	1 506 181						1 506 181
Onions and shallots, green	270	400	108 100						108 100
Onions, dry	7 629	500	3 814 571						3 814 571
Garlic	6 969	1 800	12 544 470						12 544 470
Leek, etc.	6	240	14 809						14 809
Beans, green	840	450	378 000						378 000

http://dx.doi.org/10.1787/088206155215

 ISBN: 978-92-64-03762-5 © OECD 2007

Table A.17. continued (2)

	China 1994 Production	1987 Producer Price	Gross Value of Output (1987 prices)	Output destined for use as Feed		Output destined for use as Seed		Value of Feed/Seed (1987 prices)	Final Output
	1 000 MT	Yuan per ton	thousand yuan	1 000 MT	thousand yuan	1 000 MT	thousand yuan	thousand yuan	thousand yuan
Vegetables									
Peas, green	719	450	323 471						323 471
Broad beans	91	450	40 988						40 988
String beans	22	**450**	9 744						
Carrots	3 427	300	1 028 115	99	29 701			29 701	998 414
Mushrooms	490	3 800	1 861 776						1 861 776
Vegetables, fresh NES	82 894	240	19 894 488						19 894 488
Fruit	55 923		48 680 388	1 090	308 398			308 398	48 371 991
Bananas	2 898	911	2 639 923						2 639 923
Oranges	1 680	1 080	1 814 400						1 814 400
Tangerines, etc.	4 500	**980**	4 410 000						4 410 000
Lemons and limes	155	1 100	170 500						170 500
Grapefruit and pomeloes	120	728	87 360						87 360
Citrus fruit, NES	351	**980**	343 490						343 490
Apples	11 129	1 757	19 553 653						19 553 653
Pears	4 043	1 362	5 506 471						5 506 471
Apricots	5								
Quinces	20	**980**	19 600						19 600
Peaches, nectarines	2 000	984	1 968 000						1 968 000
Plums	1 800	700	1 260 000						1 260 000
Grapes	1 522	800	1 217 664						1 217 664
Watermelons	17 396	259	4 505 691	855	221 448			221 448	4 284 243
Cantaloupes, etc.	4 842	370	1 791 417	235	86 950			86 950	1 704 467
Mangoes	950	980	931 000						931 000
Pineapples	600	984	590 400						590 400
Dates	30	**980**	29 400						29 400
Persimmons	820	**980**	803 600						803 600
Papayas	4								
Fruit tropical, NES	650	980	637 000						637 000
Fruit fresh, NES	409	980	400 820						400 820

http://dx.doi.org/10.1787/088206155215

Table A.17. continued (3)

	China 1994 Production 1 000 MT	1987 Producer Price Yuan per ton	Gross Value of Output (1987 prices) thousand yuan	Output destined for use as Feed 1 000 MT	Output destined for use as Feed thousand yuan	Output destined for use as Seed 1 000 MT	Output destined for use as Seed thousand yuan	Value of Feed/Seed (1987 prices) thousand yuan	Final Output thousand yuan
Other crops	77 219		15 689 877	16 527	1 320 568			1 320 568	14 369 309
Coffee, green	44	3 600	158 400						158 400
Tea	588	3 500	2 059 638						2 059 638
Hops	12								
Pimento, white	10								
Pimento, all spice	172	2 850	490 200						490 200
Vanilla									
Cinnamon	23	5 323	122 429						122 429
Cloves									
Anise, badian, fennel	21	2 850	59 850						59 850
Ginger	65								
Spices, NES	49	2 850	139 650						139 650
Straw, husks	40					20			
Forage products, NES	130								
Tobacco leaves	2 238	2 000	4 476 000						4 476 000
Natural rubber	374	6 176	2 309 836						2 309 836
Sugar cane	60 927	74	4 508 583	13 677	1 012 098			1 012 098	3 496 485
Sugar beets	12 526	109	1 365 290	2 830	308 470			308 470	1 056 820
Fibres	6 138		22 854 865					0	22 854 865
Cotton lint	4 341	3 558	15 445 278						15 445 278
Flax fibre and tow	250	3 500	875 000						875 000
Hemp fibre and tow	20	1 448	28 960						28 960
Jute	210	500	105 000						105 000
Jute-like fibres	170	500	85 000						85 000
Ramie	60	12 800	768 000						768 000
Sisal	16								
Fibre crops, NES	3								
Wool	255	6 200	1 581 000						
Silk worm cocoons	813	4 879	3 966 627						
Milk and eggs	23 423		52 674 100	113	59 598			59 598	52 614 502
Cow milk, whole, fresh	5 288	536	2 834 368						2 834 368
Buffalo milk	2 100	530	1 113 000	105	55 650			55 650	1 057 350
Sheep milk	801	468	374 868						374 868
Goat milk	168	470	78 960	8	3 948			3 948	75 012
Camel milk	16	470	7 426						7 426
Hen eggs	12 092	3 207	38 779 172						38 779 172
Eggs, excludng hen	2 958	3 207	9 486 306						9 486 306

http://dx.doi.org/10.1787/088206155215

ISBN: 978-92-64-03762-5 © OECD 2007

Tables A.17 continued (4) and end

	China 1994 Production	1987 Producer Price	Gross Value of Output (1987 prices)	Output destined for use as Feed		Output destined for use as Seed		Value of Feed/Seed (1987 prices)	Final Output
	1 000 MT	Yuan per ton	thousand yuan	1 000 MT	thousand yuan	1 000 MT	thousand yuan	thousand yuan	thousand yuan
Meat	46 799		123 692 734	1	1 164			1 164	123 691 570
Cattle meat	3 004	4 300	12 916 405						12 916 405
Buffalo meat	271	3 800	1 031 221						1 031 221
Sheep meat	840	3 164	2 657 760						2 657 760
Goat meat	771	3 259	2 513 973						2 513 973
Pig meat	33 250	2 150	71 487 801						71 487 801
Duck meat	1 280	3 209	4 108 483						4 108 483
Geese meat	1 166	**3 209**	3 741 373						3 741 373
Chicken meat	5 719	4 188	23 949 916						23 949 916
Horse meat	116	3 400	393 638						393 638
Ass meat	28	3 100	85 808						85 808
Mule meat	30	3 100	93 930						93 930
Camel meat	10	2 300	23 276	1	1 164			1 164	22 112
Rabbit meat	229	2 100	480 900						480 900
Meat, NES	85	2 450	208 250						208 250
Honey, beeswax	191		352 230					0	352 230
Honey	177	1 990	352 230						352 230
Beeswax	14								
Total gross value of output			604 938 636		48 495 622		7 117 589	55 613 211	549 325 425

NES = not elewhere specified

Source: See Table A.18. Those prices which are shown in bold type are shadow prices.

http://dx.doi.org/10.1787/088206155215

Table A.18. China 1987: Detailed Accounts for Quantities, Prices and Value of Farm Output

	China Production 1 000 MT	1987 Producer Price Yuan per ton	Gross Value of Output thousand Yuan	Output destined for use as Feed 1 000 MT	Output destined for use as Feed thousand Yuan	Output destined for use as Seed 1 000 MT	Output destined for use as Seed thousand Yuan	Value of Feed/Seed thousand Yuan	Final Output thousand Yuan
Cereals	356 366		160 699 261		19 378 184		4 919 398	24 297 582	136 401 679
Wheat	85 900	474	40 716 602	2 796	1 325 162	4 606	2 183 015	3 508 176	37 208 426
Rice, paddy	174 260	480	83 644 802	3 783	1 815 840	4 448	2 135 158	3 950 998	79 693 804
Barley	2 800	505	1 414 000	148	74 598	103	51 964	126 562	1 287 438
Maize	79 240	366	29 001 841	40 700	14 896 201	985	360 360	15 256 561	13 745 280
Rye	1 000	362	362 000	20	7 240	68	24 706	31 946	330 054
Oats	500	320	160 000	113	36 289	42	13 600	49 888	110 112
Millet	4 538	382	1 733 516	772	294 904	88	33 595	328 499	1 405 017
Sorghum	5 428	475	2 578 300	1 650	783 750	62	29 564	813 314	1 764 986
Buckwheat	1 600	412	659 200	350	144 200	136	56 238	200 438	458 762
Triticale	1 100	390	429 000			80	31 200	31 200	397 800
Cereals, NES									
Roots and tubers	145 655		25 361 503		9 497 144		444 715	9 941 859	15 419 644
Potatoes	26 675	180	4 801 502	9 000	1 620 000	2 470	444 630	2 064 630	2 736 872
Sweet potatoes	114 440	170	19 454 801	45 783	7 783 111	1	85	7 783 196	11 671 605
Cassava	3 300	260	858 000	312	81 198			81 198	776 802
Taro (coco yam)	1 200	200	240 000	60	12 000			12 000	228 000
Roots and tubers, NES	40	**180**	7 200	5	835			835	6 365
Pulses	5 354		2 713 596		587 866		193 494	781 360	1 932 236
Dry beans	1 454	600	872 400	45	26 825	104	62 400	89 225	783 175
Broad beans	2 200	420	924 000	615	258 300	168	70 560	328 860	595 140
Dry peas	1 652	543	897 036	525	285 075	108	58 644	343 719	553 317
Lentils	48	**420**	20 160	42	17 665	5	1 890	19 555	605
Pulses, NES				159					
Nuts/oilseeds	51 701		70 419 688		1 583 805		1 423 739	3 007 544	67 412 144
Cashew nuts	8	**2 092**	16 318		0		0	0	16 318
Chestnuts	115	2 216	253 818		0		0	0	253 818
Almonds	15	**2 092**	31 380		0		0	0	31 380
Walnuts	147	**2 092**	307 524		0		0	0	307 524
Pistachios	22	**2 092**	46 024		0		0	0	46 024
Hazelnuts	7	**2 092**	15 062		0		0	0	15 062
Areca nuts		**2 092**	0		0		0	0	0
Nuts, NES	19	**2 092**	39 748		0		0	0	39 748
Soybeans	12 184	808	9 844 672	700	565 600	852	688 496	1 254 096	8 590 576

http://dx.doi.org/10.1787/088211876788

 ISBN: 978-92-64-03762-5 © OECD 2007

Table A.18. continued (1)

	China Production	1987 Producer Price	Gross Value of Output	Output destined for use as Feed		Output destined for use as Seed		Value of Feed/Seed	Final Output
	1 000 MT	Yuan per ton	thousand yuan	1 000 MT	thousand yuan	1 000 MT	Thousand yuan	thousand yuan	thousand yuan
Nuts/oilseeds									
Groundnuts in shell	6 171	1 137	7 016 427		0	262	297 813	297 813	6 718 614
Coconuts	80	300	24 000		0	0	0	0	24 000
Oil palm fruit	500	360	180 000	0	0	0	0	0	180 000
Palm kernels	42	360	14 976		1	0	0	1	14 975
Palm oil	167	670	111 622		0	0	0	0	111 622
Castor beans	330	3 051	1 006 830		0	3	8 238	8 238	998 592
Sunflower seed	1 241	866	1 074 706		0	21	17 970	17 970	1 056 737
Rape seed	6 605	980	6 472 900	446	437 494	173	169 304	606 797	5 866 103
Tung nuts	342	735	251 180		0		0	0	251 180
Sesame seed	526	1 695	891 570		0	10	17 794	17 794	873 776
Melon seed	30	390	11 700	2	692	1	273	965	10 735
Tallow tree seeds	680	390	265 200		0		0	0	265 200
Vegetable tallow	102	390	39 780		0		0	0	39 780
Stillingia oil	102	390	39 780		0		0	0	39 780
Seed cotton	12 735	2 842	36 192 870		0		0	0	36192870
Cottonseed	8 490	650	5 518 500	841	546 751	332	215 630	762 381	4 756 119
Linseed	460	750	345 000		0	9	6 923	6 923	338 078
Hemp seed	64	700	44 800	48	33 268	2	1 299	34 567	10 233
Oilseed, NES	519	700	363 300		0		0	0	363 300
Vegetables	63 185		23 001 601		138 092		0	138 092	22863509
Cabbages	6 500	200	1 300 000	325	65 000			65 000	1 235 000
Asparagus	1 260	240	302 400		0			0	302 400
Lettuce	2 100	240	504 000		0			0	504 000
Spinach	2 145	240	514 800		0			0	514 800
Tomatoes	6 250	300	1 875 000		0			0	1 875 000
Cauliflower	1 400	200	280 000	42	8 400			8 400	271 600
Pumpkins, squash gourds	1 000	300	300 000	30	9 000			9 000	291 000
Cucumbers, gherkins	5 760	240	1 382 400	173	41 472			41 472	1 340 928
Eggplants	3 850	300	1 155 000		0			0	1 155 000
Chillies, peppers	2 200	300	660 000		0			0	660 000
Onions and shallots, green	100	400	40 000		0			0	40 000
Onions, dry	3 700	500	1 850 000		0			0	1 850 000
Garlic	3 300	1 800	5 940 000		0			0	5 940 000
Leek, etc.	25	240	6 000		0			0	6 000
Beans, green	420	450	189 000		0			0	189 000

http://dx.doi.org/10.1787/088211876788

Table A.18. continued (2)

	China Production	1987 Producer Price	Gross Value of Output	Output destined for use as Feed		Output destined for use as Seed		Value of Feed/Seed	Final Output
	1 000 MT	Yuan per ton	thousand yuan	1 000 MT	thousand yuan	1 000 MT	thousand yuan	thousand yuan	thousand yuan
Vegetables(continued)									
Peas, green	320	450	144 000		0			0	144 000
Broad beans			0						
String beans			0						
Carrots	1 580	300	474 000	47	14 220			14 220	459 780
Mushrooms	275	3 800	1 045 000		0			0	1 045 000
Vegetables, fresh, NES	21 000	240	5 040 001		0			0	5 040 001
Fruit	24 104		22 464 630		110 636			110 636	22 353 994
Bananas	2 029	911	1 848 419		0			0	1 848 419
Oranges	2 902	1 080	3 134 160		0			0	3 134 160
Tangerines, etc.	322	980	315 560		0			0	315 560
Lemons and limes	135	1 100	148 500		0			0	148 500
Grapefruit and	215	728	156 520		0			0	156 520
Citrus fruit, NES	8	980	7 840		0			0	7 840
Apples	4 265	1 757	7 493 605		0			0	7 493 605
Pears	2 489	1 362	3 390 018		0			0	3 390 018
Apricots			0		0			0	0
Quinces	3	980	2 940		0			0	2 940
Peaches, nectarines	630	984	619 920		0			0	619 920
Plums	670	700	469 000		0			0	469 000
Grapes	641	800	512 800		0			0	512 800
Watermelons	5 400	259	1 398 600	270	69 936			69 936	1 328 664
Cantaloupes, etc.	2 200	370	814 000	110	40 700			40 700	773 300
Mangoes	315	980	308 700		0			0	308 700
Pineapples	412	984	405 408		0			0	405 408
Dates	20	980	19 600		0			0	19 600
Persimmons	820	980	803 600		0			0	803 600
Papayas			0						
Fruit tropical, NES	580	980	568 400		0			0	568 400
Fruit fresh, NES	48	980	47 040		0			0	47 040

http://dx.doi.org/10.1787/088211876788

ISBN: 978-92-64-03762-5 © OECD 2007

Table A.18. continued (3)

	China Production	1987 Producer Price	Gross Value of Output	Output destined for use as Feed		Output destined for use as Seed		Value of Feed/Seed	Final Output
	1 000 MT	Yuan per ton	thousand yuan	1 000 MT	thousand yuan	1 000 MT	thousand yuan	thousand yuan	thousand yuan
Other crops	58 536		12 316 671		752 050			752 050	11 564 621
Coffee, green	26	3 600	93 600		0			0	93 600
Tea	509	3 500	1 781 500		0			0	1 781 500
Hops	5		0		0			0	0
Pimento, white	4		0		0			0	0
Pimento, all spice	150	2 850	427 500		0			0	427 500
Vanilla	0		0		0			0	0
Cinnamon	20	5 323	106 460		0			0	106 460
Cloves	1		0		0			0	0
Anise, badian, fennel	16	2 850	45 600		0			0	45 600
Ginger	20		0		0			0	0
Spices, NES	40	2 850	114 000		0			0	114 000
Straw, husks	12		0	9	0			0	0
Forage products, NES	50		0	14	0			0	0
Tobacco leaves	1 943	2 000	3 886 000		0			0	3 886 000
Natural rubber	238	6 176	1 469 888		0			0	1 469 888
Sugar cane	47 363	74	3 504 863	9500	703 000			703 000	2 801 863
Sugar beets	8 140	109	887 260	450	49 050			49 050	838 210
Fibres	6 105		25 707 807						25 707 807
Cotton lint	4 240	3 558	15 085 920						15 085 920
Flax fibre and tow	320	3 500	1 120 000						1 120 000
Hemp fibre and tow	65	1 448	94 120						94 120
Jute	300	500	150 000						150 000
Jute–like fibres	269	500	134 500						134 500
Ramie	567	12 800	7 257 600						7 257 600
Sisal	16		0						0
Fibre crops, NES	2		0						0
Wool	209	6 200	1 295 800						1 295 800
Silk worm cocoons	117	4 879	569 867						569 867
Milk and eggs	11 643		21 951 064		509 900		443 849	953 749	20 997 315
Cow milk, whole,	3 301	536	1 769 336		0		0	0	1 769 336
Buffalo milk	1 800	530	954 000	900	477 000		0	477 000	477 000
Sheep milk	487	468	227 916		0		0	0	227 916
Goat milk	140	470	65 800	70	32 900		0	32 900	32 900
Camel milk	13	470	6 298		0		0	0	6 298
Hen eggs	4 722	3 207	15 143 454		0	103	330 321	330 321	14 813 133
Eggs, excluding hen	1 180	**3 207**	3 784 260		0	35	113 528	113 528	3 670 732

http://dx.doi.org/10.1787/088211876788

Table A.18. continued (4) and end

	China Production	1987 Producer Price	Gross Value of Output	Output destined for use as Feed		Output destined for use as Seed		Value of Feed/Seed	Final Output
	1 000 MT	Yuan per ton	thousand Yuan	1 000 MT	thousand Yuan	1 000 MT	thousand Yuan	thousand Yuan	thousand Yuan
Meat	30 004		86 139 784						86 139 784
Cattle meat	6 714	4 300	28 871 920						28 871 920
Buffalo meat	1 440	3 800	5 472 000						5 472 000
Sheep meat	351	3 164	1 109 827						1 109 827
Goat meat	371	3 259	1 207 792						1 207 792
Pig meat	18 562	2 150	39 907 724						39 907 724
Duck meat	387	3 209	1 241 658						1 241 658
Geese meat	284	**3 209**	912 178						912 178
Chicken meat	1 573	4 188	6 586 179						6 586 179
Horse meat	50	3 400	169 323						169 323
Ass meat	24	3 100	74 409						74 409
Mule meat	23	3 100	69 750						69 750
Camel meat	15	2 300	35 420						35 420
Rabbit meat	101	2 100	212 104						212 104
Meat, NES	110	2 450	269 500						269 500
Honey, beeswax	217		405 960		0				405 960
Honey	204	1 990	405 960		0				405 960
Beeswax	13		0		0				0
Total gross value of output			451 181 565		32 557 677		7 425 194	39 982 872	411 198 693

Source: The quantities of output, feed and seed and the prices were kindly supplied by FAO from its data–base. Where prices were missing and where there were some grounds for assuming price parallelism, shadow prices were estimated, which are shown in bold type. There are production data for 134 items, price information for 103 of these, and 22 shadow prices, so our total is for 125 items. There are nine production items for which we had no basis for shadow prices, but these nine items are of negligible importance. NES means not elsewhere specified.

http://dx.doi.org/10.1787/088211876788

Table A.19. China 1975: Detailed Accounts for Quantities, Prices and Value of Farm Output

	China Production	1987 Producer Price	Gross Value of Output	Output destined for use as Feed		Output destined for use as Seed		Value of Feed/Seed	Final Output
	1 000 MT	Yuan per ton	thousand yuan	1 000 MT	thousand yuan	1 000 MT	thousand yuan	thousand yuan	thousand yuan
Cereals	241 250		109 036 960		11 467 927		5 772 798	17 240 725	91 796 235
Wheat	45 310	474	21 476 940	1 500	711 000	4 541	2 152 434	2 863 434	18 613 506
Rice, paddy	125 560	480	60 268 800	1 700	816 000	6 065	2 911 200	3 727 200	56 541 600
Barley	3 000	505	1 515 000	601	303 505	156	78 780	382 285	1 132 715
Maize	47 220	366	17 282 520	22 600	8 271 600	960	351 360	8 622 960	8 659 560
Rye	1 300	362	470 600	26	9 412	95	34 390	43 802	426 798
Oats	700	320	224 000	175	56 000	43	13 760	69 760	154 240
Millet	6 500	382	2 483 000	830	317 060	158	60 356	377 416	2 105 584
Sorghum	8 500	475	4 037 500	1 810	859 750	152	72 200	931 950	3 105 550
Buckwheat	2 100	412	865 200	300	123 600	179	73 748	197 348	667 852
Triticale	1 060	390	413 400	0	0	63	24 570	24 570	388 830
Cereals, NES			0						
Roots and Tubers	145 917		25 267 660		5 375 520		324 000	5 699 520	19 568 140
Potatoes	24 300	180	4 374 000	7 300	1 314 000	1 800	324 000	1 638 000	2 736 000
Sweet potatoes	118 500	170	20 145 000	23 000	3 910 000	0	0	3 910 000	16 235 000
Cassava	2 100	260	546 000	542	140 920		0	140 920	405 080
Taro (coco yam)	980	200	196 000	53	10 600		0	10 600	185 400
Roots and tubers, NES	37	**180**	6 660	0	0		0		6 660
Pulses	6 200		3 168 300		419 340		271 206	690 546	2 477 754
Dry beans	1 700	600	1 020 000	61	36 600	136	81 600	118 200	901 800
Broad beans	2 400	420	1 008 000	420	176 400	242	101 640	278 040	729 960
Dry peas	2 100	543	1 140 300	380	206 340	162	87 966	294 306	845 994
Lentils	0	**420**	0	0	0	0	0	0	0
Pulses, NES			0						
Nuts/oilseeds	25 019		35 494 075		521 568		872 668	1 394 236	34 099 839
Cashew nuts	5	**2 092**	10 460	0				0	10 460
Chestnuts	142	2 216	314 672	0				0	314 672
Almonds	11	**2 092**	23 012	0				0	23 012
Walnuts	65	2 092	135 980	0				0	135 980
Pistachios	16	**2 092**	33 472	0				0	33 472
Hazelnuts	4	**2 092**	8 368	0				0	8 368
Areca nuts	0		0	0				0	0
Nuts, NES	12	**2 092**	25 104	0				0	25 104
Soybeans	7 240	808	5 849 920	221	178 568	702	567 216	745 784	5 104 136

http://dx.doi.org/10.1787/088218408531

Table A.19. continued (1)

	China Production	1987 Producer Price	Gross Value of Output	Output destined for use as Feed		Output destined for use as Seed		Value of Feed/Seed	Final Output
	1 000 MT	Yuan per ton	thousand yuan	1 000 MT	thousand yuan	1 000 MT	thousand yuan	thousand yuan	thousand yuan
Groundnuts in shell	2 270	1 137	2 580 990	0	0	16	18 192	18 192	2 562 798
Coconuts	54	300	16 200		0		0	0	16 200
Oil palm fruit		360	0		0		0	0	0
Palm kernels	39	360	14 040		0		0	0	14 040
Palm oil	156	670	104 520		0		0	0	104 520
Castor beans	67	3 051	204 417		0	2	6 102	6 102	198 315
Sunflower seed	80	866	69 280		0	3	2 598	2 598	66 682
Rapeseed	1 635	980	1 602 300	0	0	82	80 360	80 360	1 521 940
Tung nuts	370	735	271 950	0	0		0	0	271 950
Sesame seed	208	1 695	352 560		0		0	0	352 560
Melonseed		390	0		0		0	0	0
Tallowtree seeds	104	390	40 560		0		0	0	40 560
Vegetable tallow	104	390	40 560		0		0	0	40 560
Stillingia oil		390	0		0		0	0	0
Seed cotton	7 155	2 842	20 334 510		0		0	0	20 334 510
Cottonseed	4 762	650	3 095 300	476	309 400	295	191 750	501 150	2 594 150
Linseed	38	750	28 500	0	0	3	2 250	2 250	26 250
Hempseed	57	700	39 900	48	33 600	6	4 200	37 800	2 100
Oilseed, NES	425	700	297 500		0		0	0	297 500
Vegetables	60 623		20 132 690		85 680		0	85 680	20 047 010
Cabbages	3 800	200	760 000	190	38 000			38 000	722 000
Asparagus	850	240	204 000		0			0	204 000
Lettuce	1 000	240	240 000		0			0	240 000
Spinach	1 710	240	410 400		0			0	410 400
Tomatoes	4 000	300	1 200 000		0			0	1 200 000
Cauliflower	572	200	114 400	17	3 400		3 400	3 400	111 000
Pumpkins, squash, gourds	565	300	169 500	18	5 400		5 400	5 400	164 100
Cucumbers, gherkins	4 226	240	1 014 240	127	30 480		30 480	30 480	983 760
Eggplants	2 580	300	774 000		0			0	774 000
Chillies, peppers	1 113	300	333 900		0			0	333 900
Onions and shallots, green	30	400	12 000		0			0	12 000
Onions, dry	2 330	500	1 165 000		0			0	1 165 000
Garlic	2 450	1 800	4 410 000		0			0	1 165 000
Leek, etc.		240	0		0		0	0	4 410 000

http://dx.doi.org/10.1787/088218408531

ISBN: 978-92-64-03762-5 © OECD 2007

Table A.19. continued (2)

	China Production	1987 Producer Price	Gross Value of Output	Output destined for use as Feed		Output destined for use as Seed		Value of Feed/Seed	Final Output
	1 000 MT	Yuan per ton	thousand yuan	1 000 MT	thousand yuan	1 000 MT	thousand yuan	thousand yuan	thousand Yuan
Vegetables (continued)									
Beans, green	275	450	123 750		0			0	123 750
Peas, green	186	450	83 700		0			0	83 700
Broad beans			0						
String beans			0						
Carrots	946	300	283 800	28	8 400			8 400	275 400
Mushrooms	190	3 800	722 000		0			0	722 000
Vegetables, fresh, NES	33 800	240	8 112 000		0			0	8 112 000
Fruit	9 565		7 791 546		46 250			46 250	7 745 296
Bananas	165	911	150 315		0			0	150 315
Oranges	302	1 080	326 160		0			0	326 160
Tangerines, etc.	34	**980**	33 320		0			0	33 320
Lemons and limes	35	1 100	38 500		0			0	38 500
Grapefruit & pomeloes	50	728	36 400		0			0	36 400
Citrus fruit, NES	6	**980**	5 880		0			0	5 880
Apples	1 583	1 757	2 781 331		0			0	2 781 331
Pears	1 087	1 362	1 480 494		0			0	1 480 494
Apricots			0		0			0	0
Quinces		**980**	0		0			0	0
Peaches, nectarines	331	984	325 704		0			0	325 704
Plums	331	700	231 700		0			0	231 700
Grapes	123	800	98 400		0			0	98 400
Watermelons	3 392	259	878 528	170	44 030			44 030	834 498
Cantaloupes, etc.	1 113	370	411 810	6	2 220			2 220	409 590
Mangoes	168	980	164 640		0			0	164 640
Pineapples	66	984	64 944		0			0	64 944
Dates	5	**980**	4 900		0			0	4 900
Persimmons	450	980	441 000		0			0	441 000
Papayas			0						
Fruit tropical, NES	310	980	303 800		0			0	303 800
Fruit fresh, NES	14	980	13 720		0			0	13 720

http://dx.doi.org/10.1787/088218408531

Table A.19. continued (3)

	China Production 1 000 MT	1987 Producer Price Yuan per ton	Gross Value of Output thousand yuan	Output destined for use as Feed 1 000 MT	Output destined for use as Feed thousand yuan	Output destined for use as Seed 1 000 MT	Output destined for use as Seed thousand yuan	Value of Feed/Seed thousand yuan	Final Output thousand yuan
Other crops	20 527		5 015 151		262 206			262 206	4 752 945
Coffee, green	6	3 600	21 600	0	0		0	0	21 600
Tea	211	3 500	738 500	0	0		0	0	738 500
Hops			0		0		0	0	0
Pimento, white			0		0		0	0	0
Pimento, all spice	105	2 850	299 250		0		0	0	299 250
Vanilla			0		0		0	0	0
Cinnamon	5	5 323	26 615		0		0	0	26 615
Cloves			0		0		0	0	0
Anise, badian,	6	2 850	17 100		0		0	0	17 100
Ginger			0		0		0	0	0
Spices, NES	22	2 850	62 700		0		0	0	62 700
Straw, husks			0	0	0	0	0	0	0
Forage products,			0	0	0	0	0	0	0
Tobacco leaves	960	2 000	1 920 000		0		0	0	1 920 000
Natural rubber	69	6 176	426 144		0		0	0	426 144
Sugar cane	16 667	74	1 233 358	3 343	247 382			247 382	985 976
Sugar beets	2 476	109	269 884	136	14 824			14 824	255 060
Fibres	3 152		10 569 203						10 569 203
Cotton lint	2 381	3 558	8 471 598						8 471 598
Flax fibre and tow	90	3 500	315 000						315 000
Hemp fibre and tow	94	1 448	136 112						136 112
Jute	161	500	80 500						80 500
Jute–like fibres	189	500	94 500						94 500
Ramie	25	12 800	320 000						320 000
Sisal	12		0						0
Fibre crops, NES			0						0
Milk and eggs	4 545		8 363 900		31 620		166 764	198 384	8 165 516
Cow milk, whole,	840	536	450 240		0		0	0	450 240
Buffalo milk	1 155	530	612 150	57	30 210		0	30 210	581 940
Sheep milk	250	468	117 000		0		0	0	117 000
Goat milk	58	470	27 260	3	1 410		0	1 410	25 850
Camel milk	12	470	5 640		0		0	0	5 640
Hen eggs	1 780	3 207	5 708 460		0	39	125 073	125 073	5 583 387
Eggs, excluding hen	450	**3 207**	1 443 150		0	13	41 691	41 691	1 401 459

http://dx.doi.org/10.1787/088218408531

ISBN: 978-92-64-03762-5 © OECD 2007

Table A.19. continued (4) and end

	China Production	1987 Producer Price	Gross Value of Output	Output destined for use as Feed		Output destined for use as Seed		Value of Feed/Seed	Final Output
	1 000 MT	Yuan per ton	thousand yuan	1 000 MT	thousand yuan	1 000 MT	thousand yuan	thousand yuan	thousand yuan
Meat	9 237		22 603 803						22 603 803
Cattle meat	181	4 300	778 300						778 300
Buffalo meat	54	3 800	205 200						205 200
Sheep meat	159	3 164	503 076						503 076
Goat meat	150	3 259	488 850						488 850
Pig meat	7 460	2 150	16 039 000						16 039 000
Duck meat	200	3 209	641 800						641 800
Geese meat	143	**3 209**	458 887						458 887
Chicken meat	730	4 188	3 057 240						3 057 240
Horse meat	40	3 400	136 000						136 000
Ass meat	20	3 100	62 000						62 000
Mule meat	9	3 100	27 900						27 900
Camel meat	11	2 300	25 300						25 300
Rabbit meat	45	2 100	94 500						94 500
Meat, NES	35	2 450	85 750						85 750
Honey, beeswax	88		159 200		0			0	159 200
Honey	80	1 990	159 200		0			0	159 200
Beeswax	8		0		0			0	0
Total gross value of output			247 602 488		18 210 111		7 407 436	25 617 547	221 984 941

Source: As for Table A.18. Quantity of seed cotton is shown in bold type, as it is derived from older FAO published estimates.

http://dx.doi.org/10.1787/088218408531

Table A.20. China 1952–78: Detailed Derivation of Gross Value of Farm Output

	1987 prices Yuan per ton	(000 metric tons)				(000 yuan at 1987 prices)			
		1952	1957	1975	1978	1952	1957	1975	1978
Rice	480	68 450	86 800	125 550	136 950	32 856 000	41 664 000	60 264 000	65 736 000
Wheat	474	18 150	23 650	45 300	53 850	8 603 100	11 210 100	21 472 200	25 524 900
Maize	366	16 850	21 450	47 200	55 950	6 167 100	7 850 700	17 275 200	20 477 700
Sorghum	472	11 100	7 650	10 750	8 050	5 239 200	3 610 800	5 074 000	3 799 600
Millet	382	11 550	8 550	7 150	6 550	4 412 100	3 266 100	2 731 300	2 502 100
7 Coarse Grains	432	12 050	15 050	13 600	13 600	5 205 600	6 501 600	5 875 200	5 875 200
Tubers[a]	172	81 750	109 500	142 800	158 750	14 061 000	18 834 000	24 561 600	27 305 000
Soybeans	808	9 500	10 050	7 250	7 550	7 676 000	8 120 400	5 858 000	6 100 400
Peanuts	1 137	2 316	2 571	2 270	2 377	2 633 292	2 923 227	2 580 990	2 702 649
Rapeseed	980	932	888	1 535	1 868	913 360	870 240	1 504 300	1 830 640
Sesame	1 695	481	312	208	322	815 295	528 840	352 560	545 790
Fruits (Total)	932	2 443	3 247	5 381	6 570	2 276 876	3 026 204	5 015 092	6 123 240
Sugar Cane	74	7 116	10 392	16 667	21 116	526 584	769 008	1 233 358	1 562 584
Sugar Beets	109	479	1 501	2 477	2 702	52 211	163 609	269 993	294 518
Tea	3 500	82	112	211	268	287 000	392 000	738 500	938 000
Tobacco	2 000	222	256	701	1 053	444 000	512 000	1 402 000	2 106 000
Cotton	3 558	1 304	1 640	2 381	2 207	4 639 632	5 835 120	8 471 598	7 852 506
Flax	3 500	40	53	29	26	140 000	185 500	101 500	91 000
Hemp	1 442	36	301	700	1 088	51 912	434 042	1 009 400	1 568 896
Silk Cocoons	4 879	123	112	195	228	600 117	546 448	951 405	1 112 412
Meat	2 871	3 385	3 985	7 970	8 563	9 718 335	11 440 935	22 881 870	24 584 373
Total of sample items		248 359	308 070	440 325	489 638	107 318 714	128 684 873	189 624 066	208 633 508
Total gross value of output						140 131 847	168 030 796	247 602 395	272 424 051
Ratio of sample to total						0.765841	0.765841	0.765841	0.765841

a. Chinese statistical practice converts tubers (potatoes and sweet potatoes) to grain equivalent by dividing quantities produced by 5. I have therefore multiplied the official quantities by five. I used a weighted average of FAO prices for the two categories of potato.

Source: 1987 FAO prices from Table A.18. Quantities from Table A.18. Quantities from Ministry of Agriculture, 1989,, pp. 150–241. Gross value derived by multiplying quantities by price.

http://dx.doi.org/10.1787/088283522828

ISBN: 978-92-64-03762-5 © OECD 2007

Table A.21. **China 1933–75: Detailed Derivation of Gross Value of Farm Output**

	1987 prices	Liu and Yeh 1933 quantities	1933 quantities at 1987 prices	1975 quantities	1975 quantities at 1987 prices	Perkins 1931–37 quantities	Perkins 1931–37 quantities at 1987 prices
	Yuan per ton	thousand MT	million yuan	thousand MT	million yuan	thousand MT	million yuan
Wheat	474	26 700	12 655.8	45 310	21 476.9	23 100	10 949.4
Rice	480	81 740	39 235.2	125 560	60 268.8	69 555	33 386.4
Barley	505	7 580	3 827.9	3 000	1 515.0	9 720	4 908.6
Maize	366	9 295	3 402.0	47 220	17 282.5	10 220	3 740.5
Oats	320	665	212.8	700	224.0	n.a.	
Millet	382	14 645	5 594.4	6 500	2 483.0	13 840	5 286.9
Sorghum	475	12 565	5 968.4	8 500	4 037.5	12 340	5 861.5
Buckwheat	412	450	185.4	2 100	865.2	n.a.	
Potatoes	180	4 115	740.7	24 300	4 374.0	4 115	740.7
Sweet	170	26 445	4 495.7	118 500	20 145.0	26 445	4 495.7
Broad beans	420	3 015	1 266.3	2 400	1 008.0	n.a.	
Peas	543	3 265	1 772.9	2 100	1 140.3	n.a.	
Black beans	n.a.	1 010					
Mung beans	n.a.	1 365					
Soybeans	808	11 815	9 546.5	7 240	5 849.9	8 430	6 811.4
Peanuts	1 137	3 345	3 803.3	2 270	2 581.0	2 625	2 984.6
Rape seed	980	2 100	2 058.0	1 635	1 602.3	2 540	2 489.2
Sesame	1 695	965	1 635.7	208	352.6	905	1 534.0
Tobacco	2 000	990	1 980.0	960	1 920.0	915	1 830.0
Cotton lint	3 558	950	3 380.1	2 381	8 471.6	944	3 358.8
Hemp	1 448	340	492.3	94	136.1	675	977.4
Sugar cane	74	3 930	290.8	16 667	1 233.4	2 434	180.1
Hen eggs	3 207	826	2 649.0	1 780	5 708.5	n.a.	
Cattle/buffalo	4 185	128	535.7	235	983.5	101	422.7
Sheep meat	3 164	86	272.1	159	503.1	57	180.3
Goat meat	3 259	46	149.9	150	488.9	31	101.0
Pig meat	2 150	1 863	4 005.5	7 460	16 039.0	1 814	3 900.1
Horse meat	3 400	35	119.0	40	136.0	28	95.2
Mule meat	3 100	12	37.2	9	27.9	13	40.3
Ass meat	3 100	31	96.1	20	62.0	n.a.	
Total of Liu–Yeh sample products		110 408.5		180 915.9			
Total gross value of output (Liu–Yeh)		151 105.7		247 602.5			
Ratio of Liu–Yeh sample to total		(73.07)		73.07			
Total value of Perkins sample products				171 907.9			94 274.8
Total gross value of output (Perkins variant)				247 602.4			135 785.8
Ratio of Perkins sample to total				69.43			(69.43)

Source: Prices from FAO (Table A.18); 1975 quantities from FAO (Table A.19); 1933 quantities from Liu and Yeh (1965), pp. 290, 300 and 308; I consolidated their figures for millet and proso millet, for rice and glutinous rice. They give egg production in millions, I assumed 14 630 hen eggs per metric ton; they give the stock of animals, and I assumed the same relation between meat output and animal stock in 1933 as prevailed in 1975. Figures in the sixth column are from Perkins (1969), pp. 276–87. Perkins gives a consolidated total for the two kinds of potatoes which is the same as the total of Liu and Yeh. I therefore broke down the Perkins figure as in Liu and Yeh.

http://dx.doi.org/10.1787/088305245030

Table A.22a. **China: 1987 Prices of Farm Commodities**
(a) SSB market prices; (b) SSB state prices; (c) FAO producer prices
(yuan per metric ton)

	SSB 1987		FAO 1987
	Average price in all outlets	Prices in state outlets	Producer price
Wheat	470	470	474
Rice	594	554	480
Soybeans	830	791	808
Maize	301	291	366
Pork	3 656	3 535	2 150
Beef	4 296	4 166	4 300
Mutton	4 578	4 277	3 164
White chicken	4 840	4 723	4 188
Chicken eggs	3 628	3 461	3 207
Apples	2 239	2 207	1 757
Pears	1 902	1 951	1 362

Source: SSB (1988, p. 123).

http://dx.doi.org/10.1787/088306043107

Table A.22b. **China 1987, Prices of Farm Commodities**
(a) SSB "mixed average retail prices" (b) FAO Producer prices
(yuan per metric ton)

	SSB 1987	FAO 1987
Fat pork	2 073	2 150
Beef	3 498	4 300
Sheep/goat meat	2 918	3 164
Poultry meat	4 329	4 188
Fresh eggs	3 042	3 207
Tea	5 454	3 500
Sugar cane	78	74
Sugar beets	108	109
Honey	2 144	1 990
Fruits	867	932
Mandarin oranges	1 114	1 080
Cotton lint	3 563	3 558
Flue-cured tobacco	2 485	2 000
Hemp	1 675	1 448
Ramie	5 609	12 800
Mulberry silkworm cocoons	4 617	4 879
Wool	6 285	9 200

Source: SSB, (1988, pp. 121-2).

http://dx.doi.org/10.1787/088306043107

Table A.22c. **The Structure of Chinese Farm Prices and Market Segmentation, 1987**

	Quota Price	Above Quota Price	Free Market	Quota Sales	Above Quota Sales	Total Output
	(Yuan per metric ton)			(000 tons)		
Paddy rice (indica)	349	484	553)			
Milled rice (indica)	490	680	777)			
Paddy rice (japonica)	414	535	612)	19 783	11 654	174 260
Milled rice (japonica)	582	752	860)			
Wheat	442	545	620	17 691	10 654	85 900
Maize	332	445	503	17 202	14 842	79 240
Soybeans	738	933	1 102	2 194	3 903	12 184
Cotton	3 534	3 563	3 681	4 071	0	4 240

Source: First five columns supplied by US Department of Agriculture, March 1996. Last column from Table A.18. The proportion of output taken by government purchasers was 18 per cent for rice, 33 per cent for wheat, 40 per cent for maize, 50 per cent for soybeans and 96 per cent for cotton. The residual amounts were destined for self consumption by producers and free market sales. State procurement was 96 per cent for tea, 85 per cent for fine cured tobacco, 74 per cent for sugar cane and 94 per cent for sugar beet.

http://dx.doi.org/10.1787/088306043107

ISBN: 978-92-64-03762-5 © OECD 2007

Table A.23. **United States 1987: Detailed Accounts for Quantities, Prices and Value of Farm Output**

	US Production	1987 Producer Price	Gross Value of Output	Output destined for use as Feed		Output destined for use as Seed		Value of Feed/Seed (1987 prices)	Final Output
	1 000 MT	$ per ton	$ 000	1 000 MT	$ 000	1 000 MT	$ 000	$ 000	$ 000
Cereals	280 447		21 624 070					11 479 717	10 144 353
Wheat	57 362	94	5 392 010	7 898	742 412	2 313	217 422	959 834	4 432 176
Rice	5 879	160	940 640			163	26 128	26 128	914 512
Barley	11 354	83	942 407	5 511	457 372	342	28 369	485 741	456 666
Maize	181 142	69	12 498 798	121 874	8 409 306	432	29 808	8 439 114	4 059 684
Rye	496	63	31 247	269	16 963	97	6 080	23 042	8 204
Oats	5 424	107	580 411	5 199	556 293	459	49 113	605 406	−24 995
Millet	180	61	10 980	113	6 870			6 870	4 110
Sorghum	18 563	66	1 225 185	14 105	930 930	33	2 178	933 108	292 077
Buckwheat	46	52	2 392	5	250	4	224	473	1 919
Canary seed				13					
Roots and Tubers	18 189		1 811 312					145 088	1 666 224
Potatoes	17 659	96	1 695 284	224	21 504	1 159	111 264	132 768	1 562 516
Sweet potatoes	527	220	116 028	16	3 520	40	8 800	12 320	103 708
Taracoco yams	3								
Pulses	1 479		479 498					18 551	460 947
Dry beans	1 181	364	429 793	0.5	165	45	16 345	16 511	413 282
Dry broad beans									
Dry peas	208	154	32 032			13	2 033	2 033	29 999
Dry cowpeas	13	154	2 042	0.05	7			7	2 035
Lentils	77	203	15 631						15 631
Nuts/oilseeds	70 562		19 979 506					593 327	19 386 180
Almonds	500	2 315	1 157 500						1 157 500
Walnuts	224	1 085	243 040						243 040
Pistachios	15	2 954	44 310						44 310
Hazelnuts	20	1 069	21 145						21 145
Nuts, NES	138	1 246	172 197						172 197
Soybeans	52 737	216	11 391 195	52	11 146	1 500	323 935	335 081	11 056 114
Groundnuts in shell	1 640	617	1 011 880			91	56 252	56 252	955 628
Olives	61	670	41 027						41 027
Sunflower seed	1 183	183	216 489	30	5 435	10	1 811	7 246	209 243
Safflower seed	147	190	27 930			1	198	198	27 732
Mustard seed	26	165	4 282			0	50	50	4 233
Seed cotton	8 448	610	5 153 097						5 153 097
Cottonseed	5 234	90	471 033	2 033	182 970	120	10 800	193 770	277 263
Linseed	189	129	24 381			6	731	731	23 650

http://dx.doi.org/10.1787/088324534775

Table A.23. continued (1)

	US Production	1987 Producer Price	Gross Value of Output	Output destined for use as Feed		Output destined for use as Seed		Value of Feed/Seed (1987 prices)	Final Output
	1 000 MT	$ per ton	$ 000	1 000 MT	$ 000	1 000 MT	$ 000	$ 000	$ 000
Vegetables	26 433		6 110 593						6 110 593
Cabbages	1 400	136	190 400						190 400
Artichokes	55	716	39 511						39 511
Asparagus	106	1 274	135 630						135 630
Lettuce	3 079	326	1 003 689						1 003 689
Spinach	176	348	61 248						61 248
Tomatoes	8 372	151	1 264 145						1 264 145
Cauliflower	335	549	183 641						183 641
Cucumbers, gherkins	576	190	109 529						109 529
Eggplants	35	390	13 455						13 455
Chillies, peppers, green	490	520	254 800						254 800
Onions	2 046	251	513 619						513 619
Garlic	135	490	66 150						66 150
Beans, green	116	400	46 400						46 400
Peas, green	997	247	246 259						246 259
String beans	622	403	250 735						250 735
Carrots	1 303	185	241 003						241 003
Green corn (maize)	3 311	110	364 210						364 210
Mushrooms	279	1 931	538 170						538 170
Vegetables, fresh NES	3 000	196	588 000						588 000
Fruit	27 680		7 700 053					21 871	7 678 181
Bananas	5	653	3 376						3 376
Oranges	6 983	221	1 543 155						1 543 155
Tangerines, mandarines, clementines	509	727	369 970						369 970
Lemons, limes	1 043	449	468 424						468 424
Grapefruit, pomeloes	2 346	193	452 778						452 778
Apples	4 873	209	1 018 373						1 018 373
Pears	851	214	182 200						182 200
Apricots	104	385	39 963						39 963
Sour cherries	163	172	28 088						28 088
Cherries	195	819	159 705						159 705
Peaches, nectarines	1 254	300	376 110						376 110
Plums	886	340	301 240						301 240
Strawberries	507	1 089	551 905						551 905
Raspberries	22	1 270	28 227						28 227
Currants	0	1 650	74						74
Blueberries	67	1 440	96 270						96 270
Cranberries	154	980	150 822						150 822
Berries NES	20	1 140	22 954						22 954
Grapes	4 478	274	1 226 999						1 226 999

http://dx.doi.org/10.1787/088324534775

ISBN: 978-92-64-03762-5 © OECD 2007

Table A.23. continued (2) and end

	US Production	1987 Producer Price	Gross Value of Output	Output destined for use as Feed		Output destined for use as Seed		Value of Feed/Seed (1987 prices)	Final Output
	1 000 MT	$ per ton	$ 000	1 000 MT	$ 000	1 000 MT	$ 000	$ 000	$ 000
Fruit (continued)									
Watermelons	1 130	100	113 000	63	6 348			6 348	106 652
Cantoloupes, other	1 138	230	261 694	67	15 524			15 524	246 170
Mangoes	14								
Figs	47	331	15 689						15 689
Avocados	190	827	156 799						156 799
Pineapples	628	158	99 192						99 192
Dates	17	855	14 706						14 706
Papayas	31	362	11 150						11 150
Fruit fresh NES	26	280	7 190						7 190
Other crops	52 542		3 691 262					31 349	3 659 913
Coffee, green	1	6 388	4 056						4 056
Hops	23	3 329	75 568						75 568
Pimento, all spice	8	750	5 641						5 641
Tobacco leaves	539	3 467	1 869 614						1 869 614
Sugar cane	26 506	29	768 674			1 081	31 349	31 349	737 325
Sugar beets	25 466	38	967 708						967 708
Fibres	3 252		4 589 899						4 589 899
Cotton lint	3 214	1 404	4 512 456						4 512 456
Wool	38	2 022	77 443						77 443
Milk and eggs	68 901		21 080 829					527 004	20 553 825
Cow milk, whole, fresh	64 731	276	17 865 759	725	200 100			200 100	17 665 659
Hen eggs	4 170	771	3 215 070			424	326 904	326 904	2 888 166
Meat	26 508		46 543 049						46 543 049
Cattle meat	10 734	2 435	26 137 290						26 137 290
Sheep meat	144	2 808	402 948						402 948
Pig meat	6 487	1 822	11 818 950						11 818 950
Duck meat	48	970	46 856						46 856
Turkey meat	1 679	983	1 650 654						1 650 654
Chicken meat	7 145	864	6 173 280						6 173 280
Horse meat	72	2 000	143 072						143 072
Game meat	200	850	170 000						170 000
Honey			174 928						174 928
Honey	103	1 700	174 928						174 928
Total gross value of output			133 784 999		11 567 114		1 249 793	2 816 907	20 968 092

Source: FAO data base.

http://dx.doi.org/10.1787/088324534775

Table A.24. **Detailed Matching of Farm Products, China/United States, 1987, FAO Data**

	United States Product Item	US Quantity Produced	US Value of Output	US Unit Value	US Quantity Valued at Chinese Unit Values	PPP at US Quantity Weights	China Product Item	China Quantity Produced	China Value of Output	China Unit Value	China Quantity Valued at US Unit Values	PPP at Chinese Quantity Weights
		1 000 MT	($ 000)	($)	(000 yuan)	(Yuan/$)		1 000 MT	(000 yuan)	(yuan)	($ 000)	Yuan/$
	Cereals											
1	Wheat	57 362	5 392 010	94	27 189 499	5.04	Wheat	85 900	40 716 602	474	8 074 600	5.04
2	Rice	5 879	940 640	160	2 821 920	3.00	Rice, paddy	174 260	83 644 802	480	27 881 601	3.00
3	Barley	11 354	942 407	83	5 733 922	6.08	Barley	2 800	1 414 000	505	232 400	6.08
4	Maize	181 142	12 498 798	69	66 297 973	5.30	Maize	79 240	29 001 841	366	5 467 560	5.30
5	Rye	496	31 247	63	179 545	5.75	Rye	1 000	362 000	362	63 000	5.75
6	Oats	5 424	580 411	107	1 735 808	2.99	Oats	500	160 000	320	53 500	2.99
7	Millet (sorgh)	180	10 980	61	68 760	6.26	Millet (sorgh)	4 538	1 733 516	382	276 818	6.26
8	Sorghum	18 563	1 225 185	66	8 817 621	7.20	Sorghum	5 428	2 578 300	475	358 248	7.20
9	Buckwheat	46	2 392	52	18 952	7.92	Buckwheat	1 600	659 200	412	83 200	7.92
	Total		21 624 070		112 86 999	5.22			160 270 261		42 490 927	3.77
	Roots and Tubers											
10	Potatoes	17 659	1 695 284	96	3 178 657	1.88	Potatoes	26 675	4 801 502	180	2 560 801	1.88
11	Sweet potatoes	527	116 028	220	89 658	0.77	Sweet potatoes	114 440	19 454 801	170	25 176 801	0.77
	Total		1 811 312		3 268 315	1.80			24 256 303		27 737 602	0.87
	Pulses											
12	Dry beans	1 181	429 793	364	708 45	1.65	Dry beans	1 454	872 400	600	529 256	1.65
13	Dry peas	208	32 032	154	112 94	3.53	Dry peas	1 652	897 036	543	254 408	3.53
	Total		461 825		821 39	1.78			1 769 436		783 664	2.26
	Nuts/oilseeds											
14	Walnuts	224	243 040	1 085	468 608	1.93	Walnuts	147	307 524	2092	159 495	1.93
15	Soybeans	52 737	11 391 195	216	42 611 506	3.74	Soybeans	12 184	9 844 672	808	2 631 744	3.74
16	Groundnuts in shell	1 640	1 011 880	617	1 864 680	1.84	Groundnuts in shell	6 171	7 016 427	1 137	3 807 507	1.84
17	Sunflower seed	1 183	216 489	183	1 024 478	4.73	Sunflower seed	1 241	1 074 706	866	227 103	4.73
18	Seed cotton	8 448	5 153 097	610	24 008 363	4.66	Seed cotton	12 735	36 192 870	2 842	7 768 350	4.66
19	Cottonseed	5 234	471 033	90	3 401 905	7.22	Cottonseed	8 490	5 518 500	650	764 100	7.22
20	Linseed	189	24 381	129	141 750	5.81	Linseed	460	345 000	750	59 340	5.81
	Total		18 511 115		73 521 290	3.97			60 299 699		15 417 639	3.91

http://dx.doi.org/10.1787/088330152501

ISBN: 978-92-64-03762-5 © OECD 2007

Table A.24. continued (1)

	United States Product Item	US Quantity Produced (1 000 MT)	US Value of Output ($ 000)	US Unit Value ($)	US Quantity Valued at Chinese Unit Values (000 yuan)	PPP at US Quantity Weights (Yuan/$)	China Product Item	China Quantity Produced (1 000 MT)	China Value of Output (000 yuan)	China Unit Value (Yuan)	China Quantity Valued at US Unit Values ($ 000)	PPP at Chinese Quantity Weights (Yuan/$)
Vegetables												
2	Cabbages	1 400	190 400	136	280 000	1.47	Cabbages	6 500	1 300 000	200	884 000	1.47
2	Tomatoes	8 372	1 264 145	151	2 511 546	1.99	Tomatoes	6 250	1 875 000	300	943 750	1.99
2	Cauliflower	335	183 641	549	66 900	0.36	Cauliflower	1 400	280 000	200	768 600	0.36
2	Cucumbers, gherkins	576	109 529	190	138 353	1.26	Cucumbers, gherkins	5 760	1 382 400	240	1 094 400	1.26
2	Eggplants	35	13 455	390	10 350	0.77	Eggplants	3 850	1 155 000	300	1 501 500	0.77
2	Chillies, peppers, green	490	254 800	520	147 000	0.58	Chillies, peppers	2 200	660 000	300	1 144 000	0.58
2	Onions	2 046	513 619	251	1 023 145	1.99	Onions	3 700	1 850 000	500	928 700	1.99
2	Garlic	135	66 150	490	243 000	3.67	Garlic	3 300	5 940 000	1 800	1 617 000	3.67
2	Beans, green	116	46 400	400	52 200	1.13	Beans, green	420	189 000	450	168 000	1.13
3	Peas, green	997	246 259	247	448 650	1.82	Peas, green	320	144 000	450	79 040	1.82
3	Carrots	1 303	241 003	185	390 816	1.62	Carrots	1 580	474 000	300	292 300	1.62
3	Mushrooms	279	538 170	1 931	1 059 060	1.97	Mushrooms	275	1 045 000	3 800	531 025	1.97
	Total		3 667 570		6 371 020	1.74			16 294 400		9 952 315	1.64
Fruit												
3	Bananas	5	3 376	653	4 710	1.40	Bananas	2 029	1 848 419	911	1 324 937	1.40
3	Oranges	6 983	1 543 155	221	7 541 208	4.89	Oranges	2 902	3 134 160	1 080	641 342	4.89
3	Lemons, limes	1 043	468 424	449	1 147 586	2.45	Lemons, limes	135	148 500	1 100	60 615	2.45
3	Grapefruit, pomeloes	2 346	452 778	193	1 707 888	3.77	Grapefruit, pomeloes	215	156 520	728	41 495	3.77
3	Apples	4 873	1 018 373	209	8 561 158	8.41	Apples	4 265	7 493 605	1 757	891 385	8.41
3	Pears	851	182 200	214	1 159 607	6.36	Pears	2 489	3 390 018	1 362	532 646	6.36
3	Peaches, nectarines	1 254	376 110	300	1 233 641	3.28	Peaches, nectarines	630	619 920	984	189 000	3.28
4	Plums	886	301 240	340	620 200	2.06	Plums	670	469 000	700	227 800	2.06
4	Grapes	4 478	1 226 999	274	3 582 480	2.92	Grapes	641	512 800	800	175 634	2.92
4	Watermelons	1 130	113 000	100	292 670	2.59	Watermelons	5 400	1 398 600	259	540 000	2.59
4	Cantaloupes	1 138	261 694	230	420 986	1.61	Cantaloupes	2 200	814 000	370	506 000	1.61
4	Pineapples	628	99 192	158	617 755	6.23	Pineapples	412	405 408	984	65 096	6.23
	Total		6 046 541		26 889 889	4.45			20 390 950		5 195 950	3.92
Other crop products												
4	Coffee, green	1	4 056	6 388	2 286	0.56	Coffee, green	26	93 600	3 600	166 088	0.56
4	Pimento, all spice	8	5 641	750	21 435	3.80	Pimento, all spice	150	427 500	2 850	112 500	3.80
4	Tobacco leaves	539	1 869 614	3 467	1 078 520	0.58	Tobacco leaves	1 943	3 886 000	2 000	6 736 381	0.58
	Total		1 879 312		1 102 241	0.59			4 407 100		7 014 969	0.63

http://dx.doi.org/10.1787/088330152501

Table A.24 continued (2) and end

	United States Product Item	US Quantity Produced	US Value of Output	US Unit Value	US Quantity Valued at Chinese Unit Values	PPP at US Quantity Weights	China Product Item	China Quantity Produced	China Value of Output	China Unit Value	China Quantity Valued at US Unit Values	PPP at Chinese Quantity Weights
		1 000 MT	($ 000)	($)	(000 yuan)	(Yuan/$)		1 000 MT	(000 yuan)	(Yuan)	($ 000)	Yuan/$
Fibres												
48	Cotton lint	3 214	4 512 456	1 404	11 435 412	2.53	Cotton lint	4 240	15 085 920	3 558	5 952 960	2.53
49	Wool	38	77 443	2 022	237 460	3.07	Wool	209	1 295 800	6 200	422 600	3.07
	Total		4 589 899		11 672 872	2.54			16 381 720		6 375 560	2.57
Milk and eggs												
50	Cow milk, whole, fresh	64 731	17 865 759	276	34 695 822	1.94	Cow milk, whole, fresh	3 301	1 769 336	536	911 076	1.94
51	Hen eggs	4 170	3 215 070	771	13 373 190	4.16	Hen eggs	4 722	15 143 454	3 207	3 640 662	4.16
	Total		21 080 829		48 069 012	2.28			16 912 790		4 551 738	3.72
Meat												
52	Cattle meat	10 734	26 137 290	2 435	46 156 200	1.77	Cattle meat	6 714	28 871 920	4 300	16 349 564	1.77
53	Sheep meat	144	402 948	2 808	454 034	1.13	Sheep meat	351	1 109 827	3 164	984 954	1.13
54	Pig meat	6 487	11 818 950	1 822	13 946 620	1.18	Pig meat	18 562	39 907 724	2 150	33 819 476	1.18
55	Chicken meat	7 145	6 173 280	864	29 923 260	4.85	Chicken meat	1 573	6 586 179	4 188	1 358 753	4.85
56	Duck meat	48	46 856	970	155 011	3.31	Duck meat	387	1 241 658	3 209	375 322	3.31
57	Horse meat	72	143 072	2 000	243 222	1.70	Horse meat	50	169 323	3 400	99 602	1.70
	Total		44 722 395		90 878 347	2.03			77 886 631		52 987 671	1.47
Sugar, honey												
58	Sugar cane	26 506	768 674	29	1 961 444	2.55	Sugar cane	47 363	3 504 863	74	1 373 527	2.55
59	Sugar beets	25 466	967 708	38	2 775 790	2.87	Sugar beets	8 140	887 260	109	309 320	2.87
60	Honey	103	174 928	1 700	4 204 769	1.17	Honey	204	405 960	1 990	346 800	1.17
	Total		1 911 311		4 942 008	2.59			4 798 083		2 029 647	2.36
	Total matched items		126 306 179		380 400 387	3.01			403 667 373		174 537 683	2.31
	as % of gross value of output		94.4%						89.5%			

http://dx.doi.org/10.1787/088330152501

ISBN: 978-92-64-03762-5 © OECD 2007

Table A.25. **Persons Engaged in US Farming, Forestry, Fishery and Agricultural Services, Benchmark Years, 1933–94**

(000s)

	Self Employed		Full and Part–time Employees		Total	
	Farms	F.F.A.S.	Farms	F.F.A.S.	Farms	F.F.A.S.
1933	5 857	95	2 865	130	8 722	225
1952	3 794	152	2 152	186	5 946	338
1957	3 120	143	1 932	182	5 052	325
1975	1 571	180	1 360	351	2 931	531
1978	1 455	207	1 268	495	2 723	702
1987	1 142	335	964	842	2 106	1 177
1994	1 272	407	842	1 101	2 114	1 508

Source: *National Income and Product Accounts of the United States*, N.I.P.A., vols., US Dept. of Commerce, 1992 and 1993. Vol. 1, pp. 112–4 and 121, for 1933–57, vol. 2, pp. 212–3 and 218 for 1975–87. *Survey of Current Business*, Jan–Feb 1996 pp. 75–6 for 1994. F.F.A.S. means forestry, fishery and agricultural services.

http://dx.doi.org/10.1787/088341067221

Table A.26. **Gross Value Added in US Farming, Benchmark Years, 1933–92 at 1987 Prices**

($ million)

	Farms	Farms Minus Imputed Housing Services	Adjusted Farm Product
1933	47 400	41 000	41 466
1952	44 800	37 100	37 522
1957	46 300	38 000	38 432
1975	53 100	45 900	46 422
1978	48 200	41 500	41 972
1987	66 000	61 100	61 795
1994	86 900	82 400	83 337

Source: First two columns, 1933–87 as for Table A.25 from *N.I.P.A.*, vol. l, p. 195, and vol.2, p. 342. 1987–94 volume movement from *Survey of Current Business*, August 1996, p. 154. The 1987–94 volume movement was based on the new chain index of the US Dept. of Commerce, which I linked to the figures for earlier years in 1987 prices. The third column is benchmarked on the 1987 gross value added as shown in the input–output accounts (see Table A.13 above).

http://dx.doi.org/10.1787/088370163025

Appendix B

Industrial Performance, China 1913–2003

The official measure of industrial performance (see second column of Table C.5) is made by cumulating returns from enterprises with very few independent checks. In order to measure constant prices, enterprises are given price manuals which specify the prices they are to use for benchmark years. The manual gives prices for about 2 000 items. In principle, firms estimate constant price values in years after 1990 by multiplying the volume of output of specified items in these years by their price in 1990. However, the specification manual does not cover all items produced or specify in sufficient detail. State enterprises have an incentive to mismeasure performance by understating inflation. Although there are penalties for falsification, there are substantial possibilities for exaggerating the volume of output when new products are incorporated into the reporting system at so–called "comparable" prices. In 1978 there were 348 000 industrial enterprises, but by 1996, the number had risen to 8 million. Many of these new small–scale, non–state enterprises cannot or do not bother to distinguish between current and "comparable" prices, so the tendency to understate inflation has been increased.

Wu's Alternative Estimates of Real Gross Value Added

Wu (1997 and 2002) has made alternative estimates of industrial gross value added in constant 1987 prices since 1949 which are much better than the official figures for several reasons. He has updated his estimates to 2003 for this volume (see Tables B.1 and B.2). He used time series on physical output and prices for a relatively large number of products (117) from the official *China Industrial Economic Statistical Yearbook*. Value added weights for 1987 were derived from the official. *Input Output Table of China 1987*, SSB, 1991, pp. 147–62 (see Table B.4). The exercise is fully transparent and follows methods which are used in Western countries. His procedure is rather like that which I used to measure farm output in Appendix A, except that he was unable to adjust for possible changes in input ratios over time. Wu's coverage corresponds to that in Western definitions (he excludes forestry products and repair and maintenance which are included in the official statistics). He has a breakdown for 15 manufacturing sectors, which follows the standard industrial classification and he also provides estimates for mining and utilities. His measure therefore throws a good deal of light on structural change (see Table B.1).

Wu shows significantly slower growth than the official estimates. His growth rate is 10.1 per cent a year for industry as a whole for 1952–78, compared to the official 11.5 per cent; and 9.75 per cent a year for 1978–2003 compared to the official 11.46. The profile of the two estimates is very different in the 1990s, with Wu showing a distinct slowdown of growth in 1996–98 and faster growth than the official estimates thereafter. It seems clear that the official estimates for industry involved a smoothing of the growth path in the 1990s.

 ISBN: 978-92-64-03762-5 © OECD 2007

Estimates for Prewar Years

For 1933–52, the best estimates are by Liu and Yeh (1965). Their work was done under the watchful eye of Simon Kuznets, they explain their procedures meticulously, their sources are given in detail as is their rationale for filling gaps.

The best documented part of their work is for the benchmark year 1933. They measure the structure of gross output, gross value added and depreciation in great detail exploiting survey material on Chinese and foreign–owned factories and Japanese output in Manchuria. They have 1933 price and quantity data for 61 items produced in factories (firms using power, pp. 426–8); gross output, value added and depreciation estimates for 45 handicraft items (pp. 512–3); 29 mining products (p. 569); and 3 utilities (p. 578).

Their evidence for changes in output between 1933 and 1952 is weaker than for their benchmark year. They have 16 indicators for the movement of factory output and for all their mining and utility items. For handicrafts, they had no direct indicator, but assumed that output moved parallel to the combined output of agriculture and mining, because these two sectors supplied most of the raw materials for handicrafts (p. 155).

The Liu and Yeh results are shown in Table B.3 for 1933–57 at 1933 and 1952 prices. I have used the estimates at 1933 weights as they are better documented than those for 1952. I used Wu (1997) for 1952–57 as he had many more indicators for this period than Liu and Yeh.

For 1913–33, there are estimates by Chang (1969) and Rawski (1989). Rawski's estimates for manufacturing are better documented, as he has indicators for fourteen products (p. 354) whereas Chang had only five (pp. 117–19). However, Chang has better coverage for mining and I used his estimates for this sector in Table C.1.

Table B.1. **Wu's Rates of Growth and Shares of Value Added by Industrial Branch, 1952–2003**

	Growth Rates (annual average compound growth rates)		Branch Share of Gross Value Added (per cent)		
	1952–78	1978–2003	1952	1978	2003
Food Products	6.4	9.5	6.3	2.6	2.4
Beverages	9.1	7.4	1.6	1.3	0.7
Tobacco Products	5.9	4.5	10.0	3.6	1.1
Textile Products	5.9	6.3	27.5	9.8	4.5
Wearing Apparel	3.8	16.9	5.7	1.2	5.9
Leather Goods and Footwear	8.4	10.6	1.2	0.8	1.0
Wood Products, Furniture & Fixtures	6.3	5.3	6.2	2.4	0.9
Paper, Printing & Publishing	10.0	10.1	2.5	2.5	2.7
Chemical and Allied Products	13.7	8.6	6.7	15.5	11.8
Rubber and Plastic Products	11.5	11.7	1.8	2.4	3.7
Non-Metallic Mineral Products	9.5	9.9	7.0	6.0	6.2
Basic and Fabricated Metal Products	15.7	5.7	2.5	9.0	3.5
Machinery and Transport Equipment	16.4	9.7	3.2	13.4	13.2
Electrical Machinery and Equipment	16.5	18.0	1.0	4.4	27.1
Other	9.2	13.6	4.2	3.3	7.9
Total Manufacturing	9.7	10.5	87.4	78.3	92.6
Mining	11.9	3.0	10.6	16.0	3.3
Utilities	14.7	8.4	2.0	5.8	4.2
Total Industry	10.1	9.8	100.0	100.0	100.0

Source: Wu H.X. (2002), "How Fast has Chinese Industry Grown? Measuring the Real Output of Chinese Industry, 1949-97", *Review of Income and Wealth* (48), No. 2, pp. 179-204, updated.

http://dx.doi.org/10.1787/086827837164

ISBN: 978-92-64-03762-5 © OECD 2007

Table B.2. **New Wu Estimates of Industrial Value Added 1952–2003**

	Industrial GDP in 1987 Yuan (million)			
	Manufacturing	Mining	Utilities	Total
1952	15 548	1 889	359	17 796
1953	20 246	1 916	452	22 615
1954	23 427	2 405	541	26 373
1955	23 912	3 099	605	27 616
1956	29 920	3 190	816	33 926
1957	33 116	4 155	949	38 220
1958	49 262	7 955	1 352	58 569
1959	66 796	10 717	2 080	79 592
1960	71 770	12 465	2 920	87 155
1961	36 504	8 409	2 360	47 272
1962	31 978	6 760	2 252	40 990
1963	38 100	6 930	2 409	47 439
1964	46 841	6 725	2 753	56 319
1965	57 992	8 587	3 324	69 902
1966	69 882	9 612	4 056	83 550
1967	57 385	8 433	3 805	69 624
1968	54 205	8 979	3 520	66 705
1969	71 884	10 730	4 622	87 236
1970	94 673	14 742	5 698	115 113
1971	104 960	17 672	6 804	129 437
1972	112 177	19 469	7 493	139 139
1973	123 493	20 494	8 201	152 188
1974	118 354	22 704	8 299	149 357
1975	134 009	26 670	9 627	170 306
1976	129 346	28 053	9 985	167 385
1977	147 732	31 252	10 984	189 968
1978	171 695	35 003	12 616	219 314
1979	188 271	34 803	13 865	236 940
1980	199 233	34 825	14 779	248 837
1981	204 491	33 860	15 207	253 557
1982	219 478	34 653	16 111	270 242
1983	237 326	36 455	17 277	291 058
1984	265 054	39 649	18 535	323 239
1985	302 008	41 842	20 192	364 042
1986	328 943	43 931	22 100	394 974
1987	390 072	46 420	24 450	460 943
1988	425 387	48 852	26 805	501 043
1989	437 587	51 552	28 752	517 891
1990	446 245	51 622	30 542	528 408
1991	498 600	53 056	33 310	584 966
1992	569 410	54 979	37 066	661 456
1993	655 098	56 253	41 274	752 626
1994	744 676	59 452	45 630	849 759
1995	956 156	65 472	49 510	1 071 138
1996	916 307	66 963	53 162	1 036 432
1997	965 662	68 257	55 832	1 089 751
1998	893 110	62 284	57 376	1 012 770
1999	990 267	58 789	60 931	1 109 987
2000	1 146 735	57 324	66 649	1 270 707
2001	1 356 913	61 043	72 804	1 490 760
2002	1 651 151	66 513	81 319	1 798 983
2003	2 079 632	73 222	93 935	2 246 790

http://dx.doi.org/10.1787/086836675576

Table B.3. **Liu and Yeh Estimates of Gross Value Added in Chinese Industry, 1933–57**
(billion yuan)

	1933	1952 at 1933 prices	1957	1933	1952 at 1952 prices	1957
Factories	0.74	1.35	3.12	3.71	7.46	18.31
Handicrafts	2.22	2.33	2.66	4.81	5.14	5.86
Mining	0.23	0.68	1.40	0.54	1.58	3.29
Utilities	0.16	0.39	0.89	0.19	0.41	0.94
Total Industry	3.35	4.75	8.07	9.25	14.59	28.40

Source: Liu and Yeh (1965), pp. 141, 153 and 157.

http://dx.doi.org/10.1787/086843736433

Table B.4. **Input-Output Characteristics of Chinese Industry, 1987**
(million yuan)

Gross Value of Output	1 381 300
Total Inputs	908 698
of which:	
Agriculture	136 490
Industry	651 950
Other Material Product	86 678
"Non-productive" Services	33 581
Gross Value Added	472 602
Basic Depreciation	42 462
Repair & Maintenance	20 695
Net Value Added	409 445
Gross Material Product	506 183
Net Material Product	443 026
Allocation of Gross Value Added	
Labour Income	103 502
Welfare Income	9 706
Profits & Taxes	233 781
Depreciation, Repair & Maintenance	63 156
Other	62 457
Total Gross Value Added	472 602
Gross Value of Output	1 381 300
Total Intermediate Uses	984 713
of which:	
Agriculture	61 450
Industry	651 950
Other Material Product	206 072
"Non-productive" Services	65 240
Final Uses	396 587
of which:	
Private Consumption	260 269
Social Consumption	11 523
Investment	119 792
Inventories	39 416
Net Exports	-31 915
Reconciliation Item	-2 398

Source: SSB, *Input-Output Table of China 1987* (in Chinese), 1991. This table follows the official definition of industry, which includes some forestry products, and repair and maintenance of machinery and equipment. Together these two items accounted for 12 billion yuan of gross value added in 1987.

http://dx.doi.org/10.1787/086845666832

ISBN: 978-92-64-03762-5 © OECD 2007

Appendix C

Growth and Level of Chinese Gross Domestic Product

For the period before 1890, estimates of Chinese GDP can only be very rough judgements. It seems clear that the 1890 level was below that of 1820. In the nineteenth century there were several important revolts, a major civil war and important military clashes with foreign powers, particularly the United Kingdom, Japan, Russia and France, who sought extraterritorial rights and financial indemnities from China. The Taiping rebellion devastated the most prosperous areas in the 1850s. The administrative apparatus was severely challenged and there was important damage to major waterways. The Grand Canal fell out of use; the Yellow River burst its banks and changed its course. Between 1820 and 1890 population showed no net growth, whereas it had increased by almost half from 1750–1820.

Table C.1 presents estimates of GDP for benchmark years — 1890, 1913, 1933 and 1952 — with a 13 sector breakdown in 1933 yuan. Table C.2 presents aggregate GDP estimates for 24 key years between 1 and 1952 AD in 1990 Geary–Khamis dollars. The sources are indicated in the footnotes.

These years are shown because they represent significant turning points in economic policy, are useful for purposes of international comparison, or for contingent reasons of statistical availability. is The first year for which sectoral estimates were feasible is 1890, while 1913 is a significant point for international comparison as the last normal year before a world conflict. By far the best documented prewar year is 1933 and it was investigated in detail by Ou (1947), Liu and Yeh (1965), Chang (1969) and Rawski (1989). It was the worst year of the world depression, but it was not a depressed year for China. The 1933 level of per capita income was higher than that of 1952, which is the starting year for most long–term series of the Chinese statistical office.

Official Chinese Measures of GDP for 1952–2003

The Chinese State Statistical Bureau (SSB), now renamed as the National Bureau of Statistics (NBS), has published aggregate estimates of Chinese economic performance on an annual basis back to 1952. Until the late 1980s, it used the Soviet material product system of accounts which overstated growth and excluded a large part of service activity. There were also serious deficiencies in the basic reporting system. In the turbulence of the cultural revolution, the statistical office was abolished in 1968 and its staff disbursed. It was re–established in 1972, but most of the old personnel had disappeared and many old records had been destroyed. No new graduates with the requisite training had been produced in the years when the universities were closed.

The statistical office used to publish two measures of aggregate economic performance. The "total product of society" showed an average annual growth rate in "comparable prices" of 7.9 per cent for 1952–78 (1988 Yearbook p. 28). This represented aggregate gross output of five sectors and

 ISBN: 978-92-64-03762-5 © OECD 2007

involved a good deal of double counting because each of the component sectors had significant inputs from the others. "Net material product" which the Chinese called "national income" showed 6 per cent growth for the same period at "comparable prices" (p. 42 of the 1988 Yearbook); this was better as it deducted most inputs except "non–material services".

In the early 1990s, these Soviet style measures were dropped in favour of Western concepts showing slower growth. The statistical office has stopped reporting estimates for the Maoist period 1952–78. Since 1995, the Yearbooks have only published estimates for 1978 onwards. However, there was a joint retrospective exercise by the Statistical Office and Hitotsubashi University in 1997 which provided Western type estimates for 1952–1995.

The official estimates for 1978 onwards are a great improvement on the earlier Material Product Syustem (MPS) system. They are made independently from the production and expenditure side, but the former are considered more reliable (see Xu and Ye, 2000, p. 12). They are based on the international standard United Nations System of National Accounts (SNA) guidelines, but there is still scope for improvement. The national accounts department of the NBS is of high quality, but relatively small. In 2000, there were only 26 staff members. Reports at the basic level reach the NBS through several levels of aggregation in the administrative hierarchy. This transmission route provides opportunities for officials at different levels to adjust their reports to reflect favourably on their management. The NBS makes crosschecks, but they are necessarily limited in scope. Xu and Ye give a detailed account of the procedures used in constructing official accounts. Except for two sectors (agriculture and transport), growth measures are not based on quantitative indicators of volume movement. Most sector accounts are constructed at current prices and deflated by price indices. Because of the shakiness of the price reports it receives, the NBS, until 2002, distinguished between current and "comparable" prices instead of current and "constant" prices as other countries do. State enterprises use a price manual specifying 2 000 items to help them differentiate current and constant prices. Many reporting units in the private sector cannot or do not make this distinction. This is an important reason for overstatement in the official statistics.

Table C.5 shows the annual official estimates of GDP growth from the production side. The official estimates show a breakdown by five sectors. There is also an official estimate for non–material services, but it is not shown explicitly. The NBS provide a total for the tertiary sector and a two–way breakdown between transport and commerce; the third service component, non–material services, is a residual which the reader can derive. I have done this and thus provide a six sector breakdown. For 1978–2003 the individual sector movement was derived from the volume indices for each sector in the 2006 Statistical Yearbook, p. 60. For 1952–78, I used the estimates in SSB–Hitotsubashi (1997), pp. 70–71. The official estimates of GDP level are shown in current yuan, but the official constant price estimates are only available as indices. For comparability with my alternative estimates in Table C.3, I used 1987 sector weights from the 1987 input–output table and show level estimates in 1987 yuan for all years. I derived total GDP by adding the estimates for the six sectors. In doing this, I get an average compound growth rate for GDP of 9.59 for 1978–2003, which is identical with official GDP growth estimate for this period. Following the same procedure for 1952–78, I got an average growth rate of 4.7 per cent. This is a good deal lower than the GDP growth rate of 6.1 per cent shown in the Hitotsubashi study. It is not clear why their aggregate growth rate is so different, as they give no indication of the weights they used. However, it seems possible that their aggregate GDP estimate was derived from the old net material product estimate.

ISBN: 978-92-64-03762-5 © OECD 2007

Maddison Modification of the Official Estimates of GDP by Industry of Origin for 1952–2003

In view of the problems mentioned above, I made alternative measures of GDP growth which involve significant modification of the official figures. Table C.3 provides annual estimates for all the years 1952–2003 disaggregated by six sectors. It shows slower GDP growth than the official estimates in Table C.5. So far as possible, my estimates are based on the measurement conventions of the SNA. The main adjustments to the official estimates were as follows:

i)   Maddison (1998) contained my own detailed estimate of gross value added in farming, as shown in Appendix A above. I used price and quantity data for 125 crop and livestock items, with adjustment for changes in the proportion of farm and non–farm inputs over time. I used the official Chinese series for fishery, forestry and sidelines. My estimate for agriculture as a whole showed slightly faster growth (3.25 a year from 1952 to 1990) than the official estimates (3.15 a year). In view of the close congruence of the official and Maddison estimates for this sector, I used the official estimates to update the series from 1990 to 2003. However, my estimate of the level of output in the sector is higher than the official (nearly one–fifth in 1990).

ii) In Maddison (1998), I used Harry Wu's (1997) estimates of gross value added in industry, which showed substantially slower growth than the official estimates for this sector. This was a volume index, with detailed time series on physical output and prices from the *China Industrial Economic Statistical Yearbook*. Value added was derived from the official input–output table. Wu (2002) presented a bigger sample covering 117 products and explained in detail why the official figures exaggerated growth. He provided detailed time series showing annual movement for 15 branches of manufacturing as well as mining and utilities. Here I used his revised estimates updated to 2003 (see Appendix B). He shows a growth rate of 10.1 per cent a year for industry as a whole for 1952–78, compared to the official 11.5 per cent; and 9.75 per cent a year for 1978–2003. The profile of the two estimates is very different in the 1990s, with Wu showing a distinct slowdown of growth in 1996–98 and faster growth than the official estimates thereafter. It seems clear that the official estimates for industry involved a smoothing of the growth path in the 1990s.

iii) For construction I used official estimates throughout.

iv) For transport and communications, commerce and restaurants I used the estimates of Liu and Yeh (1965) for 1952–7, linked to the official estimates for 1957–2003. It should be noted that the official estimates for growth in these two sectors were revised upwards significantly for 1993–2003 in the 2006 Yearbook (compare the NBS Yearbook, 2005, p. 53 and 2006, pp. 59–60).

v)   In the old Soviet–style national accounts "non–material services" were excluded from "material product". These are banking, insurance, housing services, administration of real estate, social services, health, education, entertainment, personal services, R & D activities, the armed forces, police, government and party organisations. They are now incorporated in the Chinese accounts, but are not shown explicitly. The NBS provides an estimate for the "tertiary" sector as a whole, with a breakdown for two component sub–sectors (transport and commerce). The estimate for non–material services is a residual which the reader has to derive for him or herself. As GDP originating in this sub–sector is bigger than in transport or commerce, the residual treatment is perhaps due to official qualms about its measure for this sector. The international standardised *System of National Accounts* (1993, p. 134), excludes any imputation of productivity growth in this sector. I therefore used employment as a proxy indicator of growth in real value added (see Table C.6 for my estimates). However, the NBS does assume substantial productivity growth (1.5 per cent per annum per person employed for 1952–78 and 5.1 per cent for 1978–2003). Thus there is a major discrepancy between my estimates in Table C.6 and the official estimates in

  ISBN: 978-92-64-03762-5 © OECD 2007

Table C.5. There is also a difference in the level of the two estimates. The official coverage appeared to be inadequate. It substantially undervalued housing and military outlays and probably did not cover welfare benefits in kind which were provided free to employees of state enterprises. I therefore augmented the 1987 weight for this sector by one third.

vi) I used 1987 gross value added weights throughout. The price structure changed drastically over the 51 years under survey. In 1952 agricultural prices were kept very low and industrial prices were relatively high. By 1987 (my weighting year), farm prices had risen more than three–fold, but the official deflator suggests that industrial prices had actually fallen. My use of 1987 prices gives a bigger weight to the slow–growing agricultural sector than if I had used 1952 weights. In fact I chose 1987 as a weighting year for two reasons: *i)* the Chinese economy was by then subject to market forces to a much greater extent than in earlier years of very tight control and regulation; *ii)* the 1987 input–output table provided a wealth of detailed information which permitted much clearer definitions of gross value added by sector than for earlier years.

My GDP estimates show lower growth than the NBS. For 1952–78, I show an annual growth rate of 4.4 against the official 4.7 per cent; for 1978–2003, 7.85 per cent a year compared with the official 9.59 per cent. Use of the Wu estimates for industry lowers the GDP growth rate to 8.8 per cent. Use of my non–material services estimate reduces the growth rate further to 7.98. Use of my estimate for agriculture reduces the GDP growth rate to 7.85 (this latter effect is not due to the difference between my estimate and the official measure of growth in the sector, but to the fact that agiculture – a relatively slow growing sector – has a bigger weight in my estimate).

Figure C.1 compares my estimates and those of the NBS. For 1952, my GDP level is 38 per cent higher than the official estimate; in 1978, 27 per cent higher; in 1987, 10.3 per cent higher; and for 2003 nearly 19 per cent lower.

Table C.4 shows the annual growth of population, GDP and per capita GDP in China and Hong Kong for 1952–2003.

NBS Estimates of GDP from the Expenditure Side

The NBS provides estimates of GDP by type of expenditure as well as by industry of origin. The leading official statisticians, Xu and Ye (2000, p. 12) say "NBS considers that its estimates from the production side are more reliable". There was a discrepancy between the annual current price estimates in the production and expenditure side of up to 4 per cent in 1978–2003 (see pp. 57 and 68 of the 2006 Yearbook); and a similar range of variance in 1952–78 (see SSB/Hitotsubashi, 1997, p. 59). However, the main problem with the expenditure estimates is that there is no explicit indication of the change in volume of output and an inadequate breakdown of investment. There is a breakdown in current prices between gross fixed investment and inventories (p. 69 of the 2006 Yearbook), but no estimates before 1981 of residential and non–residential construction. It also seems that the official investment estimates include repairs and military hardware; these items would be excluded in the accounts of OECD countries.

Table C.7 shows my estimates of the breakdown of gross investment in current prices for 1952–2003. This requires some degree of conjecture as shown in the footnotes. Table C.8 shows how I measured capital formation and the growth of the non–residential stock of fixed capital. The derivation is explained in the footnotes. I used these estimates in the growth accounts in Table 3.9

Figure C.1. **Confrontation of Official and Maddison Estimates of GDP Level, 1952–2003**

million 1990 G–K $

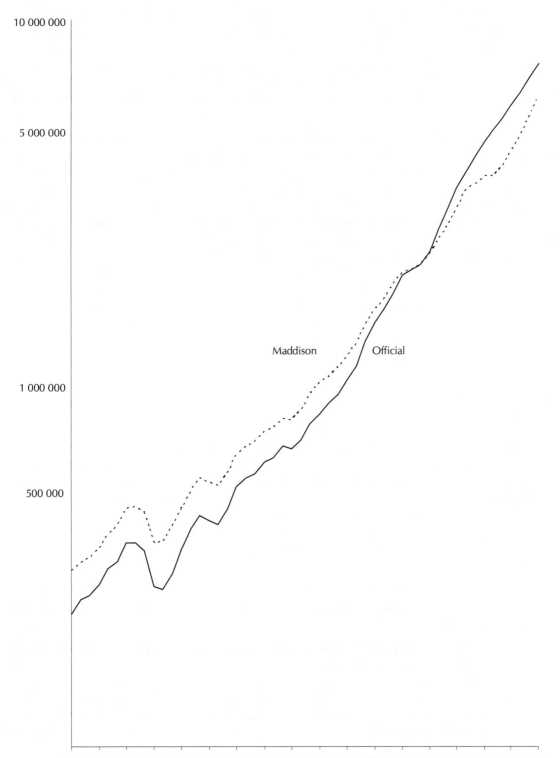

Source: Last columns of Tables C.3 and C.5.

http://dx.doi.org/10.1787/086016746264

ISBN: 978-92-64-03762-5 © OECD 2007

Conversion of Chinese GDP Estimates in Yuan into "International" Dollars

For purposes of international comparison, it is necessary to convert the estimates for China in national currency (yuan) into a numeraire which is available for other countries. Exchange rates are a misleading indicator of comparative real values. The most appropriate and convenient measure is a purchasing power comparison in terms of US dollars. The coverage of such PPP measures is best for 1990, where estimates are available for 154 countries–70 covered by the International Comparison Programme (ICP) of the United Nations and 84 by the Penn World Tables (PWT) of Robert Summers and Alan Heston (see Maddison, 2003, p. 230). China did not participate in the 1990 ICP exercise, but Ren (1997) produced an ICP–type estimate of comparative Chinese/US real expenditure levels for 1986.

Several adjustments are necessary to the Ren estimates to put them on a comparable basis to the 1990 multilateral (Geary–Khamis) purchasing power parities. Ren (1997, p. 37) had three expenditure PPP estimates for his benchmark year 1986: a Laspeyres measure with US quantity weights, a Paasche measure with Chinese quantity weights and a geometric (Fisher) average of the two binary measures. The Laspeyres PPP was the least favourable (1.5091 yuan to the dollar), the Paasche the most favourable (0.5895 to the dollar). He prefers the geometric average of 0.9432 yuan to the dollar. These were all bilateral measures, but for a multi–country comparison it is better to have a multilateral PPP which produces transitive results for all countries. Kravis (1981) who created the ICP approach and made the first ICP–type estimate for China, adjusted his Chinese/US Fisher PPP by 19 per cent as an approximation to his preferred multilateral (Geary–Khamis) converter. This was in fact the average Fisher/Geary–Khamis spread for five Asian countries in the 1980 ICP exercise (see Maddison, 1995, p. 176). I made the same proportionate adjustment to the Fisher estimate of Ren to derive a proxy Geary–Khamis PPP for China/United States of 0.7926 for 1986. This compares with an exchange rate of 3.45 yuan to the dollar in that year (see Maddison, 1995, pp. 162–78, for a discussion of these issues and examples of the range between the different kinds of PPP measure).

Ren used the official estimate of Chinese GDP for 1986, whereas my estimate for 1986 (adjusted to 1986 prices) was more than 13 percent above the official estimate because of the coverage adjustments mentioned above. Converting my estimate into 1986 dollars with the Geary–Khamis converter yields an estimate of $1 458 996 million. This needs to be updated to 1990 by my estimate of the increase in volume of Chinese GDP (24.66 per cent) and adjusted for the 16.77 per cent rise in dollar prices (US GDP deflator). These two adjustments yield a 1990 internationally comparable dollar estimate of $2 123 852 million. The 1990 conversion coefficient was then applied to all other years as can be seen by comparing the seventh and eighth columns of Table C.3. As the estimate for China in US dollars is not derived from exchange rate conversion, I refer to them as "int." (international) dollars, or "G–K $" after the two inventors, (Geary and Khamis), of this method of calculating multilateral purchasing power parities (PPPs).

For valid international comparisons of GDP performance, it is essential to use PPP converters. Exchange rate comparisons can give a very misleading picture of China's geopolitical weight. I cite three illustrations of this:

i)   Mr. Patten, the last British governor of Hong Kong, stated in an article in the *Economist* newspaper of 4 January 1997, that "Britain's GDP today is almost twice the size of China's — China's GDP is about the same as those of Belgium, the Netherlands and Luxembourg combined". If he had used my PPP converters, he might have said "Britain's GDP today is about one–third the size of China's — China's GDP is more than six and a half times as big as the combined GDP of Belgium, the Netherlands and Luxembourg".

ii) Lord Patten, in an article of 22 June 2007 in the *International Herald Tribune*, suggested that in 1997, the GDP of Hong Kong was 22 per cent of that of China. My estimate, using purchasing power parity converters, shows that Hong Kong's GDP was less than 4 per cent of China's in 1997 — see Table C.4.

iii) It is often suggested that China is especially delinquent as an emitter of greenhouse gases. In 2003, its carbon emissions were 0.63 tons per thousand dollars of GDP if the official exchange rate is used. This is very much higher than the 0.19 tons per thousand dollars of GDP in the United States. When PPP converters are used the Chinese ratio is lower than that of the United States (0.17 tons per thousand dollars of GDP).

ISBN: 978-92-64-03762-5 © OECD 2007

Table C.1. **Gross Domestic Product by Sector of Origin, Benchmark Years, China 1890–1952**
(million 1933 yuan)

	1890	1913	1933	1952
Farming, Fishery & Forestry	14 576	16 769	19 180	17 664
Handicrafts	1 646	1 932	2 220	2 330
Modern Manufacturing	26	156	740	1 350
Mining	45	87	230	680
Electric Power	0	5	160	390
Construction	364	420	480	960
Modern Transport & Communication	84	208	460	880
Traditional Transport & Communication	1 085	1 150	1 210	1 210
Trade	1 747	2 257	2 820	2 950
Government	602	692	850	
Finance	64	124	220	3 281
Personal Services	239	293	350	
Residential Services	805	926	1 060	
GDP	21 283	25 019	29 980	31 695

Source: 1933 gross value added in first eight sectors from Liu and Yeh (1965), pp. 140–41, 153, 157 and 161. For the other five sectors they give only net value added (p. 66), and an all–economy total for depreciation. Residual depreciation was 4.2 per cent of net value added in the five other branches. I assumed that this average rate applied to them all individually. For 1933 construction, Yeh (1979) raised the original Liu and Yeh figure from 380 to 480, and I incorporated his revision. 1933–52 sector movements are from Liu and Yeh in most cases, interpreting their 1952 estimate for work brigade output as part of construction activity. 1933–52 farming, forestry and fishery from Table A.3.   For other services (government, finance, personal and residential) the Liu and Yeh 72 per cent increase seemed implausibly high and was not well documented, so I assumed that value added in these services rose 32 per cent, parallel with employment (see Table D.5). 1913–33 growth rates from Yeh (1979), p. 126, for handicrafts, modern and traditional transportation, trade, government, finance and personal services. For these sectors (except government) I assumed that the 1913–33 growth rates were also valid for 1890–1913. For agriculture and construction, value added was assumed to move parallel to population in 1890–1933, and so was government product 1890–1913. Modern manufacturing 1913–33 growth rate from Rawski (1989), p. 354, and the same growth rate was assumed for 1890–1913. Mining and utilities from Chang (1969) pp. 117–19, for individual indicators, pp. 76–9, for his weights and branch indices; I assumed that his 1913–33 growth rates were valid for 1890–1913 coal, ferrous metals, other mining products and electric power.   http://dx.doi.org/10.1787/088475754840

Table C.2. **Growth and Level of GDP, Population and GDP Per Capita, 1–2030**

	GDP Level (million 1990 G–K $)	Population (000s)	Per Capita GDP (1990 G–K $)
1	26 820	59 600	450
960	24 750	55 000	450
1300	60 000	100 000	600
1500	61 800	130 000	600
1600	96 000	160 000	600
1700	82 800	138 000	600
1820	228 600	381 000	600
1850	247 200	412 000	600
1870	189 740	358 000	530
1890	205 379	380 000	540
1990	218 154	400 000	545
1913	241 431	437 140	552
1929	274 090	487 273	562
1930	277 567	489 000	568
1931	280 393	492 640	569
1932	289 304	496 307	583
1933	289 304	500 000	579
1934	264 091	502 639	525
1935	285 403	505 292	565
1936	303 433	507 959	597
1937	296 043	510 640	580
1938	288 653	513 336	562
1950	244 985	546 815	448
1951	273 733	557 480	491
1952	305 854	568 910	538
2003	6 187 983	1 288 400	4 803
2030	22 982 784	1 458 024	15 763

Source: 1–1870 from Maddison (1998, 2001 and 2003); 1890, 1913, 1933, 1952 volume movement from Liu and Yeh (1965), see Table C.1. 1929–38 movement from Maddison (1985, p. 85) and Maddison (1995), pp. 145 and 158. 1950–52 from T.G. Rawski (1989) *Economic Growth in Prewar China*, p. 336. 1952–2003 from Table C.3.

http://dx.doi.org/10.1787/086873246163

ISBN: 978-92-64-03762-5 © OECD 2007

Table C.3 **Maddison-Wu Estimates of Chinese GDP by Sector, 1952-2003**

	GDP in million 1987 yuan							GDP in million 1990 G-K $
	Agriculture	Industry	Construction	Transport & Communication	Commerce	"Non material" Services	Total GDP	
1952	127 891	17 796	3 658	5 183	14 272	45 486	214 286	305 854
1953	130 139	22 615	4 990	5 406	14 730	47 038	224 918	321 030
1954	132 229	26 373	4 821	5 679	15 173	48 014	232 289	331 550
1955	142 595	27 616	5 487	5 852	15 498	48 803	245 851	350 908
1956	149 135	33 926	9 238	6 447	16 472	53 042	268 260	382 892
1957	153 649	38 220	8 662	6 695	16 916	59 877	284 019	405 386
1958	154 538	58 569	12 993	9 827	17 522	62 512	315 961	450 977
1959	130 265	79 592	13 728	12 874	18 555	65 264	320 278	457 139
1960	109 107	87 155	13 919	14 213	16 927	68 136	309 457	441 694
1961	110 965	47 272	4 821	9 237	12 359	71 135	255 789	365 092
1962	116 172	40 990	5 970	7 488	11 865	74 266	256 751	366 465
1963	129 505	47 439	7 514	7 368	12 830	77 535	282 191	402 776
1964	146 495	56 319	9 434	7 761	14 525	80 961	315 495	450 312
1965	161 098	69 902	10 433	10 441	14 446	85 227	351 547	501 769
1966	173 034	83 550	11 413	11 521	17 398	87 610	384 526	548 841
1967	176 576	69 624	10 846	9 907	18 106	88 654	373 713	533 407
1968	174 153	66 705	8 794	9 677	16 433	90 469	366 231	522 728
1969	175 885	87 236	11 826	11 878	19 587	91 218	397 630	567 545
1970	189 751	115 113	15 422	13 871	21 417	90 673	446 247	636 937
1971	193 604	129 437	17 295	15 027	21 406	91 694	468 463	668 646
1972	192 235	139 139	16 929	16 471	23 280	94 099	482 153	688 186
1973	209 868	152 188	17 500	17 500	25 391	95 597	518 044	739 414
1974	218 892	149 357	18 583	17 555	24 874	97 548	526 809	751 924
1975	223 928	170 306	21 151	19 562	24 841	99 545	559 333	798 346
1976	220 352	167 385	22 053	19 246	23 909	103 040	555 985	793 568
1977	215 841	189 968	22 420	21 679	27 119	113 659	590 686	843 097
1978	225 079	219 314	22 292	23 617	33 383	131 448	655 133	935 083
1979	238 994	236 940	22 731	25 432	36 312	145 245	705 654	1 007 193
1980	235 798	248 837	28 810	26 876	35 841	153 277	729 439	1 041 142
1981	252 451	253 557	29 722	27 389	46 594	163 330	773 043	1 103 378
1982	281 773	270 242	30 739	30 589	48 424	169 433	831 200	1 186 387
1983	305 265	291 058	35 984	33 648	59 020	176 740	901 715	1 287 034
1984	345 075	323 239	39 891	38 695	71 704	195 369	1 013 973	1 447 262
1985	351 680	364 042	48 747	43 903	92 392	217 901	1 118 665	1 596 691
1986	363 504	394 974	56 484	49 519	102 180	226 955	1 193 616	1 703 670
1987	381 013	460 943	66 580	54 490	115 930	240 320	1 319 276	1 883 027
1988	390 373	501 043	71 899	61 756	132 475	254 910	1 412 456	2 016 024
1989	402 216	517 891	65 826	64 669	121 453	265 620	1 437 675	2 051 813
1990	431 708	528 408	66 609	70 205	115 672	275 400	1 488 002	2 123 852
1991	441 895	584 966	72 984	78 054	120 880	287 268	1 586 047	2 263 794
1992	462 722	661 456	88 321	86 249	136 670	304 853	1 740 271	2 483 921
1993	484 455	752 626	104 215	98 790	148 187	320 442	1 908 715	2 724 344
1994	503 923	849 759	118 482	110 244	162 308	355 068	2 099 784	2 997 060
1995	529 052	1 071 138	133 172	125 808	174 827	383 182	2 417 179	3 450 084
1996	555 991	1 036 432	144 497	142 883	187 345	399 815	2 466 963	3 521 141
1997	575 460	1 089 751	148 286	161 257	206 774	415 403	2 596 931	3 706 647
1998	595 608	1 012 770	161 662	178 332	222 798	433 261	2 604 431	3 717 352
1999	612 360	1 109 987	168 572	202 209	242 995	439 320	2 775 443	3 961 441
2000	627 075	1 270 707	178 135	229 793	267 498	452 984	3 026 192	4 319 339
2001	644 732	1 490 760	190 218	256 433	292 635	474 718	3 349 496	4 780 797
2002	663 522	1 798 983	206 937	281 821	321 645	492 212	3 765 120	5 374 025
2003	679 821	2 246 790	231 926	305 202	356 931	514 495	4 335 165	6 187 983

http://dx.doi.org/10.1787/087014842288

Table C.4. **GDP and GDP Per Capita of China and Hong Kong, 1952-2003**
(annual estimate in 1990 international dollars)

	China	Hong Kong	China	Hong Kongs
	GDP in million 1990 int. $		GDP Per Capita in 1990 int. $	
1952	305 854	5 054	538	2 377
1953	321 030	5 515	552	2 460
1954	331 550	6 021	557	2 546
1955	350 908	6 564	577	2 636
1956	382 892	7 136	616	2 729
1957	405 386	7 729	636	2 825
1958	450 977	8 345	690	2 924
1959	457 139	8 981	686	3 027
1960	441 694	9 637	662	3 134
1961	365 092	10 276	553	3 244
1962	366 465	12 072	550	3 652
1963	402 776	13 968	590	4 083
1964	450 312	15 165	645	4 327
1965	501 769	17 360	702	4 825
1966	548 841	17 659	746	4 865
1967	533 407	17 959	707	4 824
1968	522 728	18 557	675	4 880
1969	567 545	20 652	713	5 345
1970	636 937	22 548	778	5 695
1971	668 646	24 144	795	5 968
1972	688 186	26 639	798	6 473
1973	739 414	29 931	838	7 105
1974	751 724	30 629	835	7 091
1975	798 346	30 729	871	6 991
1976	793 568	35 716	853	7 906
1977	843 097	39 908	894	8 707
1978	935 083	43 300	978	9 277
1979	1 007 193	48 289	1 039	9 796
1980	1 041 142	53 177	1 061	10 503
1981	1 103 378	58 066	1 110	11 202
1982	1 186 387	59 662	1 186	11 333
1983	1 287 034	63 055	1 258	11 797
1984	1 447 262	69 340	1 396	12 846
1985	1 596 691	69 639	1 519	12 763
1986	1 703 670	77 122	1 597	13 960
1987	1 883 027	87 099	1 737	15 597
1988	2 016 024	94 083	1 834	16 716
1989	2 051 813	96 478	1 842	17 043
1990	2 123 852	99 770	1 871	17 541
1991	2 263 754	105 395	1 967	18 323
1992	2 483 921	112 336	2 132	19 270
1993	2 724 344	119 466	2 312	20 131
1994	2 997 060	126 016	2 515	20 770
1995	3 450 084	130 912	2 863	21 029
1996	3 521 141	136 550	2 892	21 364
1997	3 706 647	143 476	3 013	22 087
1998	3 717 352	136 347	2 993	20 834
1999	3 961 441	141 006	3 162	21 367
2000	4 319 339	155 337	3 421	22 328
2001	4 780 797	156 057	3 759	23 246
2002	5 374 025	159 003	4 197	23 513
2003	6 187 983	164 103	4 803	24 098

Source: www.ggdc.net/Maddison

http://dx.doi.org/10.1787/087017307146

 ISBN: 978-92-64-03762-5 © OECD 2007

Table C.5. **Official Estimates of Chinese GDP by Sector, 1952-2003**

	Agriculture	Industry	Construction	Transport & Communication	Commerce	Non-material services	Total GDP	GDP in million 1990 GK $
	(million 1987 yuan)							
1952	112 038	11 111	3 658	3 637	11 225	13 879	155 548	231 550
1953	114 167	15 077	4 990	4 513	15 490	16 597	170 834	254 305
1954	116 072	17 988	4 821	5 004	15 771	15 336	174 992	260 495
1955	125 259	19 177	5 487	5 128	15 749	16 877	187 677	279 378
1956	131 085	24 666	9 238	6 244	17 096	19 923	208 252	310 006
1957	135 118	27 465	8 662	6 695	16 916	21 883	216 739	322 640
1958	135 679	42 131	12 993	9 827	17 522	26 564	244 716	364 287
1959	114 167	54 409	13 728	12 874	18 555	30 870	244 603	364 119
1960	95 457	57 753	13 919	14 213	16 927	34 693	232 962	346 790
1961	96 913	35 198	4 821	9 237	12 359	27 459	185 987	276 862
1962	101 283	30 521	5 970	7 488	11 865	25 178	182 305	271 381
1963	112 711	34 587	7 514	7 368	12 830	26 294	201 304	299 663
1964	127 276	43 443	9 434	7 761	14 525	31 658	234 097	348 479
1965	139 600	54 664	10 433	10 441	14 446	37 820	267 404	398 061
1966	149 683	67 653	11 413	11 521	17 398	31 731	289 399	430 803
1967	152 484	57 409	10 846	9 907	18 106	32 983	281 735	419 394
1968	150 132	52 675	8 794	9 677	16 433	35 721	273 432	407 034
1969	151 364	70 053	11 826	11 878	19 587	38 233	302 941	450 961
1970	163 016	94 718	15 422	13 871	21 417	39 062	347 506	517 301
1971	166 041	106 384	17 295	15 027	21 406	42 481	368 634	548 753
1972	164 585	114 484	16 929	16 471	23 280	42 926	378 675	563 700
1973	179 374	124 539	17 500	17 500	25 391	44 204	408 508	608 110
1974	186 768	125 761	18 583	17 555	24 874	46 220	419 761	624 861
1975	190 577	145 871	21 151	19 562	24 841	48 770	450 772	671 024
1976	187 216	141 338	22 053	19 246	23 909	50 583	444 345	661 457
1977	183 071	161 715	22 420	21 679	27 119	53 572	469 576	699 016
1978	190 577	188 214	22 292	23 617	33 383	58 972	517 055	769 694
1979	202 341	204 513	22 731	25 432	36 312	62 290	553 619	824 123
1980	199 316	230 401	28 810	26 876	35 841	70 293	591 537	880 569
1981	213 209	234 401	29 722	27 389	46 594	74 330	625 645	931 342
1982	237 858	247 934	30 739	30 589	48 424	87 767	683 311	1 017 184
1983	247 476	272 033	35 984	33 648	59 020	100 188	748 349	1 114 001
1984	290 852	312 442	39 891	38 695	71 704	120 073	873 657	1 300 535
1985	296 118	369 339	48 747	43 903	93 392	137 697	989 196	1 472 528
1986	305 977	404 949	56 484	49 519	102 180	155 122	1 074 231	1 599 112
1987	320 430	458 580	66 580	54 490	115 930	180 240	1 196 250	1 780 751
1988	328 497	528 521	71 899	61 756	132 475	203 045	1 326 193	1 974 186
1989	338 692	555 242	65 826	64 669	121 453	228 880	1 374 762	2 046 486
1990	363 453	573 852	66 609	70 205	115 672	236 943	1 426 734	2 113 852
1991	372 006	656 490	72 984	78 054	120 880	246 481	1 546 895	2 302 725
1992	389 539	795 392	88 321	86 249	136 670	293 388	1 789 559	2 663 957
1993	407 835	955 186	104 215	98 790	148 187	330 870	2 045 083	3 044 333
1994	424 224	1 135 871	118 482	110 244	162 308	368 507	2 319 636	3 453 036
1995	445 378	1 295 289	133 172	125 808	174 827	402 118	2 576 592	3 835 543
1996	468 057	1 457 341	144 497	142 883	187 345	437 784	2 837 907	4 224 540
1997	484 447	1 622 286	148 286	161 257	206 774	480 552	3 103 602	4 620 056
1998	501 408	1 766 577	161 662	178 332	222 798	517 330	3 348 107	4 984 029
1999	515 511	1 917 148	168 572	202 209	242 995	557 416	3 603 851	5 364 732
2000	527 898	2 104 797	178 135	229 793	267 498	601 564	3 909 685	5 820 000
2001	542 763	2 287 177	190 218	256 433	292 435	661 303	4 230 329	6 297 315
2002	558 391	2 515 292	206 937	281 822	321 645	732 572	4 616 659	6 872 410
2003	572 302	2 836 009	231 926	305 202	356 901	801 926	5 104 266	7 598 267

http://dx.doi.org/10.1787/087126154476

Table C.6. **Maddison Estimates of "Non-Material" Service Employment and Output**
(employment in 000s at mid-year, and GDP in 1987 yuan)

	Civilian Employment	Assumed Military Manpower	Total Employment in sector	Sectoral GDP Maddison million 1987 yuan	Sectoral GDP Official million 1987 yuan
1952	7 023	3 000	10 023	45 486	13 879
1953	7 365	3 000	10 365	47 038	16 597
1954	7 580	3 000	10 580	48 014	15 336
1955	7 754	3 000	10 754	48 803	16 877
1956	8 688	3 000	11 688	53 042	19 923
1957	10 194	3 000	13 194	59 877	21 883
1958	17 905	3 000	20 905	62 512	26 564
1959	27 615	3 000	30 615	65 264	30 870
1960	31 515	3 000	34 515	68 136	34 693
1961	24 900	3 000	27 900	71 135	27 459
1962	15 450	3 000	18 450	74 266	25 178
1963	14 085	3 000	17 085	77 535	26 294
1964	14 840	3 000	17 840	80 961	31 658
1965	15 780	3 000	18 780	85 227	37 820
1966	16 305	3 000	19 305	87 610	31 731
1967	16 535	3 000	19 535	88 654	32 983
1968	16 935	3 000	19 935	90 469	35 721
1969	17 100	3 000	20 100	91 218	38 233
1970	16 980	3 000	19 980	90 673	39 062
1971	17 205	3 000	20 205	91 694	42 481
1972	17 735	3 000	20 735	94 099	42 926
1973	18 065	3 000	21 065	95 597	44 204
1974	18 495	3 000	21 495	97 548	46 220
1975	18 935	3 000	21 935	99 545	48 770
1976	19 705	3 000	22 705	103 040	50 583
1977	22 045	3 000	25 045	113 659	53 572
1978	25 965	3 000	28 965	131 448	58 972
1979	29 005	3 000	32 005	145 245	62 290
1980	30 775	3 000	33 775	153 277	70 293
1981	*32 990*	*3 000*	35 990	163 330	74 330
1982	34 335	3 000	37 335	169 433	87 767
1983	35 945	3 000	38 945	176 740	100 188
1984	40 845	3 000	43 845	195 369	120 073
1985	45 015	3 000	48 015	217 901	137 697
1986	47 010	3 000	50 010	226 955	155 122
1987	49 955	3 000	52 955	240 320	180 240
1988	53 170	3 000	56 170	254 910	203 045
1989	*55 530*	3 000	58 530	265 620	228 880
1990	*57 685*	3 000	60 685	275 400	236 943
1991	*60 300*	3 000	63 300	287 268	246 481
1992	64 175	3 000	67 175	304 853	293 388
1993	*67 610*	3 000	70 610	320 442	330 870
1994	*75 240*	3 000	78 240	355 068	368 507
1995	*81 435*	3 000	84 435	383 182	402 118
1996	*85 100*	3 000	88 100	399 815	437 784
1997	*88 535*	3 000	91 535	415 403	480 552
1998	*92 558*	2 912	95 470	433 261	517 330
1999	*94 065*	2 740	96 805	439 320	557 416
2000	*97 237*	2 578	99 815	452 984	601 564
2001	*102 105*	2 500	104 605	474 718	661 303
2002	*105 960*	2 500	108 460	492 212	732 572
2003	*110 870*	2 500	113 370	514 495	801 926

NB: This table corrects errors for 1981 and 1985 employment in Maddison (1998), p. 171. Until 1992, the official figures excluded the military. It was assumed that the military are included in the official figures from 1993. See source notes to Table D.3 for employment.

http://dx.doi.org/10.1787/087133035031

ISBN: 978-92-64-03762-5 © OECD 2007

Table C.7. **Official and Adjusted Estimates of Investment and GDP in Current Prices, China 1952-2003**
(billion yuan in current prices)

	Gross Fixed Investment	Adjusted Gross Fixed Investment	Housing Investment	Gross Fixed non-residential Investment	Increase in inventories	Official estimate of GDP
1952	8.07	7.26	2.38	4.88	7.30	69.22
1953	11.53	10.38	2.88	7.50	8.30	83.43
1954	14.09	12.68	3.01	9.67	8.60	87.83
1955	14.55	13.10	3.19	9.91	7.60	93.49
1956	21.96	19.76	3.60	16.16	3.80	103.42
1957	18.70	16.83	3.74	13.09	9.30	110.19
1958	33.30	29.97	3.63	26.34	9.90	129.12
1959	43.57	39.21	5.04	34.17	18.60	145.13
1960	47.30	42.57	5.10	37.47	10.20	150.80
1961	22.76	20.28	4.27	16.21	4.70	127.52
1962	17.51	15.76	4.02	11.74	0.30	117.64
1963	21.53	19.38	4.32	15.06	5.00	129.31
1964	29.03	26.12	5.09	21.03	6.00	144.18
1965	35.01	31.51	6.01	25.50	11.20	162.92
1966	40.68	36.61	6.54	30.07	16.30	182.73
1967	32.37	29.13	6.21	22.92	10.20	170.77
1968	30.02	27.02	6.03	20.99	13.20	170.87
1969	40.69	36.62	6.78	29.84	7.90	185.77
1970	54.59	49.13	7.88	41.25	19.90	220.70
1971	60.30	54.27	8.49	45.78	21.60	239.25
1972	62.21	55.99	8.81	47.18	16.90	245.38
1973	66.45	59.81	9.52	50.29	23.90	266.96
1974	74.81	67.33	9.76	57.57	18.80	273.87
1975	88.03	79.33	10.49	68.74	18.20	295.04
1976	86.51	77.86	10.30	67.56	12.50	296.83
1977	91.11	82.00	11.21	70.79	18.70	316.60
1978	107.39	96.65	23.56	73.09	30.40	360.56
1979	115.31	103.78	26.25	77.55	32.58	409.26
1980	132.24	119.02	29.59	93.43	27.73	459.29
1981	133.93	120.54	29.58	90.96	29.09	500.88
1982	150.32	135.29	35.71	99.58	28.10	559.00
1983	172.23	155.01	41.61	113.40	31.57	621.62
1984	214.70	193.23	46.56	146.67	36.81	736.27
1985	267.20	240.48	64.16	176.32	78.55	907.67
1986	313.97	282.57	72.94	209.63	80.22	1 050.85
1987	379.87	341.88	87.21	254.67	66.33	1 227.74
1988	471.19	424.07	106.70	317.37	99.83	1 538.86
1989	441.94	397.75	106.80	290.95	191.33	1 731.13
1990	482.78	434.50	116.40	318.10	191.82	1 934.78
1991	607.03	546.33	141.70	404.63	179.77	2 257.74
1992	851.37	766.23	171.70	594.63	157.26	2 756.52
1993	1 330.92	1 197.83	132.31	1 065.52	240.85	3 693.81
1994	1 731.27	1 558.14	255.40	1 302.74	302.84	5 021.74
1995	2 088.50	1 879.65	314.90	1 564.75	458.51	6 321.69
1996	2 404.81	2 164.33	321.64	1 842.69	473.68	7 416.36
1997	2 596.50	2 336.85	317.84	2 019.01	400.30	8 165.85
1998	2 856.90	2 571.21	361.42	2 209.79	274.52	8 653.16
1999	3 052.73	2 747.46	410.32	2 337.14	242.42	9 096.41
2000	3 384.44	3 046.00	498.41	2 547.59	99.84	9 874.90
2001	3 775.45	3 397.91	634.41	2 763.50	201.49	10 897.24
2002	4 363.21	3 926.89	779.09	3 147.89	193.29	12 035.03
2003	5 349.07	4 814.16	1 015.38	3 798.78	247.23	13 639.88

Source: First column, gross fixed capital formation, 1952-78 from Hitotsubashi (1997, p.84). 1979-2003 from NBS, *China Statistical Yearbook* (2006, p. 69). The figures differ slightly from those for 1995-2003 given in the same Yearbook, p. 188. In the second column above, the official fixed capital estimates are adjusted downwards by 10 per cent to remove military investment and repairs (which would not be included in Western national accounts). Housing investment for 1981-94 from *China Statistical Yearbooks* (1998, p. 493; 1993, p. 117; 1995 p. 147; 1996, p. 139); 1995-2003 from 2006 Yearbook, p. 188; for 1952-1980, it was necessary to make a rough assessment of housing investment. On the basis of information in the *Statistical Yearbook for China*, 1984, pp. 304 and 331 and Chao (1974, pp. 105 and 111), I assumed that housing investment was about 3.5 per cent of GDP for 1952-77 and rose to 6.5 per cent for 1978-80 (similar to the proportion in the 1980s). Column 4 on non-residential fixed investment is the difference between columns 2 and 3. Inventories 1952-78 from Hitotsubashi (1974, p. 84); 1978-2003 from 2006 Yearbook, p. 69. Official estimate of GDP from the expenditure side, 1952-77 from Hitotsubashi (1974, p. 59), 1978-2003 from the 2006 Yearbook, p. 68.

http://dx.doi.org/10.1787/087138036615

Table C.8. **Gross Non-Residential Fixed Investment, Annual Capital Formation and Gross Fixed Non-Residential Capital Stock, China 1952-2003**

	Investment rate % of GDP	Increment to capital stock	Capital stock end-year		Investment rate % of GDP	Increment to capital stock	Capital stock end-year
		(million 1987 yuan)				(million 1987 yuan)	
1952	7.05	15 107	254 000	1978	20.27	132 795	1 756 133
1953	8.99	20 220		1979	18.95	133 721	1 864 277
1954	11.01	25 575		1980	20.34	148 368	1 986 645
1955	10.60	26 000		1981	18.16	140 385	2 085 100
1956	15.63	41 929		1982	17.81	148 037	2 199 397
1957	11.88	33 741		1983	18.24	164 473	2 299 414
1958	20.40	64 456		1984	19.92	201 983	2 425 961
1959	23.54	75 436		1985	19.43	217 357	2 566 418
1960	24.85	76 900		1986	19.95	238 126	2 772 033
1961	12.71	32 511		1987	20.74	273 618	3 020 027
1962	9.98	25 624		1988	20.62	291 187	3 278 339
1963	11.65	32 875		1989	16.81	241 673	3 473 981
1964	14.59	46 031		1990	16.44	244 628	3 663 592
1965	15.65	55 017		1991	17.92	284 220	3 884 519
1966	16.46	63 293		1992	21.57	410 182	4 244 549
1967	13.42	50 152		1993	28.85	550 664	4 750 240
1968	12.28	44 973		1994	25.94	544 684	5 231 065
1969	16.06	63 859		1995	24.75	598 252	5 743 913
1970	18.69	85 404		1996	24.85	613 040	6 267 336
1971	19.13	89 617		1997	24.73	642 221	6 816 839
1973	19.23	92 718		1998	25.53	664 911	7 384 202
1976	18.83	97 548		1999	25.93	719 672	7 993 139
1974	21.02	110 735		2000	25.80	780 758	8 643 592
1975	23.30	130 325		2001	25.36	849 432	9 366 462
1976	22.76	126 542		2002	26.16	984 955	10 219 34
1977	22.36	132 077	1 643 558	2003	27.85	1 207 343	11 293 88

Source: Gross non–residential investment ratios in current prices are derived from the fourth and sixth columns of Table C.7. Annual capital formation is the increment in the non–residential capital stock derived by applying the ratios to the estimates of GDP in 1987 prices in the penultimate column of Table C.3. The end–year capital stock is derived by the perpetual inventory method, assuming a 25–year asset life, a uniform retirement pattern, and zero valuation of scrapped assets (see Maddison, 1995, pp. 137–166 for a detailed application of this method). The initial stock of 254 billion yuan in 1952 was estimated by conjecture. It is in principle the sum of capital accumulated in the 25 years 1928–52, but we have estimates of the GDP level for only 13 of these years (1929–38 and 1950–52), and limited information on the investment level in this period. I assumed the average GDP level in 1939–49 was 70 per cent of that in 1938, that the investment ratio was 7.5 per cent of GDP in 1928–38 and 1950–51, and 3 per cent of GDP (after allowing for war damage) in the years 1939–49 (the 7.5 per cent estimate is midway between that of Rawski, 1989, p. 260 and Liu and Yeh, 1965, pp. 66 and 228). The capital stock in 1977 is the cumulated total of investments in 1953–77; for 1978 it is the cumulative total for 1954–78. The capital stock for 2003 is the cumulative total of investment in 1979–2003.

http://dx.doi.org/10.1787/087180145300

ISBN: 978-92-64-03762-5 © OECD 2007

Appendix D

Population and Employment

Population of China

Chinese population records are more abundant and cover a longer period than those for other parts of the world. This is largely due to the bureaucratic mode of governance and its reliance on various kinds of land and poll tax, which required registration of population and land area.

The nature of the population records varied according to administrative and fiscal needs, sometimes covering households, sometimes persons and sometimes adult males. Bielenstein (1987) provides a masterly survey of the source material for the past 2 000 years. Ho (1959) gives an excellent account of the problems of comparability for the Ming and Ch'ing dynasties.

It is useful to start with the first century AD to get a point of comparison with estimates for Europe when the Roman Empire was at its peak (and for which we have the estimates of Beloch, 1886). For four different points in the first century, Bielenstein (1987, p. 12) gives very different figures; I took his estimates for 2 AD. Population in 960 is the figure given by Durand (1974, p. 15) for the early Sung. I took population in the year 1280 (the end of the Sung) to have been 100 million as suggested by Ho (1959) p. 265.

For 1380 to 1930, Liu and Hwang (1979) provide estimates at ten year intervals, which they derived from Perkins (1969, pp. 192–216). They do not indicate clearly how they filled the gaps, as Perkins gave a range of probability only for eleven benchmark years (p. 216). For some of their decade intervals, the figures of Liu and Hwang are implausible (e.g. a 45 per cent increase over the ten years 1730–40). I smoothed their estimates to eliminate implausible upward leaps of 20 per cent or more per decade. Table D.1 indicates (with an asterisk) the cases in which I modified their estimates. For 1933, I used Perkins (1969, p. 216). Thereafter from Maddison (1995a) and official figures published in the NBS, *Statistical Yearbooks*, adjusted to a mid–year basis. The projections to 2030 are from the US Bureau of the Census.

There are no reliable figures for birth and death rates or life expectancy in traditional China. Liu and Hwang speculate that the birth rate remained "quite steady" from 37 to 42 per thousand from 1380 to the 1950s, with death rates fluctuating widely from 26 to 41 per thousand. The NBS shows a birth rate of 37 per thousand in 1952 falling to 18.3 in 1978 and 12.4 in 2003. The big fall in birth rates came in the 1970s. Death rates in 1952 were 17 per thousand, had fallen to 6.3 in 1978 and

ISBN: 978-92-64-03762-5 © OECD 2007

were 6.4 in 2003. In 2003, 23 per cent of the population were aged 0–14, 69.6 per cent aged 15–64 and 7.4 per cent were 65 or older. The 2003 proportion of working age was higher than in Western Europe and the United States. The ratio of males to total population was 51.9 per cent in 1952 and 51.5 per cent in 1978 and 2003. This is unusual as most countries have fewer males than females as women have a longer life expectancy. The Chinese sex ratio suggests that there is some female infanticide or selective abortion.

Population of Macao, Hong Kong and Taiwan

As Hong Kong was re–incorporated into China on 1 July 1997, Macao in 1999 and Taiwan may also return at some time in the future, estimates for these areas are shown in Table D.2.

Employment

Estimates of employment for 1952–2003 are shown in Table D.3. The official figures excluded the military until 1992, so I added 3 million to the official figure for the "non–productive" sector for the years 1952–1992 (see Table C.6). I also adjusted the figures from an end–year to a midyear basis. For years before 1978 the official sources were very aggregative. They provided a 4–sector breakdown, showing employment in: a) the primary sector, i.e. farming, forestry, fishery and sideline activities (hunting, gathering and household handicrafts); b) the secondary sector, i.e. mining, manufacturing, utilities and construction; and c) the tertiary sector (services). There was a further two–way split within the tertiary sector, showing employment in "material production" and "non–material production". This classification is the labour counterpart to the Soviet material product concepts previously used in Chinese national accounts. The "material production" sector included transport and communications (except passenger services), commerce and restaurants, geological prospecting and water conservancy management. The "non–material" sector included other services. In the Soviet–Chinese classification system, repair and maintenance activities were treated as industrial rather than service activity and lumbering was also treated as an industrial activity. Table D.3 provides a consistent series using the old 4–sector classification for the whole period 1952–2003. Since 1978, employment figures are available in more disaggregated form for total employment and for employment in state enterprises. These more detailed figures are shown in Tables D.4a and D.4b.

The 4–sector breakdown in Table D.3 is the best we can do if we want a consistent picture for the whole period. The estimates for 1952–78 were derived from NBS, *Statistical Yearbook of China* (1993, Chinese version), pp. 100–101. For 1978–2002, much more detail was available for sixteen branches and the total coverage was consistent with the earlier estimates. In Table D.3 they are aggregated into four sectors for the whole period.

The 16–branch breakdown included a consolidated estimate for agriculture, forestry, animal husbandry and fisheries; four separate components for the secondary sector–mining, manufacturing, construction and utilities (gas, water and electricity); three components for "material" services–transport and communications, wholesale and retail trade and geological prospecting; and eight components for "non–material" activity. For 1978–85 estimates were derived from the 1994 Yearbook, p. 68; 1985–89 from the 2000 Yearbook, pp. 120–121, 1989–2002 from the 2006 Yearbook, p. 130.

An Important Incongruity in the Official Estimates of Employment

Until 1997, the NBS Yearbooks provided, in addition to the 16–branch breakdown, more aggregative employment estimates for three sectors, primary, secondary and tertiary. The figure for total employment was the same in the two tables.

In Yearbooks from 1997 onwards, there has been a discrepancy between the two tables. Total employment in the 3–sector table is much bigger than for the 16 sectors. In the 2006 Yearbook (pp. 128 and 130), the 3–sector total shown for 1990 (end–year) was 647.5 million and the actual total for the 16 sectors was 567.4 million. Hence a discrepancy of 80.1 million. For 2002, the discrepancy had risen to 99.6 million. Instead of explaining the discrepancy, the Yearbooks disguised it by showing the same "total" for the 16–sector breakdown as for the three sector aggregate.

The 16–sector series continues to be published, but the figures stop at the year 2002 in the last four Yearbooks. It would seem that the 3–sector breakdown is derived from the sample population census (see Yue, 2005) and the 16–sector breakdown from labour force statistics, but users of the employment figures are entitled to a detailed explanation or reconciliation of the two types of estimate. They are also entitled to know why the 16–sector breakdown has been discontinued. In the present situation, meaningful measurement of labour productivity is no longer possible.

Table D.5 shows the Liu and Yeh (1965) figures for 1933–57. They present a detailed and fully documented breakdown of employment which is a useful crosscheck on the more aggregative official figures. They also present a very detailed reconciliation (p. 209) of their figures with the official figures which were then available. They made three points about under–coverage of the official figures for the 1950s, which still seem valid (p. 208): "First a significant number of handicraftsmen, old fashioned transportation workers, peddlers and people in personal services and work brigades have been left out of the Communist total. Second, the Communist total figures include neither the employees in the private financial enterprises nor the temporary workers in construction". Third, the official statistics on employment excluded the military. Another reason for the higher estimates of Liu and Yeh is that their age cut–off was lower than that of SSB. They included people 7 years and older in agriculture, 12 and over in non–agriculture (pp. 86–7). Assuming that these SSB cut–offs were actually applied in the 1950s and that life expectancy was then 45 years, one can apply a rough adjustment coefficient (.86) to the Liu and Yeh estimates to get some clue as to the extent and location of official understatement. It seems clear from Table D.6 that the official figures substantially understate 1952–57 employment in traditional transport and commerce.

ISBN: 978-92-64-03762-5 © OECD 2007

Table D.1. **Chinese Population, 1–2030 AD**
(000s at mid–year)

1	59 595	1690	144 000	1940	518 770	1982	1 000 281
960	55 000	1700	138 000	1945	532 607	1983	1 023 288
1280	100 000	1710	156 600*	1950	546 815	1984	1 036 825
1380	68 000	1720	177 800*	1952	568 910	1985	1 051 040
1390	69 000	1730	201 800*	1953	581 390	1986	1 066 790
1400	72 000	1740	229 050*	1954	595 310	1987	1 084 035
1410	71 000	1750	260 000	1955	608 655	1988	1 101 630
1420	73 000	1760	274 600*	1956	621 465	1989	1 118 650
1430	77 000	1770	290 000*	1957	637 408	1990	1 135 185
1440	82 000	1780	306 250*	1958	653 235	1991	1 150 780
1450	88 000	1790	323 450*	1959	666 005	1992	1 164 970
1460	93 000	1800	341 600*	1960	667 070	1993	1 178 440
1470	104 000*	1810	360 750*	1961	660 330	1994	1 191 835
1480	116 000	1820	381 000	1962	665 770	1995	1 204 855
1490	98 000	1830	409 000	1963	682 335	1996	1 217 550
1500	103 000	1840	412 000	1964	698 355	1997	1 230 075
1510	117 000*	1850	412 000	1965	715 185	1998	1 241 935
1520	133 000	1860	377 000	1966	735 400	1999	1 252 735
1530	139 000	1870	358 000	1967	754 550	2000	1 262 645
1540	144 000	1880	368 000	1968	774 510	2001	1 271 850
1550	146 000	1890	380 000	1969	796 025	2002	1 280 400
1560	151 000	1895	390 000	1970	818 315	2003	1 288 400
1570	155 000	1900	400 000	1971	841 105	2004	1 295 734
1580	162 000	1910	423 000	1972	862 030	2005	1 303 182
1590	162 000	1913	437 140	1973	881 940	2006	1 310 824
1600	160 000	1915	446 829	1974	900 350	2007	1 318 683
1610	153 000	1920	472 000	1975	916 395	2008	1 326 856
1620	145 000	1925	480 425	1976	930 685		
1630	138 000	1929	487 273	1977	943 455		
1640	130 000	1930	489 000	1978	956 165	2030	1 458 024
1650	123 000	1933	500 000	1979	969 005		
1660	135 000*	1935	505 292	1980	981 235		
1670	148 000	1936	507 959	1981	993 861		
1680	126 000						

* Indicates where I modified Liu and Hwang to eliminate implausible leaps in their figures, i.e. growth rates more than 20 per cent per decade (see text). Their figures were 1470, 112 000; 1510, 124 000; 1660, 152 000; 1710, 149 000; 1720, 154 000; 1730, 151 000; 1740, 219 000; 1760, 268 000; 1770, 272 000; 1780, 342 000; 1790, 359 000; 1800, 340 000; 1810, 385 000.

Sources: see text above.

http://dx.doi.org/10.1787/087205141680

Table D.2. **Population of Macao, Hong Kong and Taiwan, 1850–2030**
(000s at mid–year)

	Macao	Hong Kong	Taiwan
1850		33	2 000
1870		123	2 000
1890		214	2 500
1900		306	2 864
1913		487	3 469
1920		606	3 736
1929		785	4 493
1936		988	5 384
1938		1 479	5 678
1950	160	2 237	7 882
1952	157	2 126	8 541
1960	143	3 075	11 155
1965	238	3 598	12 928
1970	208	3 959	14 565
1978	246	4 670	17 112
1980	256	5 063	17 848
1990	352	5 688	20 279
1992	375	5 830	20 687
1994	393	6 067	21 088
1995	401	6 225	21 283
1996	411	6 392	21 449
1997	417	6 496	21 629
1998	422	6 545	21 823
1999	428	6 599	21 993
2000	431	6 659	22 151
2001	434	6 713	22 304
2002	438	6 762	22 454
2003	441	6 810	22 603
2004	445	6 855	22 750
2005	449	6 899	22 894
2006	453	6 940	23 036
2007	457	6 980	23 174
2008	461	7 019	23 308
2030	524	7 294	24 678

Source: Hong Kong, 1850–1920 derived from Mitchell (1982), p. 43, 1929–38 from UN, *Demographic Yearbook 1960,* New York, 1960, 1950–78 from OECD Development Centre and Hong Kong Monetary Authority. Taiwan 1850–95 derived from Ho (1978), 1900-78 from Maddison (1995a), updated from Asian Development Bank (1997). Macao from OECD Development Centre, and SSB, *China Statistical Yearbook,* 1997. 1980 onwards for all three countries from US Bureau of the Census (see www.ggdc.net/Maddison).

http://dx.doi.org/10.1787/087207878566

      ISBN: 978-92-64-03762-5 © OECD 2007

Table D.3. **Employment by Sector, Old Classification, China 1952–2003**
(000s at mid–year)

	Farming Forestry Fishery & Sidelines	Industry and Construction	"Material" Services	"Non–Material" Services	Total
1952	171 070	14 479	11 684	10 023	207 256
1953	175 300	16 175	11 630	10 365	213 470
1954	179 455	17 895	11 055	10 580	218 985
1955	183 660	18 815	10 571	10 754	223 800
1956	185 600	21 675	10 767	11 688	229 730
1957	189 175	22 795	11 776	13 194	236 940
1958	173 900	45 745	14 305	20 905	254 855
1959	158 685	61 970	15 595	30 615	266 865
1960	166 265	47 095	15 390	34 515	263 265
1961	183 625	34 385	14 445	27 900	260 355
1962	204 940	24 255	12 860	18 450	260 505
1963	216 035	20 215	12 415	17 085	265 750
1964	223 630	20 820	12 590	17 840	274 880
1965	230 750	22 650	12 850	18 780	285 030
1966	238 225	24 715	13 130	19 305	295 375
1967	247 070	25 965	13 525	19 535	306 095
1968	255 895	26 665	14 150	19 935	316 645
1969	265 650	28 495	14 455	20 100	328 700
1970	274 390	32 355	14 560	19 980	341 285
1971	280 755	37 100	15 205	20 205	353 265
1972	283 065	40 830	15 745	20 735	360 375
1973	285 340	43 305	15 820	21 065	365 530
1974	290 000	45 410	16 200	21 495	373 105
1975	292 975	48 605	17 170	21 935	380 685
1976	294 065	53 020	18 220	22 705	388 010
1977	293 460	56 325	19 255	25 045	394 085
1978	288 060	63 405	20 220	28 965	400 650
1979	284 760	70 795	21 330	32 005	408 890
1980	288 780	74 605	22 770	33 775	419 930
1981	294 495	78 550	24 395	35 990	433 430
1982	303 180	81 745	25 840	37 335	448 100
1983	310 050	85 125	27 530	38 945	461 650
1984	310 095	91 345	30 870	43 845	476 155
1985	309 990	99 870	35 475	48 015	493 350
1986	311 920	108 000	38 840	50 010	508 770
1987	314 585	114 710	41 075	52 955	523 325
1988	319 560	119 390	43 485	56 170	538 605
1989	327 370	120 640	44 795	59 835	552 640
1990	336 710	120 490	45 120	60 685	563 005
1991	345 365	122 755	46 735	63 300	578 155
1992	348 755	126 540	49 495	67 175	591 965
1993	343 805	131 980	51 880	70 610	598 275
1994	336 760	137 395	55 825	78 240	608 220
1995	332 020	141 385	61 215	84 435	619 055
1996	329 640	143 305	65 110	88 100	626 155
1997	330 025	142 790	68 195	91 535	632 545
1998	331 635	134 310	68 735	95 470	630 150
1999	333 625	125 615	68 225	96 805	624 270
2000	334 240	124 745	68 545	99 816	627 346
2001	331 645	125 385	68 520	104 605	630 155
2002	327 305	128 245	70 150	108 460	634 160
2003	327 421	127 417	72 074	113 370	640 282

Source: 1952–77 end–year estimates from SSB, *China Statistical Yearbook 1993*, pp. 100-101; 1978–84 from 1994 *Yearbook*, p. 68; 1985–89 from 2000 *Yearbook*, pp. 120-121, 1989-2002 from the 2006 Yearbook, p. 130. Figures for 1952–77 are available only in the four-way breakdown shown above. The 1978-2002 figures are disaggregated into 16 branches, but this breakdown is not available for 2003. The figures for 2003 in the table are rough estimates derived from the three-way breakdown available for that year.. All figures are adjusted here from end–year to mid–year. No figures were available for 1951, but in order to calculate mid–year 1952, I assumed the end–year 1951–52 movement was the same proportionately in each branch as that for 1952-3. Before 1993, military personnel were excluded from the official statistics; I added 3 million each year for military personnel in "non–material" services.

http://dx.doi.org/10.1787/087218480026

Table D.4a. **Employment by Sector, New Classification, China 1978–2002**
(000s at end–year)

	1978	1995	2002
Farming, Forestry and Fishery	283 180	330 180	324 870
Mining and Quarrying	6 520	9 320	5 580
Manufacturing	53 320	98 030	83 070
Utilities	1 070	2 580	2 900
Geological Prospecting	1 780	1 350	980
Construction	8 540	33 220	38 930
Transport and Communication	7 500	19 420	20 840
Trade and Restaurants	11 400	42 920	49 690
Other Services	31 220	86 870	110 930
Total	404 520	625 870	637 790

Source: China Statistical Yearbook, 2006, p. 130. The military were not included in other services in 1978, I added 3 million for them in that year. Unfortunately, estimates showing this breakdown of employment were discontinued after 2002.
http://dx.doi.org/10.1787/087226854105

Table D.4b. **State Employment by Sector, New Classification, China 1978–2005**
(000s at end–year)

	1978	1995	2005*
Farming, Forestry & Fishery	7 740	6 340	3 927
Mining and Quarrying	5 888	8 340	2 357
Manufacturing	24 490	33 260	5 990
Utilities	1 020	2 370	2 057
Geological Prospecting	1 770	1 320	1 797*
Construction	4 470	6 050	2 503
Transport and Communication	4 650	6 770	4 218
Trade and Restaurants	9 070	10 610	2 044
Other Services	18 420	34 510	37 427
Total	77 510	109 550	62 320

*   includes scientific research.
Source: China Statistical Yearbook 1997, pp. 108–9 for 1978 and 1995; 2006 Yearbook, pp. 140-141 for 2005. The military were not included in 1978, I added 3 million for them in that year.
http://dx.doi.org/10.1787/087226854105

ISBN: 978-92-64-03762-5 © OECD 2007

Table D.5. **Liu and Yeh Estimates of Employment by Sector, 1933–57**
(000s)

	1933	1952	1953	1954	1955	1956	1957
Agriculture	204 910	199 890	203 590	208 260	210 760	214 890	215 760
Industry & Construction	19 230	18 330	19 970	21 290	20 950	21 030	22 410
of which:							
Factories, Mines Utilities	1 940	3 540	4 120	4 200	4 400	4 810	5 500
Handicrafts	15 750	13 500	14 030	15 190	14 560	13 780	14 510
Construction	1 550	1 290	1 820	1 900	1 950	2 440	2 400
Transport & Commerce	26 180	25 220	24 650	22 480	21 710	22 420	22 830
of which:							
Modern Transport & Comm.	440	730	790	960	1 130	1 320	1 430
Traditional Transport	10 860	10 900	10 080	9 670	9 630	10 200	10 000
Trade	7 490	5 140	5 040	4 390	4 160	4 510	5 010
Restaurants		1 450	1 400	1 400	1 400	1 350	1 350
Pedlars	7 390	7 000	7 340	6 060	5 390	5 040	5 040
Other Services	8 890	11 760	12 420	12 740	12 830	13 070	13 390
of which:							
Civil Govt.	5 120	3 960	4 160	4 360	4 550	4 900	5 070
Military	n.a.	3 000	3 000	3 000	3 000	3 000	3 000
Party & Other	n.a.	630	1 070	1 180	1 070	1 120	1 240
Finance	140	540	590	620	660	700	750
Personal Services	3 630	3 630	3 600	3 580	3 550	3 350	3 330
Work Brigades	0	4 080	2 520	2 880	4 920	5 310	5 560
Total	259 210	259 280	263 160	267 650	271 170	276 720	279 950

Source: Liu and Yeh (1965), p. 69 gives their aggregated results, pp. 181–212 contain more detailed figures and analyse their sources in detail. The breakdown for commerce is on p. 200, for other services on pp. 204 and 206.

http://dx.doi.org/10.1787/088478112268

Table D.6. **A Comparison of SSB and Adjusted Liu–Yeh Estimates of Chinese Employment, 1952–57**
(000s)

	1952	1953	1954	1955	1956	1957
Agriculture SSB	171 070	175 300	179 455	183 660	185 600	189 175
adjusted Liu–Yeh	175 905	179 159	179 104	181 254	184 805	185 554
Industry and Construction SSB	14 479	16 175	17 895	18 815	21 675	22 795
adjusted Liu–Yeh	16 130	17 574	18 735	18 436	18 506	19 721
Transport and Commerce SSB	11 684	11 630	11 055	10 571	10 767	11 776
adjusted Liu–Yeh	22 194	21 692	19 782	19 105	19 730	20 090
Other Services SSB	10 023	10 365	10 580	10 754	11 688	13 194
adjusted Liu–Yeh	10 349	10 930	11 211	11 290	11 502	11 783

Source: Table D.3 for SSB, Table D.5 for Liu and Yeh, adjusted by a coefficient of .86 to correct for the lower age cut–off in the Liu–Yeh estimates.

http://dx.doi.org/10.1787/087238324270

Appendix E

Foreign Trade

Table E.1. **Value of Chinese Merchandise Trade 1850–1938**
(million US dollars at current exchange rates)

	Exports of China		Imports of China		Exports of Taiwan	Imports of Taiwan
1850	50		n.a.			
1860	76		n.a.			
1870	102		89			
1880	125		96			
1890	126		139			
1900	132	of which	139	of which	8	11
1913	299	Manchuria	416	Manchuria	26	30
1929	660	210	810	147	129	94
1933	259	98	466	113	64	48
1934	302	121	518	169	91	64
1935	314	107	510	172	101	76
1936	348	137	467	187	113	85
1937	399	153	524	244	127	93
1938	324	170	607	346	125	102

Source: China and Manchuria 1850–60 from W.A. Lewis in Grassman and Lundberg (1981); 1870–1913 from Hsiao (1974); 1929–38 from League of Nations *Reviews of World Trade*, various issues. Taiwan 1913–38 from League of Nations, as above. 1900 from Ho (1978), p. 391.

http://dx.doi.org/10.1787/088480662076

ISBN: 978-92-64-03762-5 © OECD 2007

Table E.2. **Merchandise Trade of China, Taiwan and Hong Kong, 1950–2006**
(million US dollars at current exchange rates)

	China Exports	Taiwan Exports	Hong Kong Exports	China Imports	Taiwan Imports	Hong Kong Imports
1950	550		657	580		665
1952	820		510	1 120		663
1957	1 600	148	529	1 500	212	901
1958	1 980	157	524	1 890	826	804
1959	2 260	231	574	2 120	340	866
1960	1 860	164	689	1 950	264	1 026
1961	1 490	199	688	1 450	317	1 045
1962	1 490	228	768	1 170	341	1 165
1963	1 650	332	873	1 270	363	1 297
1964	1 920	434	1 012	1 550	430	1 496
1965	2 230	450	1 143	2 020	557	1 569
1966	2 370	537	1 324	2 250	622	1 767
1967	2 140	641	1 527	2 020	808	1 818
1968	2 100	802	1 744	1 950	906	2 058
1969	2 200	1 049	2 177	1 830	1 216	2 458
1970	2 260	1 428	2 515	2 330	1 528	2 905
1971	2 640	1 998	2 875	2 200	1 849	3 391
1972	3 440	2 914	3 436	2 860	2 518	3 856
1973	5 820	4 383	5 071	5 160	3 801	5 655
1974	6 950	5 518	5 968	7 620	6 983	6 778
1975	7 260	5 302	6 026	7 490	5 959	6 766
1976	6 850	8 155	8 484	6 580	7 609	8 838
1977	7 590	9 349	9 616	7 210	8 522	10 446
1978	9 750	12 682	11 453	10 890	11 051	13 394
1979	13 660	16 081	15 140	15 670	14 793	17 127
1980	18 120	19 786	19 752	20 020	19 764	22 447
1981	22 010	22 502	21 827	22 020	21 153	24 797
1982	22 320	22 075	21 006	19 290	18 827	23 475
1983	22 230	25 086	21 959	21 390	20 308	24 017
1984	26 140	30 439	23 323	27 410	22 002	28 568
1985	27 350	30 696	30 187	42 250	20 124	29 703
1986	30 940	39 644	35 439	42 900	24 230	35 367
1987	39 440	53 483	48 476	43 220	34 802	48 465
1988	47 520	60 493	63 163	55 280	49 763	63 896
1989	52 540	66 085	73 140	59 140	52 507	72 155
1990	62 090	67 142	82 160	53 350	54 830	82 474
1991	71 840	76 115	98 577	63 790	63 078	100 240
1992	84 940	81 395	119 512	80 590	72 181	123 407
1993	91 740	84 678	135 244	103 960	77 099	138 650
1994	121 010	92 847	151 399	115 610	85 507	161 841
1995	148 780	122 000	173 750	132 080	103 560	192 751
1996	151 050	116 000	180 750	138 830	102 528	198 550
1997	182 790	122 000	188 059	142 370	114 000	208 614
1998	183 710	111 000	174 002	140 240	105 000	184 518
1999	194 930	122 000	173 885	165 700	111 000	179 520
2000	249 200	148 000	201 860	225 090	140 000	212 805
2001	266 100	123 000	189 894	243 550	107 000	201 076
2002	325 600	130 600	200 092	295 170	112 500	207 644
2003	438 230	144 200	223 762	412 760	127 200	231 896
2004	593 320	174 000	259 000	561 230	167 900	271 000
2005	761 950	198 400	289 000	659 950	182 600	300 000
2006	969 000	224 000	317 000	672 000	203 000	335 000

Source: Maddison (1998), p. 176; updated from *China Statistical Yearbook* and IMF, *International Financial Statistics.*
http://dx.doi.org/10.1787/087238742425

Table E.3. **Exchange Rates, 1870–2005**
(US cents per unit of Chinese currency)

Year	Rate	Year	Rate
1870	159	1978	59.4
1880	138	1979	64.3
1890	127	1980	66.7
1895	80	1981	58.7
1900	75	1982	52.8
1905	73	1983	50.6
1913	73	1984	43.0
1929	64	1985	34.1
1932	34	1986	29.0
1933	26	1987	26.9
1934	34	1988	26.9
1935	36	1989	26.6
1936	30	1990	20.9
1937	29	1991	18.8
1938	21	1992	18.1
1939	11	1993	17.4
1940	6	1994	11.6
1941	5	1995	12.0
1942	n.a.	1996	12.0
1943	1.7	1997	12.0
1944	0.5	1998	12.0
1945	0.06	1999	12.0
1946	0.05	2000	12.0
1947	0.008	2001	12.0
1948 (August)	0.00001	2002	12.0
1952	44.2	2003	12.0
1957	40.6	2004	12.0
1970	40.6	2005	12.21

Source: 1870–1941 from Hsiao (1974), pp. 190–2, 1943–48 from Chang (1958). The Chinese currency was the Haekwan tael for 1870–1932, the Chinese dollar (yuan) for 1933–41. 1952–57 from Lardy (1992), p. 148, 1970–85 from IMF, *International Financial Statistics*, 1996–2005 from *China Statistical Yearbook*, 2006, p. 734.

http://dx.doi.org/10.1787/088503643713

 ISBN: 978-92-64-03762-5 © OECD 2007

Table E.4. **Volume of Chinese Exports, 1867–2003**
(1913 = 100)

1867	31.9
1870	33.3
1880	47.2
1890	42.0
1900	54.9
1913	100.0
1929	149.2
1932	100.8
1933	124.7
1934	118.6
1935	126.7
1936	125.6
1950	151.0
1952	192.1
1973	278.3
1978	372.6
1990	1 479.6
2003	10 812.1

Source: 1867–1936 Nankai volume indices from Hsiao (1974), pp. 274–5; 1870-2003 from Maddison (2001) p. 361, updated in Maddison (2007) chapter 3 from IMF, *International Financial Statistics.*
http://dx.doi.org/10.1787/088510301888

Appendix F

People and Places in Pinyin and Wade–Giles

This book uses the Wade–Giles system for alphabetisation of Chinese characters. This was invented by Sir Thomas Wade in 1859 and slightly modified by H.A. Giles in 1912. It is used in the *Cambridge History of China* and in Needham's encyclopaedic work on *Science and Civilisation in China* as well as in many of the historical works I have cited. In 1958 the Chinese government approved a new system called *pinyin zimu* (phonetic alphabet), and, in 1975, the State Council directed that Pinyin be the standard form of romanisation. As it is not always easy to find a Pinyin version of names from the past, Tables F.1 and F.2 compare Pinyin and Wade–Giles versions of some significant Chinese names.

 ISBN: 978-92-64-03762-5 © OECD 2007

Table F.1. **Chinese Rulers; 1368–2007**

	Pinyin	Wade–Giles
	Emperors' Reign Names[a]	
	Ming Dynasty	Ming Dynasty
1368–99	Hongwu	Hung–wu
1399–1402	Jianwen	Chien–wen
1403–25	Yongle	Yung–lo
1425–26	Hongxi	Hung–hsi
1426–36	Xuande	Hsüan–te
1436–49	Zhentong	Cheng–t'ung
1450–57	Jingtai	Ching–t'ai
1457–65	Tianshun	T'ien–shun
1465–88	Chenghua	Ch'eng–hua
1488–1506	Hongzhi	Hung–chih
1506–22	Zhengde	Cheng–te
1522–67	Jiajing	Chia–ching
1567–73	Longqing	Lung–ch'ing
1573–1620	Wanli	Wan–li
1620–21	Taichang	T'ai–ch'ang
1621–27	Tianqi	T'ien–ch'i
1628–44	Chongzhen	Ch'ung–chen
	Qing Dynasty	Ch'ing Dynasty
1644–61	Shunzhi	Shun–chih
1662–1722	Kangxi	K'ang–hsi
1723–35	Yongzhen	Yung–cheng
1736–96	Qianlong	Ch'ien–lung
1796–1820	Jiaqing	Chia–ch'ing
1821–50	Daoguang	Tao–kuang
1851–61	Xianfeng	Hsien–feng
1862–74	Tongzhi	T'ung–chih
1875–1908	Guangxu	Kuang–hsü
1909–11	Xuantong[b]	Hsüan–t'–ung
	Dowager Empress[c]	
1861–1908	Cixi	Tz'u–hsi
	Republic of China	
1912–16	Yuan Shikai	Yüan shih–kai
1916–28	various warlords	various warlords
1928–49	Jiang Jieshi	Chiang kai–shek
	People's Republic of China	
1949–76	Mao Zedong	Mao tse–tung
1976–77	Gang of Four	Gang of Four
1978–97	Deng Xiaoping	Teng tsiao–ping
1997–2003	Jiang Zemin	Chiang Tse–min
2003–	Hu Jintao	Hu Chin–t'ao

a.   Chinese emperors had personal names, reign names, and posthumous temple names. The reign name was used until the end of the lunar year following the emperor's death. Ch'ing dynasty emperors also had Manchu names, e.g. the K'ang–hsi Emperor's Manchu name was Elhe taifin.
b.   Better known by his personal name P'u–i (Henry, or Aisin Gioro, or Puyi). He ceased to be Emperor in 1912 and died in 1967. He was installed by the Japanese in 1934 as puppet Emperor of Manchukuo (Manchuria), with the reign title K'ang–te.
c.   Dowager Empress, consort of Hsien–feng, mother of T'ung chih, aunt of Kuang–hsü, and great aunt of Hsüan–t'ung.

http://dx.doi.org/10.1787/088613118240

Table F.2. **Characteristics of China's 31 Provinces in 2005***

Pinyin	Population (000s)	Gross Regional Product (million yuan)	GDP Per Capita) (yuan)	Wade–Giles
Beijing	15 360	688 631	44 843	Peking
Tianjin	10 430	379 762	35 452	Tientsin
Shanghai	17 780	915 418	51 486	Shanghai
Hebei	68 440	1 009 611	14 752	Hopei
Shanxi	33 520	417 952	12 469	Shansi
Nei Monggol	23 860	389 555	16 327	Inner Mongolia
Liaoning	42 200	800 901	18 979	Liaoning
Jilin	27 150	362 027	13 334	Kirin
Heilongjiang	38 180	551 150	14 436	Heilungkiang
Jiangsu	74 680	1 830 566	24 512	Kiangsu
Zhejiang	48 940	1 343 785	27 458	Chekiang
Anhui	61 140	537 512	8 791	Anhwei
Fujian	35 320	656 895	18 598	Fien
Jiangxi	43 070	405 676	9 419	Kiangsi
Shandong	92 390	1 851 687	20 042	Shantung
Henan	93 710	1 058 742	11 298	Honan
Hubei	57 070	652 014	11 425	Hupei
Hunan	63 200	651 134	10 303	Hunan
Guangdong	91 850	2 236 654	24 351	Kwangtung
Quangxi	46 550	407 575	8 756	Kwangsi
Hainan	8 260	89 457	10 830	Hainan
Chongqing	27 970	307 049	10 978	Chungking
Sichuan	82 080	738 511	8 997	Szechwan
Guizhou	37 250	197 906	5 313	Kweichow
Yunnan	44 420	347 289	7 818	Yunnan
Tibet	2 760	25 121	9 102	Tibet
Shaanxi	37 180	367 566	9 886	Shensi
Gansu	25 920	193 398	7 461	Kansu
Qinghai	5 430	54 332	10 006	Tsinghai
Ningxia	5 950	60 610	10 187	Ninghsia
Xinjiang	20 080	260 419	12 969	Sinkiang
Total	**1 306 280**	**18 308 480**	**14 016**	**Average**

* In fact, there are 22 provinces, 5 autonomous regions, and 4 municipalities
Hong Kong and Macao are special administrative regions.

Source: Gross Regional Product in 2005, in current prices, and population on 1 November 2005 from NBS, *China Statistical Yearbook* 2006, pp. 63 and 101.

http://dx.doi.org/10.1787/088602221626

ISBN: 978-92-64-03762-5 © OECD 2007

Map 1. Chinese Provinces and Places (*pinyin romanisation*)

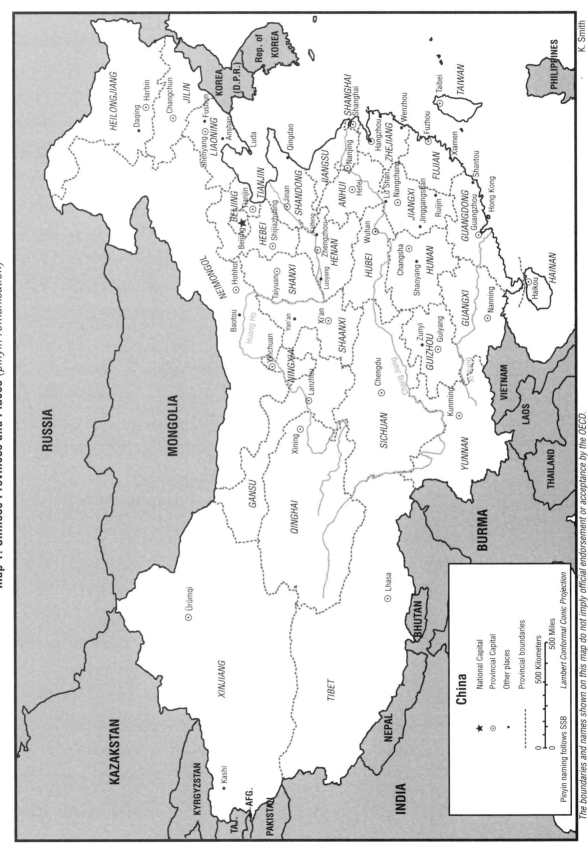

Map 2. Chinese Provinces and Places *(Wade–Giles romanisation)*

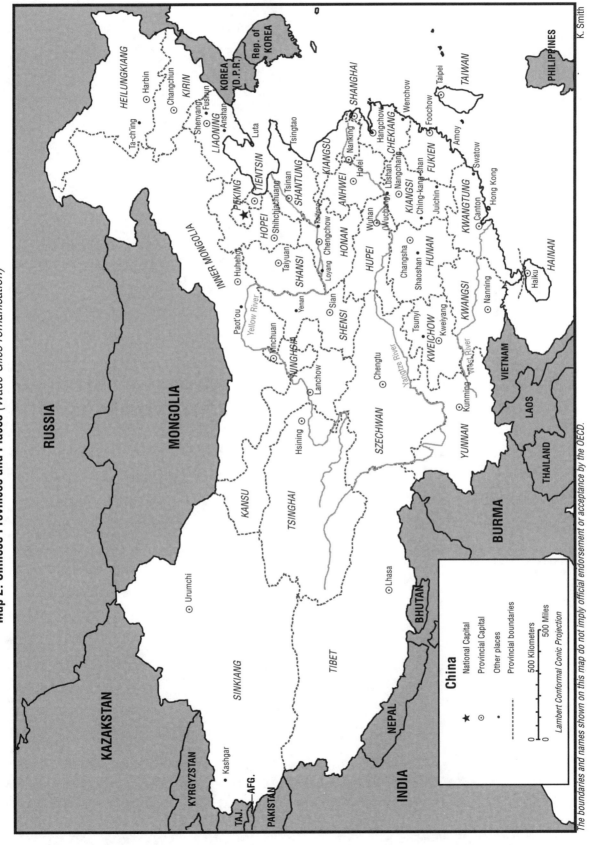

K. Smith

 ISBN: 978-92-64-03762-5 © OECD 2007

Bibliography

ABEL, W. (1978), *Agrarkrisen und Agrarkonjunktur*, Parey, Hamburg.

ALLEN, G.C. AND A.G. DONNITHORNE (1954), *Western Enterprise and Far Eastern Economic Development*, Allen and Unwin, London.

ARK, VAN, B. (1993),"International Comparisons of Output and Productivity", Ph.D. Dissertation, University of Groningen.

ARK, VAN, B. (1996), "Sectoral Growth Accounting and Structural Change in Postwar Europe" pp. 84–164 *in* van Ark & Crafts.

ARK, VAN, B. AND M. P. TIMMER (2002), "Realising Growth Potential, South Korea and Taiwan, 1960–to 1998", *in* MADDISON *et al*.ASIAN DEVELOPMENT BANK (1997), *Key Indicators of Developing Asian and Pacific Countries*, Manila.

ARK, VAN, B. AND N. CRAFTS (eds.) (1996), *Quantitative Aspects of post–war European Economic Growth*, Cambridge University Press.

BAILEY, A. AND J. LLOBERA (eds.) (1981), *The Asiatic Mode of Production*, Routledge, London.

BALAZS, S., "Beiträge zur Wirtschaftsgeschichte der T'ang–Zeit (618–906)", in *Mitteilungen des Seminars fur Orientalische Sprachen*, 34 (1931), 35 (1932), 36 (1933).

BALAZS, E. (formerly Stefan) (1952), "Les Aspects significatifs de la société chinoise", *Études Asiatiques* (VI).

BALAZS, E. (1964), *Chinese Civilization and Bureaucracy*, Yale University Press, New Haven.

BALAZS, E. (1968), *La Bureaucratie céleste; recherches sur l'économie et la société de la Chine traditionnelle*, Gallimard, Paris.

BANISTER, J. (1987), *China's Changing Population*, Stanford University Press, Stanford.

BARKER, R., R. SINHA AND B. ROSE (1982), *The Chinese Agricultural Economy*, Croom Helm, London.

BELOCH, J. (1886), *Die Bevölkerung der Griechisch–Römischen Welt*, Duncker and Humblot, Leipzig.

BENNETT, M.K. (1954), *The World's Food*, Harper, New York.

BERGSON, A. (1961), *The Real National Income of Soviet Russia Since 1928*, Harvard University Press, Cambridge, MA.

BIELENSTEIN, H. (1987), "Chinese Historical Demography AD 2–1982", *Bulletin of the Museum of Far Eastern Antiquities, Stockholm*, No. 59.

BLUNDEN, C. AND M. ELVIN (1983), *Cultural Atlas of China*, Phaidon, Oxford.

BOSERUP, E. (1965), *The Conditions of Agricultural Growth*, Aldine, Chicago.

BOSERUP, E. (1981), *Population and Technology*, Blackwell, Oxford.

BOWLES, P. AND G. WHITE (1993), *The Political Economy of China's Financial Reforms*, Westview Press, Oxford.

ISBN: 978-92-64-03762-5 © OECD 2007

BRAY, F. (1984), *Agriculture*, J. NEEDHAM (1954–97), *Science and Civilisation in China* series, Vol. VI:2.

BROWN, L.R. (1995), *Who Will Feed China?*, Norton, New York.

BUCK, J.L. (1930), *China's Farm Economy*, University of Chicago Press, Chicago.

BUCK, J.L. (1937), *Land Utilization in China*, 3 Vols., Council on Economic and Cultural Affairs, New York.

CARTER, T.F. (1925), *The Invention of Printing in China and Its Spread Westward*, Columbia University Press, New York.

CENSUS AND STATISTICS DEPARTMENT (1997), *Estimates of GDP 1961 to 1996*, Hong Kong, March.

CHANG, C.L. (1955), *The Chinese Gentry*, University of Washington, Seattle.

CHANG, C.L. (1962), *The Income of the Chinese Gentry*, University of Washington, Seattle.

CHANG, H.P. (1964), *Commissioner Lin and the Opium War*, Harvard University Press, Cambridge, MA.

CHANG, K.N. (1958), *The Inflationary Spiral: The Experience in China, 1939–1950*, MIT Press, Cambridge, MA..

CHANG, J.K. (1969), *Industrial Development in Pre–Communist China*, Edinburgh University Press, Edinburgh.

CHAO, K. (1965), *The Rate and Pattern of Industrial Growth in Communist China*, University of Michigan Press, Ann Arbor.

CHAO, K. (1968), *The Construction Industry in China*, Aldine, Chicago.

CHAO, K. (1970), *Agricultural Production in Communist China*, 1949–65, University of Wisconsin Press, Madison.

CHAO, K. (1974), *Capital Formation in Mainland China*, 1952–1965, University of California Press, Berkeley.

CHAO, K. (1977), *The Development of Cotton Textile Production in China*, Harvard University Press, Cambridge, MA.

CHAO, K. (1982), *The Economic Development of Manchuria: The Rise of a Frontier Economy*, Michigan Papers in Chinese Studies, 43, Ann Arbor.

CHAO, K. (1986), *Man and Land in Chinese History: An Economic Analysis*, Stanford University Press, Stanford.

CHEN, K., G.H. JEFFERSON, T.G. RAWSKI, H. WANG AND Y. ZHENG (1988), "New Estimates of Fixed Investment and Capital Stock for Chinese State Industry", *China Quarterly*, June.

CHEN, N.R. (1966), *Chinese Economic Statistics*, Edinburgh University Press, Edinburgh.

CHEN, N.R. AND C.M. HOU (1986), "China's Inflation, 1979–1983: Measurement and Analysis", *Economic Development and Cultural Change*, No. 2.

CHI, C.–T. (1936), *Key Economic Areas in Chinese History*, Allen and Unwin, London.

China Statistical Yearbook, (2006), China Statistics Press, Beijing.

CHINESE MINISTRY OF INFORMATION (1943), *China Handbook 1937–1943*, Macmillan, New York.

CHOW, G.C. (1993), "Capital Formation and Economic Growth in China", *Quarterly Journal of Economics*, Vol. 108, August.

CH'U, T.T. (1962), *Local Government in China Under the Ch'ing*, Harvard University Press, Cambridge, MA.

CHOU, K.R. (1966), *The Hong Kong Economy*, Academic Publishers, Hong Kong.

CIPOLLA, C.M. (1976), *Before the Industrial Revolution: European Society and Economy, 1000–1700*, Norton, New York.

CLARK, C. (1967), *Population Growth and Land Use*, Macmillan, London.

COLBY, W.H., F.W. CROOK AND S.E.H. WEBB (1992), *Agricultural Statistics of the People's Republic of China 1949–90*, Economic Research Service, US Dept. of Agriculture, Statistical Bulletin 844, Washington, D.C., December.

COLLINS, S.M. AND B.P. BOSWORTH (1996), "Economic Growth in East Asia: Accumulation versus Assimilation", *Brookings Papers on Economic Activity*, 2.

COOKE JOHNSON, L. (ed.) (1993), *Cities of Jiangnan in Late Imperial China*, State University of New York Press, Albany.

COOKE JOHNSON, L. (1995), *Shanghai: From Market Town to Treaty Port, 1074–1858*, Stanford University Press, Stanford.

CRANMER–BYNG, J.L.(1962), *An Embassy to China* (Journal kept by Lord Macartney 1793–94), Longmans, London.

DALLIN, D.J. (1950), *The Rise of Russia in Asia*, World Affairs, London.

DENG, G. (1993), *Development versus Stagnation: Technological Continuity and Agricultural Progress in Pre–Modern China*, Greenwood, Westport.

DERNBERGER, R.F. (ed.) (1980), *China's Development Experience in Comparative Perspective*, Harvard University Press, Cambridge, MA.

DNEA (Department of National Economic Accounts) (1996), *Input–Output Table of China 1992*, China Statistical Publishing House, Beijing.

DNEB (Department of National Economic Balance, State Statistical Bureau of China) and ONIOS (Office of the National Input–Output Survey) (1991), *Input–Output Table of China 1987*, China Statistical Publishing House, Beijing.

DOMAR, E.D. (1989), *Capitalism, Socialism and Serfdom*, Cambridge University Press, Cambridge.

DONNITHORNE, A. (1967), *China's Economic System*, Praeger, New York.

DUBY, G. (1998), *France in the Middle Ages, 987-1460*, Blackwell, London.

DURAND, J.D. (1960), "The Population Statistics of China A.D.2–1953", *Population Studies*, March.

DURAND, J.D. (1974), *Historical Estimates of World Population; An Evaluation*, University of Pennsylvania Press, Philadelphia.

EAST ASIA ANALYTICAL UNIT (1997), *China Embraces the Market*, Dept. of Foreign Affairs and Trade, Canberra.

EBERHARD, W.(1956), "Data on the Structure of the Chinese City in the Pre–Industrial Period", *Economic Development and Cultural Change*, October.

EBREY, P.C. (1996), *The Cambridge Illustrated History of China*, Cambridge University Press, Cambridge.

ECKSTEIN, A. (1961), *The National Economy of Communist China*, Free Press, Glencoe.

ECKSTEIN, A. (1980) (ed.), *Quantitative Measures of China's Economic Output*, University of Michigan Press, Ann Arbor.

ECKSTEIN, A., W. GALENSON AND T.C. LIU (1968) (eds.), *Economic Trends in Communist China*, Aldine, Chicago.

ECLAC (Economic Commission for Latin America and the Caribbean) (1997), *Preliminary Overview of the Economy of Latin America and the Caribbean 1997*, Santiago.

EHRLICH, E. (1985), "The Size Structure of Manufacturing Establishments and Enterprises: An International Comparison", *Journal of Comparative Economics*, 9.

ELVIN, M. (1970), "The Last Thousand Years of Chinese History; Changing Patterns of Land Tenure", *Modern Asian Studies*, 4, 2.

ELVIN, M. (1972), "The High Level Equilibrium Trap: The Causes of the Decline of Invention in the Traditional Chinese Textile Industries", *in* WILLMOTT (1972).

ELVIN, M. (1973), *The Pattern of the Chinese Past*, Methuen, London.

ELVIN, M. (1982), "The Technology of Farming in Late–Traditional China", *in* BARKER, R., R. SINHA AND B. ROSE (eds.).

ISBN: 978-92-64-03762-5 © OECD 2007

ELVIN, M. AND T.J. LIU (eds.) (1998), *Sediments of Time, Environment and Society in Chinese History*, Cambridge University Press.

ENDICOTT–WEST, E. (1989), *Mongolian Rule in China: Local Administration in the Yuan Dynasty*, Harvard University Press, Cambridge, MA.

DAVIS, K. (1951), *The Population of India and Pakistan,* Princeton University Press, Princeton.

EU, IMF, OECD, UN and World Bank (1993), *System of National Accounts*, New York.

FAIRBANK, J.K., E.O. REISCHAUER AND A.M. CRAIG (1965), *East Asia: The Modern Transformation*, Houghton Mifflin, Boston.

FAO (1994), *Production Yearbook*, FAO, Rome.

FAURE, D. (1984), *The Rural Economy of Pre–Liberation China,* Oxford University Press, Hong Kong.

FELTENSTEIN, A. AND J. HA (1991), "Measurement of Repressed Inflation in China", *Journal of Development Economics,* Vol. 36, No. 2, October.

FEUERWERKER, A. (1958), *China's Early Industrialization,* Harvard University Press, Cambridge, MA.

FEUERWERKER, A. (eds.) (1968), *History in Communist China*, MIT Press, London.

FEUERWERKER, A. (1975), *Rebellion in Nineteenth Century China*, Michigan Papers in Chinese Studies, No. 21.

FEUERWERKER, A. (1976), *State and Society in Eighteenth–Century China: The Ching Empire in its Glory,* Michigan Papers in Chinese Studies, No. 27, Ann Arbor.

FEUERWERKER, A. (1977), *Economic Trends in the Republic of China,* 1912–1949, Michigan Papers in Chinese Studies, Ann Arbor.

FEUERWERKER, A. (1995), *Studies in the Economic History of Late Imperial China,* Center for Chinese Studies, University of Michigan Press, Ann Arbor.

FEUERWERKER, A., R. MURPHY AND M.C. WRIGHT (1967), *Approaches to Modern Chinese History,* University of California Press, Berkeley.

FIELD, R.M. (1992), "China's Industrial Performance Since 1978", *China Quarterly,* September.

FINDLAY, C., A. WATSON AND H.X. WU (1994), *Rural Enterprises in China,* Macmillan, London.

FOGEL, J.A. (1984), *Politics and Sinology: The Case of Naito Konan,* Harvard University Press, Cambridge, MA.

FOGEL, R.W. (1964), *Railroads and American Economic Growth,* Johns Hopkins University Press, Baltimore.

FONG, H.D. (1975), *Reminiscences of a Chinese Economist at 70,* South Seas Society, Singapore.

FREEDMAN, M. (1958), *Lineage Organisation in South Eastern China,* London School of Economics, Monograph 18, London.

GERNET, J. (1970), *Daily Life in China on the Eve of the Mongol Invasion 1250–1276,* Stanford University Press, Stanford.

GERNET, J. (1982), *A History of Chinese Civilization,* Cambridge University Press, Cambridge.

GOLDSMITH, R.W. (1984), "An Estimate of the Size and Structure of the National Product of the Roman Empire", *Review of Income and Wealth,* Vol. 30, No. 3, September.

GRASSMAN, S. AND E. LUNDBERG (eds.) (1981), *The World Economic Order: Past and Prospects,* Macmillan, London.

GREENBERG, M. (1951), *British Trade and the Opening of China, 1800–1842,* Monthly Review Press, New York.

GRIFFIN, K. AND R. ZHAO (1993), *The Distribution of Income in China,* Macmillan, London.

HAEGER, J.W. (ed.) (1975), *Crisis and Prosperity in Sung China,* University of Arizona Press, Tucson.

HALDE DU, P.J.B. (1741), *The General History of China,* 3rd edition, translated by R. BROOKES, Watts, London.

HARTWELL, R.M. (1962), "A Revolution in the Chinese Iron and Coal Industries During the Northern Sung, 960–1126 AD", *Journal of Asian Studies,* February.

HARTWELL, R.M. (1966), "Markets, Technology and the Structure of Enterprise in the Development of the Eleventh Century Chinese Iron and Steel Industry", *Journal of Economic History,* March.

HARTWELL, R.M. (1967), "A Cycle of Economic Change in Imperial China: Coal and Iron in Northern China, 750–1350", *Journal of the Economic and Social History of the Orient,* Vol. X.

HARTWELL, R.M. (1982), "Demographic, Political and Social Transformations of China, 750–1550", *Harvard Journal of Asiatic Studies.*

HAYAMI, A. (1986), "Population Trends in Tokugawa, Japan: 1600–1868", International Statistical Institute Congress.

HERD, R. AND S. DOUGHERTY (2007), "Growth Prospects in China and India Compared", *European Journal of Comparative Economics,* vol. 4, n. 1, pp. 65–89

HIBINO, T. (1939), "To Sojidai ni ikeru Fukken no Kaihatsu", *Toyoshikenkyu,* March.

HINTON, H.C. (1970), *The Grain Tribute System of China (1845–1911),* Harvard University Press, Cambridge, MA.

HO, P.T. (1959), *Studies on the Population of China, 1368–1953,* Harvard University Press, Cambridge, MA.

HO, P.T. (1962), *The Ladder of Success in Imperial China,* Columbia University Press, New York.

HO, P.T. (1975), *The Cradle of the East: An Inquiry into the Indigenous Origins of Techniques and Ideas of Neolithic and Early Historic China, 5000–1000 BC,* Chinese University, Hong Kong.

HO, S.P.S. (1978), *Economic Development of Taiwan 1860–1970,* Yale University Press, New Haven.

HO, S.P.S. (1994), *Rural China in Transition,* Clarendon Press, Oxford.

HOLLINGSWORTH, T.H. (1969), *Historical Demography,* Cornell University Press, Ithaca, New York.

HOLLISTER, W.W. (1959), *China's Gross National Product and Social Accounts, 1950–1957,* Free Press, Glencoe.

HOU, C.M. (1965), *Foreign Investment and Economic Development in China 1840–1937,* Harvard University Press, Cambridge, MA.

HOU, C.M. AND T.S. YU (eds.) (1979), *Modern Chinese Economic History,* Academia Sinica, Taipei.

HOU, C.M. AND T.S. YU (1982), *Agricultural Development in China, Japan and Korea,* Academia Sinica, Taipei.

HSIAO, L.L. (1974), *China's Foreign Trade Statistics, 1864–1949,* Harvard University Press, Cambridge, MA.

HSÜ, I.C.Y. (1975), *The Rise of Modern China,* Oxford University Press, Oxford.

HUANG, P.C.C. (1985), *The Peasant Economy and Social Change in North China,* Stanford University Press, Stanford.

HUANG, P.C.C. (1990), *The Peasant Family and Rural Development in the Yangzi Delta, 1350–1988,* Stanford University Press, Stanford.

HUANG, R. (1974), *Taxation and Governmental Finance in Sixteenth Century Ming China,* Cambridge University Press, Cambridge.

HUCKER, C.O. (1961), *The Traditional Chinese State in Ming Times,* University of Arizona, Tucson.

HUCKER, C.O. (1978), *The Ming Dynasty: the Origins and Evolving Institutions,* University of Michigan Press, Ann Arbor.

HUCKER, C.O. (1985), *A Dictionary of Official Titles in Imperial China,* Stanford University Press, Stanford.

IBN BATTÚTA (1929), *Travels in Asia and Africa 1325–1354* in H.A.R. GIBB (ed.), Routledge, London.

IEA (2005a), *Energy Balances of OECD and Non–OECD Countries,* International Energy Agency, OECD, Paris.

IEA (2005b), CO2 Emissions from Fuel Combustion? 1971-2003, International Energy Agency, OECD, Paris.

IEA (2006), World Energy Outlook, International Energy Agency, OECD, Paris.

IMF (various years) International Financial Statistics, IMF, Washington, D.C.

Jacobs, D.N. (1981), Borodin: Stalin's Man in China, Harvard University Press, Cambridge, MA.

Jamieson, G. (1897), Report on the Revenue and Expenditures of the Chinese Empire, Foreign Office Miscellaneous Series 1415, HMSO, London.

JEC (1967), An Economic Profile of Mainland China, 2 Vols., Joint Economic Committee, US Congress, Washington, D.C., February.

JEC (1972), People's Republic of China: An Economic Assessment, Joint Economic Committee, US Congress, Washington, D.C., May.

JEC (1975), China: A Reassessment of the Economy, Joint Economic Committee, US Congress, Washington, D.C., July.

JEC (1976), China and the Chinese, Joint Economic Committee, US Congress, Washington, D.C., November

JEC (1978), Chinese Economy Post Mao, Vol. I, Joint Economic Committee, US Congress, Washington, D.C., November.

JEC (1982), China under the Four "Modernizations", 2 Vols., Joint Economic Committee, US Congress, Washington, D.C., August and December.

JEC (1986), China's Economy Looks Towards the Year 2000, 2 Vols., Joint Economic Committee, US Congress, Washington, D.C., May.

JEC (1991), China's Economic Dilemmas in the 1990s, 2 Vols., Joint Economic Committee, US Congress, Washington, D.C., April.

JEC (1996), China's Economic Future: Challenges to US Policy, Joint Economic Committee, US Congress, Washington, D.C., August.

Jefferson, G.H., T.G. Rawski and Y. Zheng (1992), "Growth, Efficiency and Convergence in China's State and Collective Industry", Economic Development and Cultural Change, Vol. 40, No. 2, January.

Jefferson, G.H. and T.G. Rawski (1994), "Enterprise Reform in Chinese Industry", Journal of Economic Perspectives, Vol. 8, No. 2, Spring.

Jefferson, G.H., A.G.Z. Hu and J. Su (2006), "The Sources and Sustainability of China's Growth", Brookings Papers in Economic Activity, No. 2, pp. 1–47.

Jones, E.L. (1981), The European Miracle, Cambridge University Press, Cambridge.

Jones, E.L. (1988), Growth Recurring, Clarendon Press, Oxford.

Keidel, A. (1992), "How Badly do China's National Accounts Underestimate China's GDP?", Rock Creek Research, mimeo.

Keidel, A. (1994), China: GNP Per Capita, World Bank, Report No. 13580–CHA, December

King, F.H. (1926), Farmers of Forty Centuries, Cape, London.

Kouwenhoven, R. (1996), "Economic Performance of Soviet Farming: A Comparison in Space and Time 1913–91", Groningen Growth and Development Centre, processed.

Kouwenhoven, R. (1997), "A Comparison of Soviet and US Industrial Performance, 1928–1990", Jahrbuch für Wirtschaftgeschichte, 2.

Kracke, E. (1953), Civil Service in Early Sung China, Harvard University Press, Cambridge, MA.

Kravis, I . (1981), "An Approximation of the Relative Real Per Capita GDP of the People's Republic of China", Journal of Comparative Economics, 5.

KRUGMAN, P. (1994), "The Myth of Asia's Miracle", *Foreign Affairs,* Vol. 73, No. 6, November/December.

KUEH, Y.Y. AND R.F. ASH (eds.) (1993), *Economic Trends in Chinese Agriculture,* Oxford University Press, Oxford.

KUHN, D. (1988), *Textile Technology: Spinning and Reeling,* Vol. V:9 *in* Needham, J. (ed.) (1954–97).

KUHN, P.A. (1970), *Rebellion and Its Enemies in Late Imperial China: Militarisation and Social Structure 1796/1864,* Harvard University Press, Cambridge, MA.

LANDES, D.S. (1969), *The Unbound Prometheus,* Cambridge University Press, Cambridge.

LARDY, N.R. (1983), *Agriculture in China's Modern Economic Development,* Cambridge University Press, Cambridge.

LARDY, N.R. (1992), *Foreign Trade and Economic Reform in China,* 1978–1990, Cambridge University Press, Cambridge.

LARDY, N.R. (1994), *China in the World Economy,* Institute for International Economics, Washington, D.C.

LEE, B. AND A. MADDISON (1997), "A Comparison of Output, Purchasing Power and Productivity in Indian and Chinese Manufacturing in the mid 1980s", *COPPAA Paper,* No. 5, Griffith University, Brisbane.

LEGGE, J. (1960), *The Chinese Classics,* 5 Vols., Hong Kong University Press (reprint of 1893 OUP edition).

LEVATHES, L. (1994), *When China Ruled the Seas,* Simon and Schuster, New York.

LEWIN, G. (1973), *Die erste Fünfzig Jahre der Sung Dynastie in China,* Akademie Verlag, Berlin.

LI, B.(1998), *Agricultural Development in Jiangnan, 1620–1850,* MacMillan, London.

LI, C.M. (1959), *Economic Development of Communist China,* University of California Press, Berkeley.

LI, C.M. (1962), *The Statistical System of Communist China,* University of California Press, Berkeley.

LI, J. et al. (1992), "Productivity and China's Economic Growth", *Economic Studies Quarterly,* December.

LIN, C.Z. (1988), "China's Economic Reforms II: Western Perspectives", *Asian–Pacific Economic Literature,* Vol. 2, No. 1, March.

LIN, J.Y. (1990), "Collectivisation and China's Agricultural Crisis in 1959–1961", *Journal of Political Economy,* Vol. 98, No. 6, December.

LIN, J.Y. (1992), "Rural Reforms and Agricultural Growth in China", *American Economic Review,* Vol. 82, No. I, March.

LIN, J.Y. (1995), "The Needham Puzzle: Why the Industrial Revolution did not Originate in China", *Economic Development and Cultural Change,* January.

LIN, J.Y. , FANG CAI AND ZHOU LI (1996), *The China Miracle,* Chinese University Press, Hong Kong.

LIPPIT, V.D. (1974), *Land Reform and Economic Development in China,* International Arts and Sciences Press, New York.

LIU, G.W. (2005, *Wrestling for Power: the State and the economy in Later Imperial China, 1000–1770,* Harvard University Ph. D. thesis.

LIU, J.T.C. AND P.J. GOLAS (eds.) (1969), *Change in Sung China: Innovation or Renovation?,* Heath, Lexington.

LIU, P.K.C. AND K.S. HWANG (1979), "Population Change and Economic Development in Mainland China since 1400", *in* HOU AND YU (1979).

LIU, T.–C. (1946), *China's National Income 1931–36: An Exploratory Study,* Brookings, Washington, D.C.

LIU, T.–C. AND K.C. YEH (1965), *The Economy of the Chinese Mainland: National Income and Economic Development, 1933–1959,* Princeton University Press, Princeton.

LIU, T.C. AND K.C. YEH (1973), "Chinese and Other Asian Economies: A Quantitative Evaluation", *American Economic Review,* May.

ISBN: 978-92-64-03762-5 © OECD 2007

LIU, T.J. AND J.C.H. FEI (1977), "An Analysis of the Land Tax Burden in China, 1650–1865", *Journal of Economic History,* June.

LIU, P.K.C. AND K.S. HWANG (1979), "Population Change and Economic Development in Mainland China Since 1400", *in* HOU, C.-M. AND T.-S. YU (eds.)

MA, L.J.C. (1971), *Commercial Development and Urban Change in Sung China,* University of Michigan Press, Ann Arbor.

MACARTNEY, G. (1962), *An Embassy to China, being the Journal kept by Lord Macartney, 1793–1794,* edited by J.L. Cranmer–Byng, Longmans, London.

MADDISON, A. (1970), *Economic Progress and Policy in Developing Countries,* Norton, New York.

MADDISON, A. (1971), *Class Structure and Economic Growth: India and Pakistan Since the Moghuls,* Allen and Unwin, London.

MADDISON, A. (1985), *Two Crises: Latin America and Asia 1929–38 and 1973–83,* OECD Development Centre, Paris.

MADDISON, A. (1987), "Growth and Slowdown in Advanced Capitalist Countries: Techniques of Quantitative Assessment", *Journal of Economic Literature,* June.

MADDISON, A. (1998a), *Chinese Economic Performance' in the Long Run,* first edition, OECD Development Centre, Paris.

MADDISON, A. (1998b), "Measuring the Performance of a Communist Command Economy: An Assessment of the CIA Estimates for the USSR", *Review of Income and Wealth,* Vol. 44, No. 3, September.

MADDISON, A. (1989), *The World Economy in the Twentieth Century,* OECD Development Centre, Paris.

MADDISON, A. (1991a), *Dynamic Forces in Capitalist Development,* Oxford University Press, Oxford.

MADDISON, A. (1991b), *A Long Run Perspective on Saving,* Research Memorandum 443, Institute of Economic Research, University of Groningen.

MADDISON, A. AND ASSOCIATES (1992), *The Political Economy of Poverty, Equity and Growth: Brazil and Mexico,* Oxford University Press, Oxford.

MADDISON, A. (1995a), *Monitoring the World Economy, 1820–1992,* OECD Development Centre, Paris.

MADDISON, A. (1995b), *Explaining the Economic Performance of Nations: Essays in Time and Space,* Elgar, Aldershot.

MADDISON, A. (1997), "The Nature and Functioning of European Capitalism: A Historical and Comparative Perspective", *Banca Nazionale del Lavoro Quarterly Review,* December.

MADDISON A. (2001), *The World Economy: A Millennial Perspective,* OECD, Paris.

MADDISON A. (2003), *The World Economy: Historical Statistics,* OECD, Paris.

MADDISON A. (2006), "Do Official Statistics Exaggerate China's GDP Growth? A Reply to Carsten Holz", *Review of Income and Wealth,* March, pp.121-126.

MADDISON A. (2007), *Contours of The World Economy, 1-2030 AD; Essays in Macroeconomic History,* Oxford University Press.

MADDISON, A. AND ASSOCIATES (1992), *The Political Economy of Poverty, Equity,and Growth: Brazil and Mexico,* Oxford University Press.

MADDISON, A., D. S. PRASADA RAO, AND W. F. SHEPHERD (eds.) (2002), *The Asian Economies in the Twentieth Century,* Elgar, Cheltenham.

MADDISON, A. AND H. VAN DER WEE (1994), *Economic Growth and Structural Change: Comparative Approaches over the Long Run,* Proceedings, Eleventh International Economic History Congress, Milan, September.

MADDISON, A. AND H. X. WU (2007), *"China's Economic Performance: How Fast has GDP Grown",* forthcoming.

MALENBAUM, W. (1982), "Modern Economic Growth in India and China: the Comparison Revisited", *Economic Development and Cultural Change*, No. 1, October.

MAYERSON, P. (1981), "Wheat Production and its Social Consequences in the Roman World", *Classical Quarterly*, 31(ii).

McNEILL, W.H. (1977), *Plagues and People*, Anchor Books, New York.

McNEILL, W.H.(1982), *The Pursuit of Power*, Blackwell, Oxford.

METZGER, T. (1973), *The Internal Organisation of the Ching Bureacracy*, Harvard University Press, Cambridge, MA.

MINISTRY OF AGRICULTURE (1988), *China Agriculture Yearbook*, SSB, Beijing.

MINISTRY OF AGRICULTURE PLANNING BUREAU (1989), *Zhongguo Nongcun Jingji Tongji Ziliao Daquan, 1949–1986*, (Comprehensive Book of China Rural Economic Statistics, 1948–86), Agriculture Press, Beijing.

MITCHELL, B.R. (1982), *International Historical Statistics: Africa and Asia*, Macmillan, London.

MIYAZAKI, I. (1976), *China's Examination Hell: The Civil Service Examinations of Imperial China*, Weatherhill, New York and Tokyo.

MIZOGUCHI, T. AND M. UMEMURA (1988), *Basic Economic Statistics of Former Japanese Colonies, 1895–1938*, Toyo Keizai Shinposha, Tokyo.

MOKYR, J. (1990), *The Lever of Riches*, Oxford University Press, Oxford.

MOTE, F. W. (1999), *Imperial China, 900-1800*, Harvard University Press.

MYERS, R. (1970), *The Chinese Peasant Economy: Agricultural Development in Hopei and Shantung 1890–1949*, Harvard University Press, Cambridge, MA.

MYERS, R. (1977), "The Chinese Economy during the Ch'ing Period", manuscript.

NAKAYAMA, S. AND N. SIVIN (eds.) (1973), *Chinese Science: Exploration of An Ancient Tradition*, MIT Press, Cambridge.

NAQUIN, S. AND E.S. RAWSKI (1987), *Chinese Society in the Eighteenth Century*, University of Yale, New Haven.

NATH, P. (1929), *A Study in the Economic Condition of Ancient India*, Royal Asiatic Society, London.

NAUGHTON, B. (1988), "The Third Front: Defence Industrialisation in the Chinese Interior", *China Quarterly*, September.

NAUGHTON, B. (1995), *Growing Out of the Plan: Chinese Economic Reform 1978–1993*, Cambridge University Press, Cambridge.

NBS, *Statistical Yearbook of China*, Beijing, various annual issues.

NEEDHAM, J. (1954–97), *Science and Civilisation in China*, 50 major sections, many co–authors, many volumes, Cambridge University Press, Cambridge.

NEEDHAM, J. (1958), *The Development of Iron and Steel Technology in China*, Science Museum, London.

NEEDHAM, J. (1969), *The Great Titration: Science and Society in East and West*, Allen and Unwin, London.

NEEDHAM, J. (1971), *Science and Civilisation in China*, vol. IV:3, *Civil Engineering and Nautical Technology*, Cambridge University Press.

NEEDHAM, J. (1981), *Science in Traditional China: A Comparative Perspective*, Harvard University Press, Cambridge, MA.

NGUYEN, D.T. AND H.X. WU (1993), "The Impact of Economic Reforms in Chinese Agricultural Performance", Chinese Economy Research Unit, Adelaide, December.

NOLAN, P. (1995), *China's Rise, Russia's Fall*, Macmillan, London.

ISBN: 978-92-64-03762-5 © OECD 2007

NORTH, D.C. (1981), *Structure and Change in Economic History,* Norton, New York.

ODAKA, K., Y. KIYOKAWA AND M. KUBONIWA (eds.) (2000), *Constructing A Historical Macroeconomic Database for Trans–Asian Regions*, Institute of Economic Research, Hitotsubashi University.

OU, P.–S. *et al.* (1946), "Industrial Production and Employment in Prewar China", *Economic Journal,* September.

OU, P.–S. (1947), *1933 Chung–Kuo Kuo–min So–te* (China's National Income 1933), 2 Vols., Shanghai.

PERDUE, P.C. (1987), *Exhausting the Earth: State and Peasant in Hunan, 1500–1850,* Harvard University Press, Cambridge, MA.

PERKINS, D.H. (1966), *Market Control and Planning in Communist China,* Harvard University Press, Cambridge, MA.

PERKINS, D.H. (1969), *Agricultural Development in China, 1368–1968,* Aldine, Chicago.

PERKINS, D.H. (ed.) (1975), *China's Modern Economy in Historical Perspective,* Stanford University Press, Stanford.

PERKINS, D.H. (1988), "Reforming China's Economic System", *Journal of Economic Literature,* Vol. 26, No. 2, June.

PERKINS, D.H. AND S. YUSUF (1984), *Rural Development in China,* Johns Hopkins University Press, Baltimore.

PILAT, D. (1994), *The Economics of Rapid Growth: The Experience of Japan and Korea,* Elgar, Aldershot.

POMERANZ, K. (2000), *The Great Divergence*, Princeton University Press.

POWELL, R.L. (1955), *The Rise of Chinese Military Power 1895–1912,* Princeton University Press, Princeton.

PURCELL, V. (1965), *The Chinese in Southeast Asia,* Royal Institute of International Affairs, London.

PYO, H.K., K.H. RHEE AND B. HA (2006). *"Estimates of Labor and Total factor Productivity by 72 industries in Korea (1870–2003)"*, paper presented to OECD Workshop, Paris, October 16th

QIAN, W.Y. (1985), *The Great Inertia: Scientific Stagnation in Traditional China,* Croom Helm, London.

RAWSKI, E.S. (1972), *Agricultural Change and the Peasant Economy of South China,* Harvard University Press, Cambridge, MA.

RAWSKI, E.S. (1979), *Education and Popular Literacy in Ch'ing China,* University of Michigan Press, Ann Arbor.

RAWSKI, T.G. (1979), *Economic Growth and Employment in China,* Oxford University Press, New York.

RAWSKI, T.G. (1989), *Economic Growth in Prewar China,* University of California Press, Berkeley.

RAWSKI, T.G. AND L.M. LI (eds.) (1992), *Chinese History in Historical Perspective,* Berkeley.

RAYCHAUDHURI, T. AND I. HABIB (1982), *The Cambridge Economic History of India,* Vol. 1, Cambridge University Press, Cambridge.

REISCHAUER, E.O. AND J.K. FAIRBANK (1958), *East Asia: The Great Tradition,* Houghton Mifflin, Boston.

REMER, C.F. (1933), *Foreign Investments in China,* Macmillan, New York.

REN, R. (1997), *China's Economic Performance in International Perspective,* OECD Development Centre, Paris.

RISKIN, C. (1975), "Surplus and Stagnation in Modern China", *in* PERKINS (ed.) (1975).

RISKIN, C. (1987), *China's Political Economy,* Oxford University Press, Oxford.

ROPP, P.S. (ed.) (1990), *Heritage of China,* University of California Press, Berkeley.

ROWE, W.T. (1986), "Approaches to Modern Chinese Social History" *in* ZUNZ, O. (ed.) (1986).

ROZMAN, G. (1973), *Urban Networks in Ch'ing China and Tokugawa Japan,* Princeton University Press, Princeton.

SALTER, W.E.G. (1960), *Productivity and Technical Change,* Cambridge University Press, Cambridge.

SCHIROKAUER, C. (1989), *A Brief History of Chinese and Japanese Civilisations,* Harcourt, Brace, Jovanovich, New York.

SCHMOOKLER, J. (1966), *Invention and Economic Growth,* Harvard University Press, Cambridge, MA.

SCHURMANN, H.F. (1967), *Economic Structure of Yuan Dynasty,* Harvard University Press, Cambridge, MA.

SHIBA, Y. (1970), *Commerce and Society in Sung China,* Center for Chinese Studies, University of Michigan, Ann Arbor.

SHIBA, Y. (1977), "Ningpo and Its Hinterland", *in* SKINNER (ed.) (1985).

SICULAR, T. X. YUE, B. GUSTAVSSON AND S. LI (2007), "The Urban–Rural Income Gap and Inequality in China" *Review of Income and Wealth*, March, pp. 93–126.

SKINNER, G.W. (1964–1965), "Marketing and Social Structure in Rural China", *Journal of Asian Studies,* November, February and May.

SKINNER, G.W. (ed.) (1977), *The City in Late Imperial China,* Stanford University Press, Stanford.

SKINNER, G.W. (1985), "The Structure of Chinese History", *Journal of Asian Studies,* February.

SLICHER VAN BATH, B.H. (1963), *The Agrarian History of Western Europe AD 500–1850,* Arnold, London.

SMITH, A. (1976), *An Inquiry into the Nature and Causes of the Wealth of Nations* (1776), University of Chicago, reprint.

SNOOKS, G.D. (1993), *Economics Without Time,* Macmillan, London.

SPRENKEL, VAN DER, O.B. (1963), "Max Weber on China", *History and Theory*, Vol. II.

SSB (STATE STATISTICAL BUREAU) (1960), *Ten Great Years,* Foreign Languages Press, Peking.

SSB (annually, from 1981 onwards), *Zhongguo Tongji Nianjian* (China Statistical Yearbook).

SSB (1985), *Zhongguo Gongye Jingji Tongji Ziliao 1949–1984* (China Industrial Economic Statistics Data 1949–1984), Industry, Transport and Materials Statistics Dept., Beijing.

SSB (1988), *Zhongguo Wujia Tongji Nianjian* (Price Statistical Yearbook of China), Beijing.

SSB (1990), *Lishi Tongji Ziliao Huibian* (Historical Statistical Data Compilation 1949–1989), Beijing.

SSB (1991), *Zhongguo Touru Chanchu Biao* (Input–Output Table of China 1987), China Statistical Publishing House, Beijing.

SSB (1995 and 1996), *Zhongguo Gongye Jingji Tongji Nianjian* (China Industrial Economic Statistics Yearbook), Beijing.

SSB (1997), *The Gross Domestic Product of China 1952–1995,* Dongbei University of Finance and Economics Press, Beijing.

SSB and Hitotsubash University Institute of Economic Research (1997) *The Historical National Accounts of the People's Republic of China, 1952–199, Tokyo*.

STAVIS, B. (1982), "Rural Institutions in China" *in* BARKER, SINHA AND ROSE (1982).

STERN REVIEW (2006), *The Economics of Climate Change,* UK Treasury, London

SUTO, Y. (1969), *Sodai keizai shi kenkyu* (Studies on the Economic History of the Sung Dynasty), Toyo Bunko, Tokyo.

SWAMY, S. (1973), "Economic Growth in China and India, 1952–1970: A Comparative Appraisal", *Economic Development and Cultural Change,* Vol. 21, No. 4, July.

SWAMY, S. (1989), *Economic Growth in China and India,* Vikas, New Delhi.

ISBN: 978-92-64-03762-5 © OECD 2007

SUMMERS, R. AND A. HESTON (1995), "Penn World Tables (Mark 5): An Expanded Set of International Comparisons 1950–1988", *Quarterly Journal of Economics,* May, supplemented by PWT 5.5 diskette of June 1993 and PWT 5.6 diskette of January.

SZIRMAI, A. AND R. REN (1995), "China's Manufacturing Performance in Comparative Perspective, 1980–1992", Research Memorandum 581, Groningen Growth and Development Centre, June.

TAEUBER, I.B. AND N.C. WANG (1960), "Population Reports in the Ch'ing Dynasty", *Journal of Asian Studies,* August.

TAEUBER, I.B. (1958), *The Population of Japan,* Princeton University Press, Princeton.

TANG, A.M. (1979), "China's Agricultural Legacy", Economic Development and Cultural Change, October.

TAWNEY, R.H. (1932), *Land and Labour in China,* Allen and Unwin, London.

TENG, S.Y., J.K. FAIRBANK *et al. (eds.) (1954), China's Response to the West: A Documentary Survey 1839–1923,* Harvard University Press, Cambridge, MA.

TORBERT, P.M. (1977), *The Ch'ing Imperial Household Department,* Harvard University Press, Cambridge, MA.

TSIEN, T.H. (1985), *Paper and Printing,* Vol. V:1, *in* NEEDHAM, J. (ed.).

TWITCHETT, D.C. (1963), *Financial Administration Under the Tang Dynasty,* Cambridge University Press, Cambridge.

TWITCHETT, D.C. (1968), "Merchant, Trade and Government in the Late T'ang", *Asia Major.*

TWITCHETT, D. AND J.K. FAIRBANK (1978 onwards), *The Cambridge History of China*, Vols. 10, 11, 12, Cambridge University Press, Cambridge.

URLANIS, B.T. (1941), *Rost Naselenie v Evrope,* Ogiz, Moscow.

VRIES DE, J. (1984), *European Urbanization 1500–1800,* Methuen, London.

WADE, T.F. (1851), "The Army of the Chinese Empire: Its Two Divisions, the Bannermen or National Guard, the Green Standard, or Provincial Troops", *The Chinese Repository,* Canton.

WAKEMAN, F. JNR. (1975), *The Fall of Imperial China,* Collier–Macmillan, London.

WANG, Y.C. (1973), *Land Taxation in Imperial China 1750–1911,* Harvard University Press, Cambridge, MA.

WARD, B. JNR. (1966), *Social Origins of Dictatorship and Democracy,* Beacon, Boston.

WEN, G.J. (1993), "Total Factor Productivity Change in China's Farming Sector: 1952–1989", *Economic Development and Cultural Change,* Vol. 42, No. 1, October.

WEBER, M. (1964), *The Religion of China,* Collier–Macmillan, London.

WHITE, L. (1962), *Medieval Technology and Social Change,* Oxford University Press, Oxford.

WILES, P. (1962), *The Political Economy of Communism,* Harvard University Press, Cambridge, MA.

WIENS, T.B. (1982), Micro-economics of Peasant Economy: China 1920–1940, Garland, New York

WILLMOTT, W. (ed.) (1972), *Economic Organisation in Chinese Society,* Stanford University Press, Stanford.

WITTFOGEL, K.A. (1931), *Wirtschaft und Gesellschaft Chinas,* Hirschfeld, Leipzig.

WITTFOGEL, K. (1957), *Oriental Despotism,* Yale University Press, New Haven.

WONG, R.B. (1997), *China Transformed,* Cornell University Press, Ithaca and London.

WOOD, F. (1995), *Did Marco Polo Go to China?,* Secker and Warburg, London.

WORLD BANK (1981), *Statistical System and Basic Data,* Annex A to China: *Socialist Economic Development,* Washington, D.C.

WORLD BANK (1983), *China, Socialist Economic Development,* 3 Vols., Washington, D.C.

WORLD BANK (1985), *China: Long Term Development Issues and Options,* Washington, D.C.